ITALIAN MOTHERS NEVER DIE

They Just
Get Louder
from the
Other Side

MARC BARONE

Outkirts Press, Inc.
Denver, Colorado

The opinions expressed in this manuscript are solely the opinions of the author and do not represent the opinions or thoughts of the publisher.

Italian Mothers Never Die
They just get louder from the Other Side
All Rights Reserved
Copyright © 2007 Marc Barone
V 2.0

Cover Image © 2007 JupiterImages Corporation
All Rights Reserved. Used With Permission.

This book may not be reproduced, transmitted, or stored in whole or in part by any means, including graphic, electronic, or mechanical without the express written consent of the publisher except in the case of brief quotations embodied in critical articles and reviews.

Outskirts Press
http://www.outskirtspress.com

ISBN-10: 1-4327-0524-5
ISBN-13: 978-1-4327-0524-4

Library of Congress Control Number: 2007924935

Outskirts Press and the "OP" logo are trademarks belonging to
Outskirts Press, Inc.

Printed in the United States of America

In loving memory of my mother Joia Barone, who from the Other Side still verifies the validity of an adage she occasionally spoke in life: "Nothing is impossible!!! Improbable perhaps...but *not* impossible!"

Marc Barone
July 30th 2006

Early Praise for Italian Mothers...

"Marc Barone's raconteur orchestration resonates in the heart as a masterpiece of love. His brilliant other worldly connections with his Mother are as heart-warming as they are amazing! The very real voice of Joia from the Other Side is alive and well in these pages, and gives credence not only to a son's everlasting love, but credibility and validation to the Soul's survival of the very death so many of us fear. This is a story of pure joy and unconditional love, a love that undeniably transcends death.

I feel grateful having glimpsed into the soul of this gifted writer.

Patricia Artes, Ph.D.
Philosopher, Author and founder of <u>Sense of Soul</u>

"Marc Barone has written a book that will doubtlessly entertain you to no end. His relationship with his mother who is now gone... well, not really...is funny and poignant at the same time and each astonishing chapter makes you wish the story would never end! If you believe there's life beyond death, this book will truly inspire you; if you are one of those who snicker at the thought of communications with the Other Side, you'll snicker no more because timeless and charming Joia will set you straight!

I loved this book and recommend it to everybody!"

Christina Brett
Author of: <u>Murder in Mind</u> a BBC Movie and numerous novels including: <u>A Nice and Quiet Place</u>, <u>Dark Moon Over Berlin</u> and <u>Old Sins Cast Long Shadows</u>; currently being made into a major motion picture.

This book touched me on so many levels; I've read it 3 times and I will read it again and again! To sum it up in a few lines is impossible so a slew of heartfelt adjectives will have to do: Unflinchingly honest, addictively entertaining, tearfully funny, touchingly sad, triumphantly inspiring, spiritually uplifting, and my list could go on and on. Perhaps, due to my own profession, I can sum it up best by saying that it is an invigorating massage of the heart, mind, and soul.

Jodi Jenkins
Massage Therapist
Green Valley Ranch Resort
Las Vegas, NV.

The Obligatory Foreword

    Though I suspect it may be accurate, a ***very unscientific*** poll has shown that many readers skip the <u>Foreword</u> and begin reading at Chapter One. Only if they've really enjoyed the book and are craving more information, do they return and read the <u>Foreword</u>.
    I wouldn't even write one at all except that a few things *must be clarified beforehand* in order to fully experience this ***true story***. Therefore, in the interest of full disclosure, and also because I don't ever want to be "Frey-ed" into *a million little pieces* on **Oprah**, the following notes apply.

1) ***<u>This is a true story</u>.*** All of the events actually happened and all quoted dialogue is as accurate as possible.

2) **Joia Barone** is my mother's true maiden name. I've decided to use mom's surname as my own, for reasons that will become evident in the course of this story.

3) With the exceptions of Rex, Megan, Fiona, and The Fisher Family, the rest of the names in this book ***<u>are the actual names</u>*** of the people portrayed.

This book is my true story from cover to cover. I swear on my…

(Honest Oprah)

"You may say I'm a dreamer, but I'm not the only one..."
-John Lennon

Joia "Joy" Barone

Baby Grand
(Part One)

As we stood surveying the spacious empty living room of the brand new home I'd just purchased, I said to my best friend; "Someday, a white baby grand piano will sit right there." I pointed to a vacant area of white carpet flowing in between two white ceramic lions, each of them sitting on opposite sides of a cathedral window that gloriously showcased the virgin plains and desert mountain range in the distance.

Nine years later, in November of 2004, the only virgin spaces left in and around my house were that piano-free stretch of white carpet between the two lions, along with the desolate and barren landscape of my front and back yards.

I'd looked at a fleet's worth of white baby grand's over the years, but the expenditure was far too extravagant for my restaurant server tips and regrettably, much lower on my long list of more urgent necessities.

For instance, I knew for a fact that my neighbors were tired of looking at the nine-year-old non-existent landscape of my property. *I* was certainly sick of looking at the boring parcel of desert clay, how could they not be? My front and back yards were the blight on the block alongside their emerald green lawns, swaying palm trees, rose blossomed trellises and garden fountains. My home exterior still looked brand new, but the terrain surrounding it was without a doubt, Home Depot deprived. I'm lucky a Homeowner's Association didn't govern the neighborhood for they would've been at my door with torches years ago! None of them ever said anything negative to me about it, they didn't have to, I could feel the vibe.

My suspicions of their secret silent scorn were confirmed very early one morning as I sat sipping coffee in a spare room on the second floor of my home, next to a window overlooking my front yard and the sidewalk. A large Irish Setter, tethered loosely to its elderly male owner, was territorially sniffing the group of mailboxes outside my open window. I'd never seen this duo before because I'd only had my morning coffee two or three times in this seldom used guest room, in the all the years I'd lived here. The only reason I'd chosen to wake up with my coffee in this room today was because it is the only room in the house with a complete view of the front yard and I was finally going to draw a garden plan.

The elderly gentleman stood silent and still, waiting for his mailbox sniffing dog, both completely unaware of my quiet presence a mere twenty feet away. I could see them both clearly, but they would have to look up to my second floor across the yard before they could see even a faint outline of me sitting behind the dark solar screened window.

Breaking the early morning silence, in a low growling voice the man disgustedly said to his dog, "Now **this** guy needs to get off his ass and shape up! He's done **nothing** to this yard after all these years!"

I instantly started choking on my coffee from the laughter I was forcing myself to stifle! Perilously close to spraying the coffee out of my mouth, I somehow managed to swallow and muffle the cough that was mixing with my choking giggles as the grumpy old man continued disparagingly: "*What kinda guy* leaves his front yard bare like this!?" He grimaced and shook his weary head at the panting open-mouthed strawberry haired Setter, who stared blankly back at him.

I covered my mouth tightly with both hands as my tearfully convulsing laughter escalated. I didn't want him or the dog to hear me so that he'd continue his rant! I felt my face flush with redness as I held my breath, and at the same time I imagined myself possessing ventriloquist skills so I could throw my voice into the panting Irish Setter's mouth so the dog could respond: "The kinda guy that barely has enough money for *living expenses*, let alone landscaping! Care to cough up funding for the front yard "kitty?" **Dawg**!!??"

I pictured the Irish Setter hysterically bark-laughing at its own kitty/dawg pun, which only made me quiver and shake harder as I struggled to stop myself from bursting into the loudest laugh of my life! Fortunately, the man tugged on the leash and they resumed shuffling down the sidewalk. I allowed them to get a full three houses away before I broke into such a rollicking, howling laughter; I nearly fell out of the chair with my dizzying hysterics.

Gradually I began to regain some composure and I chuckled in between sips of coffee for several minutes, wiping off my face flooded by the tears of laughter that had me wide-awake in record time! The wildly amusing scene I'd coincidentally just had a front row center seat for, must be a good omen, I supposed. A brief moment later, like a bold colored cartoon spelling scene from Sesame Street, the following musical sentence danced through my brain: "**A...mused...** is **all**...ways...a good omen." I curiously contemplated this as I replayed in my mind the comical scene I'd just witnessed, and thoughtfully settled into a peacefully contented smile.

I hadn't been remotely impressed, let alone amused, at most of the scenes in my life for the past several years. I deserved this morning's laughter, even if it was at my own expense. Aside from the eyesore of my landscape-challenged property, the rocky terrain of my last broken heart had finally healed.

It had taken nearly two years for me to get over another "love of my life" who turned out to be just another faux dreamboat afloat in neurosis, idling in the **No Long Term Docking** zone. Not only had I paid an enormous emotional price for that ill fated foray, this time there had been an oil spill of debt for me to clean up. I'd been slowly climbing out of a fiscal fiasco for the past eight years, and after this last relationship I'd quit dating altogether. After more than 20 years of having my head and heart decimated by freakazoids of one sort or another, I'd pretty much had my fill of "falling" in love, the inevitable resounding thud was getting harder to handle, as I got older. Also, I had too many other personal projects and everyday issues to deal with that left little time for nurturing another relationship; I had barely enough time to properly take care of myself, let alone the needs and desires of someone else.

Instead of pursuing my lifelong search for a "soul mate", to my own astonishment, I've ended up thoroughly falling in love with my solitude! I've happily discovered how much I thoroughly enjoy being alone where I can write songs, listen to music, read a book, watch a movie, etc…etc… and do whatever I please, whenever I please, instead of being the personal custodian of somebody else's unusually warped emotional baggage, which in the past has always been my pattern. I've managed to attract the most unstable and neediest souls all my life and I'm **so** over it!!! I want to be somebody's equal partner, not their chosen all-purpose savior.

I'm sure the instability factors in my history of lovers is at least partially due to the volatile archetypes of love I witnessed in my parents, who were both physically violent and emotionally abusive to me and my four siblings, along with the same violence inflicted (in the name of God's love) by my 12 year Catholic school education, the numerous sexual molestations that traumatized my teen years, coupled with the lies, fantasies, myths, and half-truths of love that my ex-wife Megan perpetuated during our 18-year union. Primarily the purveyors of love in my life have been the most messed up people I've ever known. I've finally had enough of that neurotic breed. It's taken me a long time to discover, but I've definitively learned that I don't have to coddle somebody's fragile neurosis, or fulfill someone's dreams and desires just because they *need* or want me to. I'm no longer willing to be someone's co-dependence enabler.

I also have dreams and desires and I'm pursuing them instead.

There is a wide array of artistic, intellectual, and creative pursuits that fulfill me; so quite truthfully, I'm never bored or lonely. In addition, no one else is influencing, manipulating, or controlling what I should think, how I'm supposed to feel, or what I should be doing. My solitary ***refinement*** has been so liberating! I wholly embrace and cheerfully live the axiom: "I'm alone, but I'm not lonely."

My heart is still open to being in love, and of course I'd like to be in love, but if and when I take that step again, it will be with very deliberate and careful consideration, for I'm much more inclined to be protective of my heart these days. Moreover, while I know "falling in love" is one of the most pleasurable aspects of being human, I will not allow myself to blindly <u>fall</u> in love as I used to. I've lost the ***spirit of myself*** in those falls too many times already. One song lyric, among several others that I've written on this subject, clearly illustrates my resolve.

<u>If I'm Gonna Love Somebody</u>

If I'm gonna love somebody/it's gotta be somebody who/ won't manipulate or trick me into something I don't wanna do/Someone who will stand beside me when all the sunny skies turn grey/If I'm gonna love somebody I want a love that's true in every way/If I'm gonna love somebody/If I'm gonna love somebody

Some people love for money/material security/ and some people love some "body"/just because they feel lonely/Some people love the power an influential mate can bring/well even in its darkest hour/love shouldn't become an investment scheme/If I'm gonna love somebody/If I'm gonna love somebody

Now if I'm gonna love somebody/honestly and intimately/well then I'm gonna find somebody/who's intimately honest with me/Somebody I can believe in/someone who believes in me/If I'm gonna love somebody/oh that's the only way it's gonna be/Yeah if I'm gonna love somebody/ well that's the only way it's gonna be/If I'm gonna love somebody

    I continued sipping my coffee, with an element of pride for having finally regrouped my life, from the previous eight year cycle of chaos, into a comfortable balance, in the last year and a half.
    Emotionally my heart, soul, and spirit were fully recovered, and my credit cards were soon to be paid off for the first time in 15 years. Actually, now that I think about it, I was finally going to be debt free (aside from my home mortgage) for the first time since I was a teenager. I even had a couple of thousand dollars in a savings account earmarked for landscaping improvements.
    Also, and certainly **much** more critical to my emotions than a broken heart or financial instability, four years ago, I'd ***physically*** managed to escape being a lifetime paraplegic, due to a herniated disc pressing against my spinal cord, that within 24 hours, paralyzed me from the neck down.
    Thank God for Doctor Derek Duke! He is the same neurosurgeon who saved Roy Horn (of the Las Vegas duo: Siegfried and Roy) after his tiger attack. I am forever in debt to Dr. Duke for saving me as well.
    After the surgery, Dr. Duke told me that I was a "very lucky man."
    Groggy from pain meds, confined to a hospital bed, numb from neck to toe and wearing a catheter as well as a metal neck brace, I asked him how, in this condition, he figured I was "lucky."
    Dr. Duke explained that since it had taken several doctors nearly ten hours to correctly diagnose my condition, by the time he'd been called in to operate, there was only an hour or so window left to get the proper bone transplant and begin the operation before the damage was irreversible. I undoubtedly would've been in a wheelchair for the rest of my life.
    As things stood now, there was still a reasonable chance that I could walk again, and even possibly regain all of the normal

sensations of my body, but no concrete assurances of a full and complete recovery were forthcoming from the good doctor.

As if I wasn't stunned enough by my condition, his new matter of fact revelations shocked me even further!

I considered his daunting assessment briefly before I replied; "Well, if I'm going to be as numb as I am now for the rest of my life, I'm gonna have to get someone to drive me out to the cliffs up at Red Rock and push me over because I won't live like this.
Lucky that I still have a chance, duly noted, and thank you very much doctor for at least giving me the *possibility* to overcome this, but "lucky man" at this point, may be a bit premature."

He didn't disagree, he only said; "We'll have to wait and see."

On the tenth day of my hospital confinement, Dr. Duke and my posse of physical therapists scheduled me to go to a medical rehab facility for an undetermined length of time. I knew that if the disgusting hospital food didn't kill me first, the drab surroundings of illness and suffering would only fuel the depths of depression I was already feeling.

I earnestly pleaded with my team of specialists to let me go home and recover on my own. All of them were skeptical that I'd be able to manage. In the previous ten days I'd only regained some partial mobility, and it was still unclear whether or not my bone transplant would prove successful. My nerve endings had all been fried, leaving me unable to feel anything except a cold numbness.

Undeterred by my physical limitations, I didn't care about the new hardships I was going to face without nursing assistance, I was certain I'd manage fine on my own.

Some very dear friends kindly offered their beautiful home and caretaking assistance to me, and though I loved them all the more for their generous support, I appreciatively declined.

I knew myself better than anybody else, and just as cats retreat to somewhere private when they are sick, the "Leo" lion in me is no different. I don't want to be seen or cared for by others when I'm ill; I prefer to be left alone to heal. I know that I will do whatever it takes to set things right.

Perhaps my vain pride is responsible for that, or maybe it's just that I've always fully embraced the astrological motto of my sun sign Leo: "I Will."

My medical team questioned who would do my cooking, cleaning, grocery shopping, etc…and I easily answered "I will" to every dubious look cast my way.

Fortunately I was able to persuade them all that I was up to the challenge. After all, "Leo" is also the sign of: The Actor…

I continued to wear a neck brace for the next seven weeks and was on medical leave from work. It wasn't a work related injury so I wasn't entitled to any money from disability insurance, nor any federal, state, or local social assistance. I had absolutely no funds coming my way to cover any of my expenses.

I was so glad I'd started saving all of my spare change a couple of years before, in a large restaurant industry butter container. During my lengthy convalescence, I was of very little use other than taking care of everyday chores, doing my in home rehab exercises, and counting, labeling and rolling those accumulated years of spare change to pay all my bills.

Miraculously, like the Biblical story of loaves and fishes, there had been more than enough "spare" change to pay the mortgage, the minimums on my credit cards, and all of my other living expenses, until I finally returned to my restaurant server position at the Fiesta Hotel and Casino, in Henderson Nevada, eight weeks later.

Though I managed to make myself look, move, and *act* like there was nothing wrong, the facts remained that I was still physically numb from my neck to the tips of my toes.

My outside body temperature was normal, but inside it felt like my flesh was filled to capacity with ice water. Occasionally, to test the extent of my cold numbness, I'd place my hands on the searing hot marble counter top where the dinner plates of the restaurant sizzled. It never *felt* like my skin was burning, (though the charring of my skin evidenced otherwise) the insides of my hands remained frozen and unfeeling.

Italian Mothers Never Die

I now fully realize from neck to toe what a paralyzed person feels like; a human pin cushion.

That needles and pins numbness, wrapped up in a frozen mass of fabric, formerly identified as their own flesh, newly recognized as a shell of themselves, void of any sensation.

It was sixteen months before nearly all of my nerve endings were able to repair themselves. All of my normal sensations returned, except for the freezing numbness remaining in my hands.

Dr. Duke had patiently explained that the hands are comprised of the highest concentration of nerves to regenerate, and there were no guarantees on the horizon that mine would ever be physically normal again.

The doctor had been right about everything else. It turned out that I had been a "very lucky man" to make the miraculous recovery I'd made. I wasn't confined to a wheelchair for the rest of my life, nobody was called in to assist my suicide, and the only sensation lacking in my body was my sense of touch. Important as that fifth sense is, I'd learn to get by on the remaining four. To expect a more complete miracle seemed worse than ungrateful, it was downright greedy. Inwardly I was casually resigned to my cold and numb, hands of fate.

I'd stopped trying to play my double keyboard synthesizers after a year into my recovery. Granted, I'd only been a marginally talented pianist before my surgery, but I couldn't play at all anymore because my frozen hands couldn't *feel*.

There was no point in trying to play, it was far too frustrating watching my fingers flail along the light touch plastic keyboards, let alone subject myself to the mocking, discordant results of my clumsy and pathetic attempts. Any dreams I'd ever had about owning a white baby grand piano, were entirely pointless now.

Instead, I was on the verge of fulfilling my impatient neighbor's fantasies with shrubs, trees and flagstones. I laughed again at the memory of the Irish Setter, the old man's disgust, and his need for me to "shape up!" If he'd only known the truths of my life, perhaps he wouldn't have been so callously judgmental.

I became intrigued with the fact that I'd witnessed his hysterical outburst on the very day that I sat in this seldom used room, with the perfect vantage point, to specifically look at my yard and draw design plans, and how I had physically, spiritually, financially, and emotionally, *truly had* "shaped up!" and the ironic synchronicity of it all.

I was in the middle of drawing a Zodiac theme inspired garden when the phone rang; it was my forty-two year old "baby" brother.

After our conversation, my morning of free spirited laughter became a morning of agitated and worried silence.

Depression had long been a factor in our family DNA, but this time, my brother's was over the top. He'd hated his job for years, and who could blame him. As an Auto Repair Service Advisor who had to listen to every one's car problems, twelve hour days, 6 days a week, with most of the customers angry, rude, suspicious, and sometimes threatening, I would've *run myself over* years ago!

He'd been in the same business for the past seventeen years and bounced around auto dealerships trying to find the right fit, only to find that this career choice was never going to fit, and now he hated it so much he'd quit his latest job, with no plans to look for work of any kind.

He was completely broke and owed a mountain of debt. "I'm tired of dealing with life." he said; in a tone of finality that had rolled off of my own tongue enough times over the years to recognize the seriousness of his depressed state.

He'd called to request that I cash in his one fifth of the family portion of Bank Of New York stock, left to us as part of an inheritance by our mother, that I as Executor controlled, so that he could use the money to do a bit of traveling and have a good time before he enacted his: **Get out of emotional jail free** card, by killing himself.

Mamma Leone
(Italian translation: Mother Lion)

Of course I was hardly going to finance my beloved brother's lowly aspirations with mother's money, she would've found a way to reach down from the heavens and smack me upside the head! If I'd learned nothing else since my mother's passing 18 years ago, I'd most definitely learned that Italian mothers never die; they just get louder from the other side! This had been confirmed to me on numerous occasions since her death, so many times in fact that I completely feel much closer to her now, more than I ever did when she was alive.

It wasn't that she hadn't been a good mother, but we'd never been close. In retrospect I realize there were too many similarities between us to allow a comfortable mother/son bond.

Both astrologically "Leos' " (Leone's) like cats, we had fiery temperaments. Just as lions can be aloof to one another, if only to show who is boss, we could look at each other and know we'd better look away before some fire erupted.

Of course in the jungle it is the female lion that is the fiercest, and she was no exception. She, along with my critical and crabby "Cancer" (Sign of the Crab) Dad, could be both physically and emotionally terrifying! He, with his petty critical outbursts and out of control physical violence, and her, with her scathing verbal assaults, coupled with a backhand that could knock you into next month!

Astrologically speaking, their very specific combination of the elements, Fire and Water, and of the signs Cancer and Leo, are too opposite for comfort. This is not to say that all couples with this combination are doomed (too many other societal and astrological variables apply within the chart of each individual.) but my parents were constantly "steaming" over something and were certainly far from the Ward and June Cleaver examples of parenting that we idealized in prime time back in the early 1960's.

As a matter of fact, back in those monochrome days of television, there was a spin-off of the Tarzan genre, another "nature man" who in every episode wrestled with lions, alligators, tigers, cobras, and other fierce wild animals in the jungle, known as; <u>Bomba!</u> Among my three brothers and one sister, this was our secret nickname for mother.

Wide eyed terrified whispers of "Bomba!" would pass between us if we knew mother was in a bad mood, and all of us quickly scattered for cover! Just the sound of her slippers on the carpet as she came down the hall, could send shivers of absolute terror in our hearts!

Invariably I was the slowest trailing gazelle in the pack and she'd viciously pounce on me first. She might work her way up to my other siblings when she'd finished with me, but like the Leo lioness she was, her first gashes were the deepest.

I realize now that she was toughest on me out of her brood of five, because I was the most openly cat like curious, and sensitive; a very dangerous combination. She could see that I would be eaten alive by the world if she didn't toughen me up, and like a true lioness, she took her role of "Mother of the Pride" as a serious charge.

She wasn't an easy going woman in many ways, but she was so overbearing with me, that at age-15 I took a job bussing tables in a restaurant, in order to buy the proper house wares for my future apartment, so that when I was of legal age, I could finally get away from both of my parents. I knew early on that I was living in an emotional insane asylum and I'm sure I must be the only teenage male in history who ever started his own "hope chest"!

Little did I know then that I would escape from mom's lions den, and run straight into the dark confines of a much more ferocious, oppressive, and emotionally overbearing woman, a sly and cunning predator of Mary K Letourneau's ilk. (Three decades before Mary Kay Letourneau became an infamous household name.) My "Mary Kay" was named Megan and I ended up married to her for 16 years. More on that later...

I realize now, nearly twenty years after her death, that mom was way ahead of her time, and was a forerunner of "Tough Love" long before that concept became a media cliché.

Fortunately, my resentments against her were laid to rest many years before she died. We actually began forming a better relationship from the day I left home.

As I grew older, I looked upon her great multitude of accomplishments, in her all too short fifty six years of a very complicated, hard, and emotionally tragic life, with awe and utter admiration. I was now fully able to understand and appreciate her many triumphs, as well as the tragedies she suffered, because I'd garnered a similar list of my own. I'd since walked in her shoes of misery and heartache in many comparable ways, and when I looked in the mirror of my life, (aside from her violent temper) I found that I was more like her than anyone else in our family, and I'm certain my Dad and siblings would be the first to agree. However, mom had one special talent in our family that was distinctly hers and hers alone.

Mother possessed a keen psychic awareness while she was alive. She wasn't into any form of occult practices; those were strictly forbidden in her Italian Catholic mindset. She just *knew* things ahead of time. She would dream it, speak it, and it would happen. I'd witnessed her sixth sense awareness a few times, but none of her children possessed the same gift.

My three brothers and one sister had more of our fathers Dutch looks, staid sensibilities, and sports interests. Similar to my dad, they were better at concealing their true emotions and were much more secretive about whatever trouble they were up to on the sly.

I couldn't have been more different. Never afraid to open my big mouth and speak my truth; this made me the most difficult child to raise. I was always getting into some kind of trouble with my parents, or with the priests and nuns at school, because I was too brazenly defiant about expressing myself, and too careless about covering my tracks if I was up to no good. Lying was always a bad option for me because I could never effectively hide the truth; guilt was too easily written all over my face.

I was the obvious emotional "Deigo" of the clan, the only child who looked Italian, right down to mother's Roman nose. We were both "Leo's," with finicky gourmet appetites, fine clothing and furniture tastes, strongly opinionated with regard to political and social injustices, and a passionate love for most things artistic. (Like: Jackie Onassis, Sean Penn, Madonna, Julia Child, and Martha Stewart, all Leos.)

Unlike the staunchly silent-type, covert Dutch emotional makeup of my dad and siblings, like mom, I was the hand talking, in your face, easily emoting lion. I believed our similarities ended there. I didn't possess an ounce of mom's clairvoyance. At least, that's what I thought until the day before her funeral, when my sister Liz arrived at mother's apartment a few hours before the viewing service, carrying a bag of bagels and a large carton of chopped liver.

"O-weem-o-wey-o-weem-o-wey"
(The Lion Sleeps Tonight, but the lioness is wide awake!)

Like the proverbial Taurus Bull in a china shop, my sister Liz (a Taurus) burst into our mother's small apartment. "I don't know why I brought you this, but here!" She said as she rushed passed me, thrusting the deli items at me like she was handing off a football.

I didn't know why she'd brought them either as I'd never even eaten chopped liver in my life, nor was I sure I wanted to! I knew that mom liked chopped liver, though I'd never seen her buy or eat it, but she'd mentioned many times that it was one of her favorites. However, I not only had never tried it, I hadn't been able to eat anything at all for the previous two days, due to the shock of mother's unexpected death.

Suddenly, what looked and slightly smelled like mashed up Fancy Feast cat food, spread over the thick doughy bagels, held enormous appeal. Like a nervous cat, I sniffed, and then hesitantly took my first bite. It was delicious! Before I knew it I was ravaging the open faced sandwiches like a lion on a fresh kill, stopping briefly in between bites to wash them down with club soda. My three item meal not only tasted wonderful and satisfied me, it felt as though it was nourishing the very marrow of my soul and it became the only thing I wanted to eat, or would eat, over and over again, for the next 48 hours.

That same evening, my three brothers and I viewed mother's body in the chapel for the last time. She'd left specific instructions for a closed casket ceremony, and in a way, that was a shame because I have to say she looked more beautiful and radiantly peaceful than I'd seen her in years.

She was very elegantly dressed in a simple black gown and wore a large bulbous strand of bluish black freshwater pearls around her neck. She'd very conspicuously left this ensemble prominently on display in the closet of her bedroom. Obviously she'd known she was going to die, (She told me she'd dreamt her death, two months ***before she'd been diagnosed*** with cancer, five months ago.) but the last time we'd spoken, she assured me that the doctors said she had successfully battled the cancer into remission. Only a week after she'd told me this, she was gone.

Kneeling before her coffin, I looked at her radiant glow of serenity and thought to myself; "I sure hope its better on the *Other Side* of life mom because you certainly deserved better than you got on this side."

I stayed there for a few minutes before my three brothers, Jim, Kevin and Tony, each took their turns. My sister Liz declined the viewing all together, saying it was too much for her to deal with.

After we'd said our goodbyes, my brothers and I started to file out of the chapel. The mortician asked us before closing the casket: "Do you boys know that these black pearls are genuine and are worth a lot of money?"

We honestly didn't have a clue about their value, but we all agreed instantly that we wanted them to remain with her.

The mortician's face blanched slightly as he said; "Well, alright."

His tone suggested that we were very foolish to bury such expensive gems. My brothers and I knew that we were doing it because we loved her, and we couldn't have cared less about their monetary value. We had lost her, and no precious pearls of any kind would be worth more than having her still with us. The pearls were hers in life; they belonged with her for eternity. She had given us the pearls of her wisdom and love in our lives, the very best she knew how, and that was enough.

Lost in our grief, my brothers and I continued to solemnly file out of the chapel, when suddenly mothers' distinct and unmistakable voice entered my head; *"Marc Anthony! Get back here and make sure this guy locks the casket!"*

Before I had even a moment to digest this, in a very "Stepford" mode, I spun around and went back up the aisle to the casket as the mortician clicked the lid closed.

I looked him directly in the eyes and said, "Is there any way this casket can be re-opened?"

His brown eyes mirrored mine as he replied, "Not without a court order."

Using my mother's fiercest tone, as well as one of her direct quotes, I felt her life force energy barreling through me as I replied; *"I'll advise you to remember that!"*

I could feel her lioness eyes boring through mine into his as I spoke, and I saw him quiver. I knew the fear of my mother had seized him, and I left him standing there trying to control his now obvious trembling.

I walked away quickly trying to catch up with my brothers, somewhat shaken from the experience of feeling her presence and hearing her voice, telling myself that what had just happened, *did not just happen*, and instantly put it out of my mind. It was a foolish assumption on my part to think this message from her was to be an isolated, freak incident. Or, to use an expression she often used when making a point; *"This ain't no chopped liver baby!"*

Actually, her afterlife connections *had begun* with chopped liver, but it was only the very beginning of her communications. They were to become stronger, and more frequent, in the coming months and years.

"ice…ice…ice…ice"
(From Yoko Ono's 1981 Grammy Nominated song: Walking On Thin Ice)

In 1986 I was living in rural Oregon, on the verge of ending my then 14 year marriage, when my mom died. The call came a few minutes after midnight on October 1st. My wife Megan and I were still up, as September 30th was her forty-second birthday, and I'd put aside our problematic marriage blues, in order to give her a happy occasion. We'd just finished having cake and ice cream when the phone rang.

Shortly after I'd told Megan the sad news, true to her "it's all about me" attitude, she replied; "This means that *my* birthday will always be attached to sadness from now on!"

She pouted her "Comfort me!" face, with the proper swell of tear welling eyes, which had been a reliable staple in her vast arsenal of manipulating emotional torrents throughout our marriage. I had no strength or desire to point out her selfish insensitivity, and gave her the worn Pavlovian response of dogged reassurance that she required.

I find it ironic that mother died minutes after my wife's birthday, for though Megan was fighting hard to keep our marriage from falling apart, I knew in my heart that it was also dead. We'd managed to carry on the illusion that our marriage might be saved, for the next several months, as I dealt with the deluge of hospital and personal paperwork that comprised mother's estate issues. I had no strength to argue with Megan during this time, the wind had been knocked out of me by mother's unexpected death and so our marriage issues simmered on the back burner.

In April of 1987, seven months after mom's death, I needed a break from *everything* in my life and decided to go to New York City to visit a friend who'd recently moved there.

I'd been to New York state twice in my life; once in 1965 when my Dutch Grandfather flew our entire family to Long Island for a family reunion.

It was my first time on a plane, and I was hoping we would be landing on the same tarmac as The Beatles. They were arriving in New York on the same day as we were, for their first concert at Shea Stadium on August 15, 1965, the day before my 11th birthday.

My parents gave me my gift early in order to keep me occupied on the plane. I remember getting a Timex wristwatch with the new stainless steel "twist o' flex" band, and proudly showing it off to all the stewardesses who in those days, looked more like fashion models. Being a stewardess was considered a glamorous career then, and you had to be a young and beautiful single woman to be accepted for the "exciting and rewarding" position. Certainly *those* times have changed!

Anyway, we flew across the country on American Airlines. In those days it was more like a classy, important social event, requiring everyone on the plane to dress up as if they were going to church or out to dinner.

Upon our arrival, our family went from the recently named J.F.K. Airport, directly to Long Island, where we stayed in a motel for a week.

We ventured out for several occasions including the 1964/1965 Worlds Fair in Queens, a trip to New Jersey where we had our very first McDonalds hamburgers, and of course the Family Reunion at my Dutch Grandparents.

We never spent any time in New York City on our vacation, and I was very disappointed that I didn't even get a glimpse of The Beatles, but the experience remains a happy memory.

The second time I went to New York was in August of 1970, without my family.

I'd just turned 16 and was returning from a summer in Europe where I'd traveled with 200 other high school kids, chaperoned by priests and nuns, paid for with a years worth of money I'd earned, and wanted to buy a car with, but at mother's express demand, was spent instead on this summer excursion.

I can still recall her prophetic words: "You will have *plenty* of chances to buy a car in your life, but you *may never* have the opportunity to go to Europe again, so just forget about the car Mister!"

Of course she was right; I've had nearly a dozen cars since then, but I haven't returned to Europe!

I stopped in New York on my way back, and again went out to Long Island to spend a week with my relatives, before finally returning home to Southern California.

Life had been more idyllic in those days. Though I was living in an oppressive, volatile environment with my parents and attending an equally oppressive, and violently disciplined Catholic high school, I still had hopes for a brighter future.

The "Summer of Love" had happened last year, and while I never hung around with the "hippies" I'd managed to incorporate their message of Peace and Love firmly into my consciousness, as well as my heart and soul.

The Beatles had been my spiritual guru's when I wasn't being violently disciplined into embracing my Catholicism, and their songs of love made more sense than the "Love of God" the clergy beat into me.

Somehow amid the chaos of my home and school life, I truly lived and believed The Beatles lyrical sentiments of: <u>All You Need Is Love.</u>

That innocent era was now long gone, the mood and "movement" of the mid-eighties was All You Need Is More Money, and instead of marijuana, apparently the new "yuppie" mantra was: "Things go better with Coke." (And I emphatically don't mean the soft drink!)

I never got hooked into this greedy, cocaine fueled movement, it had nothing of honorable substance to offer, but I was still trying to define my place in this world, one where I could be myself. A place where I felt free to live my life on my own terms, without someone or some religion deciding what was best for me. I'd allowed myself to be held captive for most of my life by the judgments and dictums of others, and it had gotten me nowhere.

Instead, I was consumed in depression by my unhappy marriage, my shock and grief over mother's recent death, and the avalanche of paperwork I'd been wading through for the past seven months to settle her affairs. I really began to feel that the sign **Dead End**, that stood at the beginning of the street Megan and I were living on, (ironically named: Cemetery Hill Road) was the only metaphor suitable for my state of mind.

I was looking forward to leaving it all behind. This would be the first time I would be staying in Manhattan instead of the suburbs of Long Island, and the constant atmosphere of my stressed out life in Oregon would not be missed.

I joked with my New York City friend Bill over the phone that we'd have to go and say hello to Yoko Ono as soon as I arrived.

Having been a lifelong Beatle fan, and most likely still *the* most ardent Yoko Ono supporter, (three decades before she was considered "hip") meeting her was an obvious pipe dream that Bill and I enjoyed laughing over. We giddily made up a list of questions to ask her, knowing full well it was nothing more than a frivolous endeavor.

Imagine
(Words and music by: John Lennon and Yoko Ono)

I met Bill and his room mate Dan at La Guardia airport and from there we dropped my bags off at their apartment in Columbus Circle.

The three of us then jumped on the subway and headed straight for 72nd street and Central Park West, where Yoko lives at The Dakota.

I posed as Bill took pictures of me in front of the famous landmark building where the classic movie Rosemary's Baby had been filmed.

We loitered for a few minutes in the cold and dark cavernous entryway where John Lennon had been murdered.

Bill, Dan and I waved up at the gothic windows that graced the building, laughing at our utterly ridiculous and impossible hope of Yoko seeing us, and waving back.

Afterwards, we went across the street to Central Park, entered Strawberry Fields, and took pictures of the black and white tiled, Italian crafted Imagine mosaic, a dedication plaque mounted on stone, and the rest of the tranquil surroundings.

We continued sauntering through the park until we crossed over into the city at Fifth Avenue, with its spotless sidewalks and high end shops. Finely tailored men and designer clad women mixed easily with the rest of the sidewalk parade. There were young mothers and nannies with strollers, alongside a roaming gaggle of punk rock musicians, sidewalk briefcase vendors selling faux Gucci and Rolex watches, smartly uniformed doormen hailing taxicabs, street corner three card Monty hustlers and a slew of "yuppie" business men/women looking important as they quickly moved up and down the avenue.

When I'd been to Europe as a teen, I was too young to appreciate or even notice the diverse spiritual energies of Paris, London or Rome.

I couldn't help noticing the energies here, they were reflecting off of the faces of people and storefront windows as we walked along upper Fifth Avenue.

It seemed as though I'd stepped out of the black and white movie of my dreary Oregon life and into a world bursting with color. For the first time in nearly two decades I felt truly alive!

After a few blocks we came upon a Psychic shop and for the fun of it, I decided to go in. The elegantly dressed woman said she couldn't read for me at the moment, but to come back the next day at 9am. I made the appointment, and rejoined Bill and Dan waiting for me on the sidewalk. We continued to walk down Fifth Avenue until we ended up on 34th street, where hanging above the sidewalk was a sign for an antique store with one word on it: "**Joia**".

My mother's first name was Joia, the Italian word for joy. Prior to this moment, I'd never seen that word in print anywhere other than in mother's personal papers. I *had* to be photographed beneath it.

Bill and I were still talking about strange it was to see such a sign when we rounded a corner, and saw the green and white block lettered sign for the department store: Gimbel's.

I vaguely recalled mother saying that she worked there in her youth, as both of my parents were native New Yorkers. I insisted we go inside to check out the store.

Bill, Dan, and I, walked in the lobby door and got on the first escalator in our path. We resumed talking about how weird it was to see my mom's name on the antique store sign and when we got to the top of the escalator, we were greeted by a large neon sign over a ladies cosmetics counter that simply read; **Barone**.

I slid off the escalator and stopped dead in my tracks.

"That's mother's maiden name!" I nearly shouted, incredulously.

"Now that *is* bizarre!" Bill chimed in.

"Welcome to New York!" We said simultaneously to each other, laughing.

I wanted a picture but was out of film. I'd already used up the twelve shots on the **Joia** sign, 5th Avenue, The Dakota, and Strawberry Fields.

I bought more film while we were in Gimbel's but forgot to go back to the **Barone** counter. After we shopped for a while, we were ready to go somewhere for dinner.

We resumed walking along 34th street and I had to make a call so I ducked into a phone booth. I was busy talking away to my Aunt Marilyn in Long Island, making plans for a visit later in the week.

Suddenly, Bill was tapping hard on the glass booth and was frantically pointing at something, I couldn't tell what because the sidewalk was bustling with people.

I was miming "What?" at his excited pointing and couldn't for the life of me figure out what had him so animated.

I finished the call, and swinging open the booth door I said; "What on earth were you pointing at?"

He practically shouted, "Did you see the priest walking by?!"

Puzzled, I replied, "Priest? What priest?"

"The priest who looked exactly like your mom!" he bellowed.

"What do you mean?" I pressed.

"I swear to God Marc, there was a priest walking by while you were on the phone and he looked *exactly* like your mom! Right down to the beauty mark on her lip!!! Didn't you see him?!"

Further confused, I replied, "No, I couldn't figure out *what* you were pointing at! Mother? As a priest? That *is* scary!!! But it would be just like her to masquerade as a priest on the streets of New York where she knows she'd blend right in! She already posted **Joia Barone** for us; she just hadn't gotten around to explaining that she'd returned as a priest!!!" I explained jokingly.

Bill, Dan, and I laughed the three "signs" off as merely funny coincidences. It was just the universes way of saying: "Welcome to the Big Apple!"

The following morning, I left Bill and Dan's apartment and headed for the Fifth Avenue psychic. I arrived at five minutes to nine. I got a cup of coffee from the sidewalk vendor and sat on the stoop outside of her locked office door. I was glad she hadn't yet arrived; I still hadn't concretely formed the questions I was going to ask her. I had so many! Where would I begin? But then, I figured if she really was psychic, she would already know my questions and give me the answers.

Bill had asked me to bring some of my song lyrics upon my visit to New York, he believed they were worthy of being published.

This morning he'd suggested I bring them to the psychic, and ask her what publisher I should bring them to. I thought that was a good idea, so I'd brought a collection of fifty pieces that I hoped were good enough.

I was leafing through them, waiting for her arrival. Fifteen minutes later she still hadn't shown up, and though I was getting impatient, I was determined to wait for my reading. I began reminiscing about the only time I'd ever been to a psychic before.

The year was 1969; I was 15 years old and a busboy at Sir Georges Smorgasbord in Southern California.

Diana, a very beautiful waitress, wanted to visit a psychic and had taken me with her one afternoon to a dirty white 1950's travel trailer, parked on a small concrete slab, in a dirt yard surrounded by a chain link fence, in the middle of nowhere.

There were several large dogs in the yard and the rusted door of the trailer was wide open. The dogs were barking and growling at us and I was hesitant to open the gate. I hadn't come because I believed in psychics; I barely knew what a psychic was. I'd come only because Diana wanted a reading, and I wanted to be with her wherever she wanted to go!

Now I wasn't so sure. The dilapidated trailer and its surroundings were scary enough; I certainly didn't want to be devoured by dogs!

An old haggard looking woman wearing a tattered 1960's "mod" housedress appeared at the dirty trailer door. She had two cans of dog food that she quickly shook, and the large rounds of brown solidified glop shot out of the cans and onto the pavement. The dogs immediately rushed to the food and the old woman, in a weak and cragged voice said; "Come on now children, come quickly!"

I felt like Diana and I were Hansel and Gretal rushing into the witch's hovel! Inside the cramped 8x10 trailer, the old woman sat behind a rickety rusting fold out metal counter. Diana and I sat on two small stools, and the witchy looking woman shuffled some ordinary playing cards and proceeded to "read" Diana.

I don't remember hearing anything she said to Diana, I was too petrified of the large drooling dogs who kept sticking their noses into my lap as I sat by the open door. Thankfully the old woman kept hurtling cans of dog food past me and the dogs would excitedly retreat momentarily.

The only thing I can recall about my reading was that the old woman squawked like a crow at me; "Paaaa-perwawk! Paaaaaaa-perwawk! I see you surrounded by lots of paaaa-perwawk! Why so much paaa-perwawk for such a young child?!"

I was too terrified of the dogs to answer her, but I remember thinking: "Paperwork? What paperwork? Aside from my high school homework I don't have much paperwork and besides, you're the "psychic" you tell me!" But, I really didn't believe or care what she had to say, and I paid her no mind. I just wanted to get the hell out of there alive!

Now, seventeen years later I was sitting on the stoop outside the New York City psychic's office, chuckling over the vivid memory, very glad that no cans of dog food were flying past my face onto Fifth Avenue.

I was thinking of the many years that had since past, and how completely accurate the dog food slinging psychic had been. My life since seeing her certainly had developed into an endless stream of "paaa-perwawk."

I was still recalling the crow-like squawking of the psychic's prediction, looking at the bundle of lyrics, my current "paaa-perwawk!" Thinking of the mountain of paperwork I'd been wading through since mother's death.

Suddenly, a crow's cawing caught my attention. I smiled to myself as I followed the reverberating echo of it's squawking to a building it was perched on across the street. It sounded like it was cawing: "Paaa-perwawk! Paaa-perwawk!!!"

This continued for a few minutes and as the crow eventually quieted down, a distant, gentle, soft, and unrecognizable voice began stirring inside me. The ethereal voice said; *"It's time to go to Yoko's".*

Unaccustomed to voices other than my own speaking from within, I was startled. I found myself quite inexplicably answering back: "Go to Yoko's? For what? I went there yesterday and already got the pictures I wanted."

My statement shut the faint voice within me up for a moment, and I continued thinking hard about my questions for the psychic. I was right in the middle of forming another question when the voice returned, an octave louder: ***"It's time to go to Yoko's".***

"For what!?" I countered under my breath impatiently.

Up until this point, I'd not heard from mom since the incident regarding her pearls at her funeral, and that had been seven months ago. I'd managed to dismiss it at the time, but this time, there was no denying it when her voice unmistakably vibrated within me, dripping with her special tone of sarcasm: ***"How psychic could this woman possibly be, she's a half hour late! It's time to go to Yoko's!"***

Before I realized how strange it should seem that I was hearing mother's voice, I vehemently argued back: "But *I don't want* to go to Yoko's! There's ***no*** reason for me to go there, I got the pictures I wanted yesterday! Besides, I don't have time and ..."

I continued arguing as I mechanically rose from the stoop and started walking towards the park. I literally felt like there was something *forcing* me to walk, and I was *trying* to make myself stop, turn around, and return to the psychic's storefront, but I couldn't!

As I continued through the park, I was getting all worked up, asking myself; "Why am I doing this? I don't want to do this! I've already been to Yoko's! I'm not even sure **how to get there!** I've been in the city less than 24 hours! I don't even know my way around! What if I'm walking completely in the wrong direction?!! Why the *hell* am I doing this at all???!!!"

Mom's voice remained silent during my tirade and I continued bitterly wailing against my actions until twenty minutes later, I found myself exiting the park and coming to a stop on 72nd street, in front of The Dakota.

"I'm here! *Now what?!*" I angrily said in a low voice.

Patiently sweet, mom's voice filled my head, and said; **"Well honey, for starters, you could put some film in the camera."**

"*Fine!!!*" I, by now definitely pissed off, shot back.

I crouched down on the sidewalk, opened the case, and slid the Polaroid film into the camera. I'd just clicked the camera closed, it started whining and whirring noisily, when I noticed out of the corner of my eyes, a small pair of baby blue tennis shoes walking by, inches from my sidewalk crouching position.

I looked up to see Yoko Ono's face looking over her shoulder at me.

Instantly I stood up, looked into those famous sunglasses, and was only able to silently mouth the word: "Please?"

She smiled shyly and said; "Okay."

Jauntily she stepped up on to the raised sidewalk that bordered the building, smiled, and I snapped the shot.

"Thank you!" I gushed.

"You're welcome." she replied still smiling, and started walking away.

I stood in awestruck abandon...frozen. I scarcely assimilated what had just happened as I stood watching Yoko reach the nearby corner, where she met up with a tall, stout, semi-uniformed woman whom I assumed was a bodyguard.

Dumbstruck, I continued watching them as they began walking

towards 73rd street.

Abruptly a man and woman were standing in front of me and the man said to his companion: "Hey isn't that Yoko Ono? Honey, get her picture!" His lady friend replied: "She's moving too fast, it's too late for a picture!" The man responded: "Follow her!" But they both continued to stand in front of me, partially blocking my view.

Up until that moment I'd remained cemented in my spot, but the minute the man said: "Follow her!" I found myself moving towards the corner to cross the street, and in an instant I was standing at the tree lined park entrance of Strawberry Fields.

I wasn't following Yoko; she and the bodyguard were walking up Central Park West, towards 73rd street, *away* from the park entrance.

Suddenly, they both made a u-turn on the sidewalk and started walking towards me.

I was petrified! Afraid that Yoko would think I was some weirdo stalking her. I hadn't planned on her turning around, but in a few moments she was an arms length away, looking directly at me again.

"I love you Yoko." I heard myself say.

"Thank you." she replied with a sincere smile as she walked into the park.

I couldn't resist getting another picture of her; walking past the Strawberry Fields sign five feet between us, but the second the noisy Polaroid began to whine, I became embarrassed because I knew she realized I'd just photographed her back.

I remained steadfast in my spot as I watched her stroll with her bodyguard into the park.

A few yards in, they paused to look at the large round, black and white tiled <u>Imagine</u> mosaic that is embedded into the pavement, where flowers, incense, and burning votive candles scented the air. They stood there for a few moments, talking and pointing at a picture of John that was wreathed in roses, and then slowly continued walking along the path, leading up a gentle slope where Yoko stopped in front of a large rock that bore a bronze plaque of the names of 211 nations who contributed trees and shrubs to the green landscape of Strawberry Fields. The plaque designated this portion of the park as a: "Garden of Peace."

Her bodyguard had wandered out of sight, and I found myself mesmerized by Yoko's prayer like stillness. I wanted so badly to take another picture but I knew it would disturb her very obvious meditative state.

I realized I'd walked further into the park unconsciously, and then, mom's voice returned: *"Take the picture! It's too beautiful of a moment not to capture! Take the picture!"*

I firmly resisted, answering back in my head: "I can't take another one! It's so rude! I'm gonna piss her off if I keep this up!"

My argument with mom continued briefly, and then, the moment was over. Yoko slowly and thoughtfully started to walk away.

I began silently chastising myself for missing the picture perfect photo op, when suddenly Yoko turned around and returned to the same spot, same stance, as if she knew I'd missed the perfect shot, and mom's voice commanded: *"Take the picture!!!"*

Click…phhhsssstt…ker-thunk…whirrrrrrrrrr. Yoko clearly was disturbed by the noise and quickly walked away. I remained immobilized, in stark, astonished embarrassment.

I saw her bodyguard rejoin her on the path as they continued further into the park. I knew I should turn around and go the other way, they were certain to think I was a stalker if I continued following them. They turned a corner and were out of my sight.

I wanted to walk away but found myself going in their direction instead. I purposely let them get a long distance ahead of me. I walked very slowly because I really was trying hard not to follow them, when gradually I found myself engulfed by a huge swarm of middle school students who'd come up behind me on the path.

Suddenly I was forced into walking faster as the racing crowd of 100 or more kids swept me into their motion. Caught up in the stampede of their tennis shoes, and blue plaid school uniforms, they forced me in the center of their crowd, to follow. I couldn't move left or right, only forward. If I'd stopped I'd have been

Italian Mothers Never Die

trampled. It was ludicrous! I started laughing at the preposterousness of my speeding captivity! All of us raced in the same direction as Yoko but over the blond, black, brown and red headed bouncing teens, I'd completely lost sight of her. I felt like I was trapped on a runaway train, rollicking along the tree and shrubbery lined path, until we came to a clearing, where the kids swarmed to the right, and as I struggled to stay on the path, I heard several kids holler: "Hi Yoko! Hi Yoko!!! We love you Yoko!!!"

Yoko, standing just a few yards away replied with a broad smiling: "Thank you!!! I love you too!!!"

The kids trailed away and Yoko, her bodyguard and I, were near Bethesda fountain, the very large Angel fountain depicted in so many movies with Central Park as the backdrop. I was completely shocked to see them; they seemed equally surprised to see me.

Embarrassed to be facing her again I blurted; "I'm so sorry if I'm disturbing you, I really didn't mean to follow you, and yet here I am again! I'm so sorry!"

Yoko smiled and said; "Is there something you want?"

In a nanosecond, before I had a chance to consider her question, I excitedly exclaimed; "Yes! I'd love to have a picture *with* you!!!"

"Well, alright then." she graciously replied.

I thrust the camera into the bodyguard's hands, and over excitedly started rattling away: "Yoko, I've got to tell you *thank you* for everything your music has given me!!! I have all of your albums; With John and without him! Your last song with John, Walking On Thin Ice is one of my all time favorites!!! I was so upset that you lost the Best Female Rock Vocal Performance Grammy for it to Pat Benetar in 1981!!!

Yoko's smile grew wider as I prattled on, and I could clearly see through her light tinted glasses, her eyes were smiling too.

Her bodyguard interrupted my effusive babbling; "How do you operate this thing?"

"Oh, that's right, you're really a photographer don't you know?" Yoko joked to the puzzled faced bodyguard.

I quickly showed the bodyguard how to operate the ancient Polaroid, and returned to Yoko for the pose.

"May I put my arm around you?" I reverently asked.

"Yes, that's fine." she said with a twinkle in her voice.

As we stood there, in that moment, shivering goose bumps covered my flesh. I continued telling her how much I admired her music, stage work, and films. I was looking directly into her eyes and it was obvious to me that she hadn't expected to hear such high praise for **her** work. Certainly she was used to hearing accolades for John Lennon's, but not hers.

The bodyguard interrupted my praise: "Ready?"

Yoko and I turned and faced the camera, the bodyguard snapped the shot.

As I released her, I said; "Thank you so much!!! I won't bother you anymore I promise!!!"

"You're welcome, and thank you too!" Yoko said smiling as the bodyguard handed me my camera, and the two of them continued on their way.

I stood there, trembling, holding the film in my hand as it developed into the moment of clarity that had just been captured. Me with my arm around Yoko, both smiling, and through her large light shaded glasses, the camera had captured her smiling eyes as well.

I could scarcely believe what had just happened. In shocked amazement I stood staring at the photo, as tears of joy began streaming down my face.

"Now aren't you glad you listened to me?" Moms comforting voice ethereally returned.

"Yes! Yes I'm glad! Thank you! Thank you!" I said out loud before I realized I was not only answering her, but I was accepting her presence as *real*, for the very first time.

The funny thing was that it didn't feel strange that I was talking back, it felt entirely appropriate. That, in and of itself *should've* seemed strange, and it might have under more normal circumstances, but what had just transpired in the past hour was *far* from normal! Paranormal? Evidently! Normal? No.

Mom didn't say anything more, but I had a crystal clear image of her in my mind, wearing a very wide, satisfied smile. The image lived and breathed her for a long moment before it faded, and I realized I was standing in the park, with tears streaming down my face.

The focus of the photograph came back into blurry view. My smiling face remained covered with tears as I walked out of the park, leaned against a building and shivered with goose bumps as the springtime sun shone warmly upon me. I stood there laughing at the absurdity of it all. How I'd fought against mother's prodding in the beginning, and argued against her all the way from the Fifth Avenue psychic's office to The Dakota, and how ultimately it had led me to fulfill a dream I'd previously thought was not only ridiculous, but completely impossible!

A phrase mom used to say suddenly came to mind: "Nothing is impossible!!! Improbable perhaps...but *not* impossible!"

Considering all that had happened in the less than twenty-four hours since my arrival in New York City, I was inclined to agree. I didn't consider how that very wise maxim of hers was only *just beginning* to reveal its true unlimited potential but three days later, the "improbable but not impossible" happened again.

"Root beer, through a straw, no ice…ice…ice"
(Joia Barone)

Mark Twain once said: "Houseguests are like fish, after three days they begin to stink."

Possessing the sensitivity of that logic, I decided to spend a couple of nights in a hotel, in order to give Bill and Dan their small apartment space back, houseguest free.

We made plans to meet up that night for dinner as I got into a cab at Columbus Circle.

I'd no sooner checked in to my hotel room, when I started unpacking and realized that my wallet was missing! I hadn't needed it at the check in desk and the last time I'd used it was when I paid the cab driver.

Had it fallen silently out of my pocket it onto the sidewalk? Did I leave it in on the seat of the cab? Had I absent-mindedly stuffed it into my luggage, jacket, or briefcase?

Frantically I started searching through my blazer pockets; nothing but a Chap Stick, some cash, my Walkman, and a bag of cashews.

I emptied the contents of my briefcase on the desk; cassette tapes, cigarettes, some paperwork, but no wallet.

Tearing open my suitcase, I began whining to myself aloud: "Where is it... Where is it??!!"

I started shaking out my clothes and tossing them on the bed; still no wallet!

Splashing the clattering collection of my grooming kit across the floor, getting more and more anxious by the minute, I started distractedly praying a prayer I'd known since childhood: "Dear Saint Anthony please come around, something's lost that must be found!"

I'd always felt connected to this verse, partially because my middle name is Anthony, but more importantly, whenever I lost something and said the prayer, I'd *find* whatever I'd been looking for within a few minutes.

I began consciously chanting the prayer fervently. Rummaging through my belongings for the third time, I was near tears as I continued whining and begging: "Saint Anthony *please* come around..."

Engulfed in an unrelenting manic panic, in the middle of turning everything inside out and upside down yet *again*; mom's faint voice stirred within me: ***"Calm down son, you're going to get your wallet back tomorrow."***

I instantly stopped in my tracks, shocked at the absurd dialogue that had just invaded my fear crazed spirit.

"Ha! That's a *good* one!" I sarcastically said out loud. "I'm going to get it back tomorrow? Yeah, right!!! ***That's*** really gonna happen!!!

Apparently I've not only lost my wallet, now I'm losing my mind!!!" I sneered back at her.

The vibration of her voice stirred louder within me: ***"Marc, calm down! You're going to make yourself sick if you don't!!! You need to go eat something before your stomach does that thing..."***

I knew what "that thing" was. For the past ten years I'd suffered with a chronic stomach ailment that cropped up at the most unexpected moments. A knotting and twisting, debilitating torturous stomach cramping would overtake me into such spasms of excruciating pain; I would be reduced to being doubled over on my hands and knees on the floor, completely unable to stand firmly, lie down, or be touched by anyone and barely able to walk.

I'd be petrified to eat anything but chicken broth, for an average duration of 72 hours, until finally the gut wrenching agony would gradually begin to subside.

I'd seen a country bumpkin doctor in Oregon who limply diagnosed my condition as "Colic" which by its very definition means: abdominal pain. (Duh, *yeah*…) "That's why I'm here doctor…and besides, I thought only babies and horses got colic…"

His prescription was: "Try and ride it out."

Obviously he hadn't seen the monsters birth in the movie: Alien!

"Ride it out?" I'm spawning a demon from hell in my gut and he wants me to "ride it out"?

As I limped out of his office I thought to myself: "Thanks for nothing Doc!"

Elsewhere I had the upper G.I. series to search for an ulcer or gall stones, but the tests proved negative.

I'd tried antacids, club soda, 7-Up, ginger ale, Metamucil, hot tea and prayer, but nothing could turn me loose from the torturous agony once it took hold.

Finally one doctor prescribed Bentyl, a stomach relaxant that proved to be of no relief whatsoever during my episodes. I would take far more than the prescribed amount, and still be writhing in agony on the floor. Several times I hoped I'd overdose on the pills, just to never experience such pain again, but I'd always live through it, and would return to normal painfully slow, exhausted from the outbreak.

Mother had worked in a hospital for the last 14 years of her life, and with all of the cutting edge medical knowledge at her disposal; even she was unable to discover any sufficient diagnosis or medication to cure my symptoms.

Now she'd just loudly interrupted my panic attack to sell me the preposterous hope of somehow getting my wallet back "tomorrow" as well as forewarning me of stomach trouble?

"Great! I don't have enough problems at the moment and now you're gonna threaten me with illness?!" I despairingly moaned back at her.

Her reply was immediate, sternly she echoed within me: ***"I'm not threatening you, I'm informing you! If you don't go get something to eat, you won't be able to go out tonight with your friends. Stop this nonsense; it's only making you crazy! Go get something to eat and stop worrying, you're going to get your wallet back tomorrow."***

"Fine! Whatever!" I spat out loud in a huff. I'd had enough of this fevered frenzy, this tumultuous activity had garnered nothing but anger, confusion and worry. The last thing I needed was my stomach demon from hell.

I called American Express to cancel my travelers checks. Thank God I still had some cash.

Disgustedly I abandoned my trashed hotel room and ran downstairs to the sidewalk. There was a Deli directly across the street and I angrily swung the door open. The large menu board stared me in the face upon entering. The first words I saw were: Chopped Liver on Bagel $2.25

"Fine!!! Chopped Liver it is!" I seethed under my breath. I hadn't eaten, or even thought of chopped liver since mother's funeral, and I certainly wasn't craving it now, it just seemed like the right choice.

I went to the beverage case and grabbed a club soda. "Are ya happy now ma?!" I sarcastically said in my head.

"You'll thank me later..." She responded and quickly trailed off.

Back in my hotel room, I ate the sandwich as I cleaned up the mess I'd made. Afterward, I took a nap, trying to sleep away my worried agitation, and fitfully slept until it was time to get ready to meet my friends for dinner.

As I glumly showered, the whole trauma replayed itself over and over in my head, and I scoffed at the whole idea that I would somehow, by some miracle, be getting my wallet back *"tomorrow."* This was New York City! I had to be realistic; it was not some cornfield town in Oregon that I was used to. Fat chance some stranger would find my wallet and return it!

I'd clearly been feeding myself some delusional and wishful thinking.

As for the chopped liver saving me from my stomach cramps, that was apparently a self imposed ruse as well. I could feel the slight beginnings of the demonic torture starting to rumble.

I gulped down three Bentyls and managed to go out to dinner with my friends, but stuck with chicken broth and club soda for my meal. I kept pretending to myself that I was keeping the beginnings of my cramps at bay, when after two hours of building physical anguish and shifting uncomfortably in my chair, I realized I'd better get back to my hotel before the ravaging illness arrived at full tilt.

I bid my friends goodnight, and hailed a cab. On the ride home, I found myself absentmindedly praying to my mom.

"Please, I can't go through this right now! Tell me what to do! I need an answer!"

The knotting and twisting had started churning in earnest; I was already doubling over as the cab bounced up and down on the pot holed Manhattan streets.

By the time we stopped in front of my hotel, I knew it was too late; the gut wrenching pain had taken over. I trembled as I paid the cab fare, lurching out of the car as if I'd been shot. Through the dizzying torment, the message from her came through loud and clear: ***"Root beer! Through a straw! No ice...ice...ice...ice..."*** She faded into silence.

I didn't have the strength to argue. I stumbled on the sidewalk into the deli, grabbed two bottled root beers and straws.

On my way back to the hotel I was forced to stop and painfully lean against various walls and railings, moaning in excruciating pain, before I finally reached my room, where I wearily fell to my hands and knees on the floor in agony, and began to sip the root beer.

Though I thought I must be crazy to think root beer was going to cure a decade long battle, one that emergency rooms, medications, and doctors had failed to salvage me from, I resignedly continued sipping. I managed to slowly consume one bottle, and it was forcing me to belch, which only hurt *more* as I wrestled with the torture overtaking my body.

Thirty minutes later, I was half way through the next bottle, when much to my great astonishment, the sharp knife twisting pain peaked, then released, and I could feel the knotting starting to reverse and slowly begin to unravel. This was <u>*so not*</u> par for the course! In <u>*every*</u> previous episode of the past decade, the pain garnered strength and momentum for a minimum of 48 hours before it peaked and painfully began receding. It had only been three hours of pain and it was retreating instead of advancing, I could hardly believe it!

I clung to the root beer and sipped away. I was still feeling pain, but it was on a much lighter scale than I'd ever felt it before, and I managed to get off the floor and crawl into bed, which was usually unthinkable in my previous episodes.

I curled into a fetal position, which seemed able to contain the echoes of my fading cramps, and shortly fell asleep.

The next morning I was suddenly awakened by the alarming sound of a loudly ringing telephone inches from my head. I bolted up, fumbled for the receiver and drowsily mumbled into it: "Mm... huh-lo?"

"Mr. Barone?" An unfamiliar voice on the other end inquired.

"Mm... Yes?" I answered sleepily.

"This is the front desk. A man is here; he has your wallet and would like to return it to you."

"Really? I replied groggily, completely worn out from the torture of the night before. "What man? Did he give you his name?"

"His name is Diego; he was your cabdriver yesterday. He said a woman found your wallet in the back of his cab and gave it to him. He remembered dropping you off here. Would you like to come down and get it now, or shall we hold it for you at the front desk?"

Completely stunned I could barely speak: "Um... uh... Okay...that's fine. Hold it at the desk. Please thank him for me, and could you also get his name and address so I can send him a reward?"

"Yes sir, we will take care of that for you."

"Thank you so much!" I replied in wide eyed shock.

The clerk cheerfully replied: "You're welcome sir!"

I hung up the phone. Dazed, confused, and instantly delirious with happiness!

"**What?!!** I shouted out loud; are you *kidding me??!!* Somebody has returned my wallet??!!! You *must* be kidding me, I can't believe this! This is *too much!!!* This can't be happening!!! You mean to tell me that not one person, but *three* people (the woman, the cabbie and the hotel clerk) have handled my wallet, and it's coming back to me?!! In the middle of New York City?!! *Are you freakin' kidding me?!!!"*

Waves of prickly goose bumps began racing all over my body, increasing in velocity and intensity until it felt like I'd just been shot out of a cannon! I burst into rollicking laughter as I looked up and raised my hands at the ceiling.

"**Thank you!!! Thank you!!! Thank you!!!**" I hollered in between my irrepressible laughter, as my body continued to arc and shiver with a current so powerful, I could *see* and *feel* the whitest light rocketing out of every pore of my body.

"Thank you Mom!!! Thank you God!!! Thank you Saint Anthony and who ever!!! **Thank you, thank you, thank you for fixing this!!!**"

Tears had already begun mixing with my laughter; joyful, incredibly grateful fountains of release were streaming down my face. I felt as though I'd left my body, my spirit remarried with its source, in an all encompassing embrace of purest love. I paced the room with unsettling energy, my climbing spirit filling the space with boundless, shivering gratitude, and joy. This continued unceasingly for the next ten minutes or so before I was able to contain myself, wash my face and throw some clothes on.

I wildly raced to the elevator, wondering if it was possible that all of my cash, travelers' checks and drivers' license would still be intact.

Three people (that I knew of) had a chance to take whatever they wanted. How long had my wallet been in the back of the cab before "some woman" gave it to Diego? Certainly another passenger could've rifled through it and left it on the floor of the cab before the woman found it.

For the first time it dawned on me what a long shot it was that anything worthwhile was left. Grimly I prepared myself to face the worst case scenario as the elevator descended…

Rubber Soul

Jousters of fresh doubt thrust and parried in my mind as I stared vacantly at the 8...7...6...lights of the eerily quiet elevator terminally flickering by. "What if somebody's using my identification to cash my travelers checks right now, or has already spent them!??!! I didn't own a credit card and I didn't have enough cash to get home. I won't last a day in this city without money, who am I going to call for help? Bill?? Megan?? American Express? 5...4...3... I'd been so overjoyed about having my wallet returned; I hadn't had time to think it through. Fixating my logic, I told myself: "Don't get your hopes up. Mom said I'd get my wallet back, *she didn't say anything would be in it!*" 2...1...Ding!

The elevator slowly settled and as it did, from the formerly silent metallic speaker in the ceiling, the first gentle notes of The Beatles song, (From the album: *Rubber Soul*) In My Life, began to play…

"There are places I remember/all my life/though some have changed…" I steadied my composure as John Lennon's sweet and loving voice continued… "Some forever/not for better/some have gone/and some remain…"

The elevator opened and I walked out, facing the front desk a few yards away. As I approached the counter, the elevator door

Italian Mothers Never Die

remained open, sending the song out into the lobby ..."All these places have their moments/with lovers and friends/I still can recall/some are dead and some are living/in my life/I've loved them all..."

As calm and beautiful as the music was, I didn't find it even the slightest bit reassuring. "I don't know about loving *this place* yet..." I thought to myself as I gave a half worried smile and opened my mouth to speak to the man at the front desk, but before I could utter a single sound...

"Mr. Barone! How nice to see you this morning!" The clerk smiled cheerfully and continued: "I'm sure you're anxious to retrieve your wallet and I have it right here!"

He turned his back and took a manila envelope out of the mail slot to my room. Turning back around, he handed it to me saying; "The cab drivers information is in the envelope. Is there anything else I can do for you this morning sir?"

I hadn't said a word. "Um...no...I guess not...thank you very much."

I took the package and returned towards the still open, empty elevator. "In my life/I love you more..." echoed Lennon, as I entered.

"The jury's still out on loving *anything* just yet!" I cynically thought as I pushed the button to the 9th floor. Anxiously I waited for the door to close before tearing open the manila envelope.

The elevator started rising and my heart climbed into my throat as I reached in the envelope and pulled out my wallet. I opened it and started riffling through it as John Lennon, in his purest falsetto, finished the song ... "In my-I-I-I-life/I love you more..."

I stared at the open folds of my wallet, blankly registering the contents before crying out in utter astonishment: "My travelers' checks! They're here! They're all here!!! I can't believe it!" I yelped happily as I began counting the obviously untouched bundles.

The elevator stopped at my floor as I continued thumbing through the cash that remained, every bit of it was still here! I was stunned to find my drivers' license along with everything else, completely undisturbed. It was scarcely believable and yet it was staring me in the face.

"Too much!" I bellowed, as the beige doors started to open, where a finely tailored woman, who at first glance strikingly resembled Jackie Onassis, stood facing me.

I'm sure she thought I meant that *she* was "Too much!" She broke into a wide smile below her large dark sunglasses and gingerly stepped aside for me to exit.

"Excuse me..." I giggled, racing past her, entirely unembarrassed, and began laughing all the way down the hall at myself, and at the cyclone of irrepressible joy pervading my spirit.

I entered my room and burst out laughing harder, in ecstatic, unbridled disbelief as I spread out the contents of my wallet on the bed.

"Thank you Mom!!!" I hollered, in the early morning silence of my room.

I couldn't contain my overwhelming emotions! I felt the same way I'd felt after the phone call from the desk clerk twenty minutes ago, but this time my euphoria was even more over the top!

I thanked my list of miracle sponsors all over again with boundless gratitude; **"Thank you God! Thank you Mother! Thank you Saint Anthony! Thank you Diego! And you, "woman in the backseat of the cab!" who ever <u>you</u> are! Thank you, thank you!!!"** I blissfully shouted, as I looked at the piece of paper with Diego's name and address.

And then the flood of tears began, mixing with my now fully shuddering goose bump covered flesh, and my mantra of thanks continued aloud with my half-laughing-half crying, spine tingling quivers.

"All of this *and* my stomach demon is gone too!!?? **Un-be-lievable!!!**" My words blubbered through my elated tears.

Suddenly, long beaming cylinders of speeding white light filled the room, ricocheting off the walls, throwing prisms of faint, diamond faceted rainbows through the air, engulfing me in the most wondrous awe. Faster than any modern laser light show I'd ever witnessed, the rockets of light electrifyingly raced through me, bouncing off the ceiling, floors, windows and walls. It felt as though the energies of the lights were embracing me, in a palpable, all encompassing explosion of love, and then mother's voice vibrated through me, like a voltage of music does as it vibrates the flesh when the volume is too loud.

Inserting an extra word into the lyric while staying true to Lennon's delivery she sang: *"In my **new** life, I love you more."*

Instantly I collapsed on the bed, amid my sweet and unabashed joyous tears, and the now scattered contents of the envelope. Within a few moments I became very calm and still as I began reveling in the most perfect state of bliss, a nirvana completely beyond space and time. This all encompassing wholeness of Spirit lovingly continued cradling my entire essence of energy to its own, until at some point, my slowly reawakening, ordinary *human* consciousness, reluctantly allowed the radius of *its* connection to this Perfect Oneness, to recede.

With haunting tinges of regret over an all too soon farewell, I felt like I'd seamlessly shifted from a weightless body of harmonious light, and gradually re-materialized, into the dense matter of the present moment. I began to digest *this* entire experience, in reverently awed silence.

Ultimately, my perfect contentment gave way to the more mundane reality of my surroundings. My curiosity about all that had transpired was even more intrigued as I mentally went over the finer details I'd previously overlooked.

The delirium over my lost wallet, that brought on my stomach illness, that led to the deli across the street with chopped liver on bagels; I hadn't seen or even thought of that combination, let alone eaten it, since moms' funeral.

As for the Jackie Onassis (Leo/Leone) look alike at the elevator…Why hadn't I looked closer at *her*! There were times in the Sixties when mom had looked like, and dressed herself, to resemble Jackie O. She'd find it fun to reprise the guise I'm sure.

And then…what about the thoughtful and honest cabdriver, Diego? Concerned enough to remember where he'd dropped me off *the day before*. Diego, obviously a Latin name… Spanish? Italian? Or rather, mother's most oft used self deprecating Italian slang; "Deigo." Only one letter of spelling reversed from the name

Diego; Mom would appreciate the ironic pun.

I wondered just who exactly the "woman in the backseat of the cab" was and what did *she* look like?

And finally of course, I pondered mother's other calm instruction: ***"Root beer through a straw, no ice... ice...ice."*** She'd healed my chronic ailment in less than an hour with one sentence!

Marveling again at the chain of events since my arrival in the city (72 hours ago) beginning at the Dakota, (on 72nd Street) I smiled serenely to myself, more than grateful for the continuation of undeniably miraculous events of the more immediate past twenty four hours.

I'd only been in the city a few days and I'd been showered with *so many reasons* to be thankful. Too many reasons to chalk things up to mere coincidence, mom's celestial fingerprints were noticeably visible everywhere, and I'd grown completely at ease with her now very tangible, otherworldly presence.

For the first time in my life the light of my Spirit was revived into a state of *be-ing* that made me feel *truly alive,* and mom appeared to be workin' it, in overdrive!

"Goodbye sadness, goodbye, goodbye..."
From: Goodbye Sadness on the album: Season of Glass by: Yoko Ono
This album rated Five Stars (the highest honor) from Rolling Stone Magazine

The next day, I had lunch with Bill and Dan before taking the Long Island Railroad out to West Islip to stay a week with my Aunt Marilyn.

I'd seen Marilyn briefly at mom's funeral, but prior to that I hadn't seen or spoken to her in 17 years. She and mom were close, but I really knew nothing much about her other than, she used to own an antique store, and according to mom, Marilyn and her first husband Joe, (my Dads brother) and their kids, once lived in a large house full of antiques that unfortunately burned to the ground due to a careless ashtray.

Marilyn and Joe were divorced about 15 years ago, around the same time as my parents were, so mom and Marilyn were even closer "sisters in arms" than they'd ever been.

I was also aware that mother used to fly from California to Long Island each September to stay with Marilyn and her second husband Vince, for a week or two, but that was about all I knew.

My first visit with Marilyn and Vince was very pleasant and insightful. I learned things about my mom I'd never known. For example, evidently she was a gifted violinist as a young woman. I knew her most prized possession was an antique violin that she'd left to me in her Will, but I assumed it was merely a family heirloom. It never occurred to me that she'd played it all that much, I'd never heard her.

Also, she was blessed with literary talents and had aspirations to become a writer. Of course that never happened because instead, she ended up with five rambunctious kids to raise with an often absent, philandering husband, whose moody and violent temper, fueled by other vices, eventually moved into his "well to do" middle-aged mistress's house, a block away from our own.

Almost overnight our family's upper middle class lives were transformed into destitution. Our family home was taken away, and my emotionally shattered siblings moved to a rundown house on the outskirts of town where mom was forced to accept welfare.

It was still the early 1970's, long before Prozac, Paxil, and the now seemingly endless list of medications for depression were available. With the loss of her husband and home, mom suffered a clinical nervous breakdown. She was diagnosed as a paranoid schizophrenic, and treated with Thorazine and Lithium, until, like the mythical Phoenix; she eventually rose from the ashes, started a new life and created a better one for herself and her family.

I'm certain she had several books within her; she just never got a chance to write them.

Marilyn gave me a letter that mom had written to her in 1963, in much happier times. The language and style of the letter was identical to my own. The pages were long and rambling, full of colorful verbiage, dryly humorous, with any necessary seriousness written blatantly, as well as, in between the lines.

Among other things in mom's letter, she glowingly praised a recent third grade singing performance I'd given. There are very few times I can recall mom praising me in my youth, she was more likely to be critical, so this ancient letter of loving validation became instantly treasured.

There was a free spirited humor imparted in the letter, a side of mom I'd very rarely seen.

Also, because Marilyn, like mom and I, was astrologically a Leo, I inwardly chuckled over the obvious resemblances of regal tastes in arts, food, passions, concerns and ideals expressed in the letter, and present in the personalities of the three of us. There were some differences to be sure, but with Marilyn I knew I was in the presence of another lioness, and I recognized with comfort the kindred spirits we shared.

I was free to roam the island on a bicycle during the day as Marilyn and Vince were at work until 3:30 pm. When they came home we leisurely sat around reminiscing about the family over cocktails from 4pm through dinner at 7, and then retiring to our rooms for the evening at 9.

The only television in the house was in their bedroom, so there was little for me to do except to read the only reading material in Marilyn's spare room, Whitley Strieber's Non-fictional accounts of his extraterrestrial abductions, spookily described and recorded in his book, Communion. Considering the close encounters of the Mothering kind that I'd been experiencing, this seemed entirely appropriate! It's not a book I'd ever have normally read, let alone purchase, but here it was, a story of other worldly communications, in the room that mom used to stay in, and what else was there to do? Though its depictions of "other beings" were creepy and scary in many ways, some of the dates of Mr. Strieber's abductions had a resonance of familiarity with important dates in my mom's life. He was certainly convincing in his very detailed accounts of his communications with another dimension, and I could not dismiss my own, I was just grateful that mine were blissful encounters, with an entity of pure overwhelming love, rather than the portraits of his terrifying experiences.

My two weeks of vacation time, sadly, were coming to a close. The thoughts of returning to my "Dead End" life on Cemetery Hill Road with Megan loomed ominously on the horizon. Whitley

Strieber's abductions seemed preferable to my only option of returning home!

I stayed again with Bill and Dan for the remaining two days, and on my last day, I went alone to Strawberry Fields for my final visit.

I'd written a short story for Yoko, (I still have a copy of it somewhere amid my annals of overflowing "paaaperwawk!") that I intended to leave with the doorman at The Dakota. Fat chance I would be having another happenstance with Yoko.

I was lying on the grass, reviewing the pages of my story for her, thinking of the remarkable time I'd had while I'd been here. A scruffy looking guitarist was playing arguably *the* most loved and revered Lennon song a few paces from the Imagine mosaic.
I laid my head down and languished in the warm spring sunlight with my eyes closed, listening to the music. "Imagine all the people/living life in peace/ you-hoo...ooh...ooh...ooh/you may say I'm a dreamer/but I'm not the only one..."

I lay there listening, wishing, dreaming, and looking for someway out of my Oregon life that wouldn't bring the emotional storm clouds of Megan tumbling down on my newfound happiness. I'd allowed her to manipulate and control me far too long. Partially due to her nine year age advantage, as well as her skilled "drama queen" routines, she'd easily exploited me in my youth, but now I was nearly 34 and I'd finally grown wise to her childish unrelenting neurosis. Still, I didn't want to hurt her, and every time I'd tried to leave her before, she grew more aggressively possessive and cunning.

She'd trained me well to suffer in silence, to with hold the truths of my feelings for her benefit. As long as I faked my happiness, she was fine.

My melancholy thoughts of returning home, to be emotionally buried again in that all too familiar tomb, threatened to unsettle my new found serenity. I forced myself to focus on the peaceful, liberating moments I was experiencing in the here and now.

I felt a lazy smile come upon my face as I lay in the soft, warm, shimmering sunlight. The scruffy guitarist segued from singing <u>Imagine</u>, into <u>Fixing a Hole</u>, one of my favorite songs from The

Beatles album: <u>Sergeant Peppers Lonely Hearts Club Band</u>. "I'm fixing a hole/where the rain gets in/and stops my mind from wandering/where it will go...oh..." In his finest Paul McCartney imitation, the musician lulled me into a weightless state of consciousness. I allowed my mind to wander along with the melody and lyric, smiling wider as he sang: "and it really doesn't matter if I'm wrong/I'm right/where I belong/I'm right/where I belong..." I pondered those words, knowing that I truly felt I ***am*** right where I belong, here in New York City, not in the boondocks on the edge of a cornfield, in a no opportunity, unsophisticated, nothing going on nothing doing small town, living a life of soul numbing quiet desperation with Megan, figuratively and literally, on a Dead End street.

My wandering thoughts were interrupted by silence, in mid-song, of the musician. I lay there for a moment with eyes still closed, figuring he'd broken a string. The lyric of Lennon's song <u>Strawberry Fields Forever</u>, floated into my head; "living is easy with eyes closed/misunderstanding all you see/it's getting hard to be someone but it all works out..."

After a few minutes of silence, I wondered what was taking the sidewalk singer so long to resume his impromptu performance. From my lying down position, I rose up on to my elbows and squinted through the glare of sunshine in the direction of the guitarist. He was standing with his guitar dangling on his chest, talking to a Policeman who was writing him a ticket!

A ticket!? For playing music?! I sat up fully and took in the scene. The musician was packing up his gear as the cop scribbled away. I was immediately incensed! This was outrageous! The scruffy street musician getting a ticket that he probably couldn't afford to pay, despicable!

The cop tore the ticket off his pad, gave it to the sidewalk performer, and with a casual, self important strut, continued his beat through the park.

I decided then and there that I wanted to pay for the musicians' ticket; he'd brought me such pleasure. I quickly gathered my stuff and approached him as he was strapping his guitar case onto his back.

"Excuse me..." I began.

"Hey man, what's up!" he said with a friendly smile.

"I just noticed you were getting a ticket for playing music in the park, and I enjoyed your performance very much so I'd like to pay the ticket for you."

"Ah, no sweat man, but thanks for the offer!"

"Yeah, but I really don't think you should have to pay a fine for playing music! I'm more than happy to..."

"Nah, don't sweat it man, I'm not going to pay for it anyway, I gave the cop all false information! I get tickets all the time, no big deal!" he chuckled.

"You a musician?" he asked.

"Well, more of a lyricist than a musician." I replied. "I play a bit of piano but I'm only so-so, I mostly write lyrics. I wish I could play and sing like you, you were really excellent!"

"Yeah? Well thanks man! Listen, I just finished recording some songs that I've written, wanna come to my place and check 'em out?"

I was caught completely off guard! I hadn't been looking for an invitation to hang out with anyone; I wanted to spend my last few hours alone in the park before going to the airport with Bill and Dan later. Besides, I didn't know this guy from Adam, and I was apprehensive in my reply: "Well...what time is it? ...I don't know if I have time because I have a plane to catch...Where do you live?"

I stalled, as my mind scrambled for a polite way to refuse. He could be some tricked out weirdo! Did I want to spend my last few hours with a complete stranger? What if he lived in the Bronx, or Queens, or some drug den somewhere...what if...? I didn't know what to think, except that I should be cautious here, this was New York City after all! I'm sure he read the volumes of blossoming apprehension as it spread across my face. I was still stuttering for a reply when he said: "I live right across the street man, less than 5 minutes, no travel required!"

He smiled reassuringly, and instantly I felt at ease. The only buildings across the street were expensive high rises. This was a

Italian Mothers Never Die

multibillion dollar, swanky, neighborhood; festooned grandly on the corner by the mammoth Dakota, where not only Yoko lived, but also, Lauren Bacall, Rex Reed, Roberta Flack, and many other notable celebrities, certainly this guy wasn't a dangerous waif.

"Well, alright. I've got a few hours before I have to catch my plane, I'd love to hear your songs."

"Where are you off to on a plane then?" He asked as we left Strawberry Fields.

We continued chatting as we crossed the street, and I dared not let myself even start to believe that he could live in The Dakota. He didn't, he lived in the even taller building that stood beside it, The Mayfair Towers. We rode the elevator up and entered his apartment, which was parallel with the highest levels of the Dakota. As soon as we entered his apartment, I spied two windows that faced windows of The Dakota. I could see directly into an elegantly decorated apartment.

"Is that the Lennon's apartment?!" I asked incredulously.

"Yeah man, but don't get too close to the windows, Yoko doesn't like it when my friends stare across."

"Yeah I'm sure she doesn't!" I replied with curious awe.

We sat and talked, he looked over some of the lyrics I had in my briefcase, and told me they were really good. One in particular he said he wanted to record, but told me to get it copyrighted first, because he wasn't looking for trouble. We both found this funny because the title of the song was: <u>Looking For Trouble</u>!

We began listening to his music, and he asked me if I wanted to do some Peyote, (That sounded like looking for trouble to me!) I politely declined. He didn't get high; we just listened to his wonderful songs and talked.

After an hour or so had passed, I decided it was time to leave. I did have a plane to catch. I thanked him and we exchanged addresses.

Once I was in the elevator, I couldn't resist going to the roof top of the Mayfair, which towered a few floors above the Dakota, to take some pictures of the Dakota's turquoise colored, gothic roof. My "baby" brother is a much more avid Beatle freak than I ever was, and I knew he'd love to have actual pictures of the buildings peak.

After taking the photos, I rode back to the street level, all set to drop my story off for Yoko with the doorman at The Dakota, before I entered the 72nd Street subway.

Just as I was approaching the sentry booth on the sidewalk in front of the building, I heard the jarring sound of a shrill metal whistle; I looked to my right and noticed the Dakota's doorman in the street, hailing a cab. I was busy taking the story out of my briefcase as I watched him and continued slowly walking; when out of the dark cavernous entrance of the building on my left, Yoko was suddenly in my path. I practically collided with her on the sidewalk!

"Excuse me! I'm so sorry! I didn't see you!" I stammered.

"Oh, it's okay!" She said with a shy smile.

"Yoko…" I nervously paused, and spoke again: "I very unintentionally… kind of …stalked you in the park two weeks ago, and you were so very sweet to me. In fact, I've written a story for you that out lines my embarrassing behavior, and my gratitude for how gracious you were. I was just now going to leave it with the doorman…but here you are!" I thrust the envelope at her.

"Well how nice then! Please leave it with him, I have an appointment and I can't take it with me now." She said as the doorman, standing at the curb, opened the car door.

"I'm going back home to Oregon tonight, so I'm sure I won't be seeing you again. I hope you like my story and…"

"Why are you living in Oregon? She said with a puzzled expression. "You seem like an artist to me, you belong here. There's a lot more happening for artists here than there is in Oregon."

"Well…yeah…but I'm married and I own a house there and have a life there and…well… it's kind of complicated."

"Well, alright then." She shrugged with an understanding look on her face. "If you have to go…"

"Yeah, I do. But thanks again for everything! You've been so very kind, thank you!"

"You're welcome. Goodbye then…" She smiled warmly, as

she climbed into the waiting car.

Disoriented by this most unexpected encounter, I blankly handed the doorman my story and then stumbled my way towards the subway station. I couldn't believe what had just happened! I'd just been an alley's distance from her personal living quarter windows, and then I was within an arms length of her again! Yoko had just called *me* an artist! One of my favorite artist's saw the artist in me, and had just said I belonged *here*.

I knew she was right but what could I do, I was catching a plane in two hours. I'd have rather cut off my left arm than get on that plane! That was *it*! I had to call Megan and my employers and tell them I was staying another week! I wasn't ready to let go of all the positive energies that had rejuvenated my spirits.

The ensuing extra week passed quickly, and while I spent a lot of time exploring the city further on my own and with my friends, I found one more chance for the opportunity to go to Strawberry Fields on my final day. This time I knew it was really going to be the last time, and I wanted to leave the city with a boost of the positive energy I always felt when I'd been in the park.

I'd just finished buying a soda from the hot dog vendor at the corner of 72nd and Central Park West when out of the Dakota's entrance stepped Yoko! I could scarcely believe it and stood there stunned! How was I running into her every time I was in the neighborhood?

She smiled when she spotted me and said; "Oh! So you didn't leave after all!"

I was completely surprised and excited to see her but managed to calmly convey that I'd stayed an extra week, and had a great time, but I was definitely going back to Oregon tonight.

She looked at me thoughtfully and replied; "Well, that's too bad. I have a feeling you'll be back." she said smiling, as a Lincoln Town Car driver at the curb opened the car door for her.

"Yeah, well maybe you're right. I hope so! But I guess its goodbye for now." I replied with sad resignation.

She paused before getting into the car, and gave me a look that I could only surmise by her facial expression was saying; Why? And then she said; "Well, okay then I guess, goodbye." She climbed into the car.

"Goodbye." I said with a wave as she looked at me before the driver closed the door, and then I watched the Lincoln drive away.

Yoko's touching song about strength returning after adversity, began playing in my head; "Goodbye sadness/goodbye/goodbye/ I don't need you anymore…" I leaned against the lion faced black ironwork railing bordering The Dakota, wondering why *that* song came to me because it's about leaving sadness behind, and I was going home, *back to my sadness*.

The last place I wanted to go was Oregon but I had no unrealistic thoughts of staying longer. I knew from our phone calls that Megan was jealous of the great time I'd been having, and was impatient for my return. She'd made it clear that now I owed it to her to come back and make a more committed attempt to make our marriage work. Megan pointed out how patient she'd been with my state of unhappiness; she'd "allow" no more talk of divorce. We'd work on our marriage because "that's what couples do" and "we will find a way to *make* it work." She also reminded me that my employers had been very patient and generous to let me stay this long, but she knew they wanted me back, and I couldn't afford to jeopardize my job.

And, just to drive her point all the way home, she prompted me with extra guilt saying that we were barely able to afford my extended stay already.

I felt the appropriate chasm of shame and responsibility in my soul, and dutifully complied reassuringly with her logic. I hated more than anything to leave, but I'd accepted this trip as just a fortunate series of dreams and miracles coming true. Now the dreams were over, it was time to get back to the realities of whatever life was going to continue for Megan and me. There were no serious thoughts or illusions of ever moving here. As much as I agreed that Yoko was correct about the lack of artistic opportunities in Oregon, I saw no way out of my life there, and I'd just promised Megan that I would come back and work harder on making our marriage work. For better or worse, it was the only home I had, the only home I knew.

Approximately Infinite Universe

I'd been back in Oregon for two months before the cosmic high of my New York vacation wore off. I'd managed to reclaim some slight new hope for a better future with Megan, but the dullness of the secluded, emotionally crippled, everyday life of fulfilling her requirements for happiness, while my dreams and spirits withered, infested my illusions once again. I was doing my best, forcing myself to *make* our marriage work, and that's precisely why it wasn't working. I'd been forcing it because I didn't want to hurt Megan, she wanted us to be together forever more than anything, but I was dying inside. I couldn't shake the feeling that as long as I remained with her, my purpose in life would never be fulfilled. I didn't know what that purpose might be, I only knew that it had to be more than being a slave to her needs, and as I looked back over the years, I realized that's all I'd ever been. Nothing more than a puppet on a string to dance and sing to whatever tune *she* decided was my life's path.

"In this approximately infinite universe/I know I'll go through some constant hell..." echoed Yoko from the record player in my music room. Each day my growing depression surfaced with strengthened regularity. My isolated small town surroundings, suffocated me with viscously taunting reminders of my shattered dreams, lost hopes, dysfunctional marriage, and completely joyless life. I continued to finalize all of mom's estate issues, went to work each day, then came home and put on my best phony face of satisfied stability for Megan. I'd promised to work harder and I had been. She was happy and content, why wasn't I? The walls of my frozen soul began to crack and crumble, and before long I was retreating more and more into myself.

I'd heard nothing from mother since I'd been back. It was as though the black clouds hovering over me were too dark to let her vibrations come through.

I avoided Megan as much as possible, but my distance and resistance only made her more firmly determined to cling harder. It was as though her happiness was all that mattered. I couldn't take our forced lives together anymore. The whole holiday atmosphere felt plastic and vacant. The only thing I wanted for Christmas was my freedom.

After a horrible afternoon of joylessly schlepping through a mall, with her prattling on and on about her Christmas plans for us, while my thoughts fantasized of killing myself, just so I wouldn't have to wear a counterfeit face of contentment for one moment longer, on the drive home I told her I wanted a divorce.

"I love you as a person, and I'll always love you, but I'm not *in love* with you. I'm not happy, and I can't live this lie any longer."

She argued that lots of people feel that way but they don't leave each other because of it. I knew she had a valid point for "lots of people" but I also knew my heart, and if I wasn't in love with her now, I would never be. I'd been trying hard to deny that I'd always felt suffocated by her. She'd forced our relationship from the beginning, and I'd forced myself to believe that I loved her because it's what she wanted. I realized that I could no longer continue to play the dutiful husband role Megan required of me just because she *needed* me to. No matter what it looks like on the outside, lions are never happy when caged, and I'd been trapped in her emotional unrelenting possessiveness for 15 years.

She knew she was fighting a losing the battle as we continued quarreling for weeks. I would go out at night with my friends just to get away from her. She'd whine, complain and cajole but my ears were deaf to her pleadings. I didn't care when she turned on her faucet of tears anymore. I'd dried rivers of them for her over the years to placate her insecurities, now her whining about me not loving her was finally valid, I couldn't stand being in the same room with her.

True to her Chameleon archives of self-serving neurosis, she transformed her long suffering patience completely overnight, into slick, venomous, indignant anger.

One day she absolutely hissed at me: "Go ahead and leave! I don't care! I'll be fine! Oh, and by the way, I'm pregnant!" Then, as bitchy as she could spit it out, added; "Don't worry, I'll raise the baby all by myself!" and she left the room.

I was utterly and overwhelmingly devastated. My hope for a better life on my own dropped dead at that moment. I could scarcely believe she was pregnant because we'd always used protection. It was even more ironic because we hadn't had sex for the last two months, and the last time we did, I couldn't finish the act, for the very reason that it was just that, an act, put on for her benefit because she'd initiated her wanton desire. I knew the moment I drew away from her, it would be the last time I'd allow her to control me physically or emotionally. She'd begun our relationship with a physical and emotional molestation, and she'd just used up her final opportunity. I was not in love with her, and I would not pretend for the sake of both of our hearts that I was. Now she was pregnant? After all these years of deliberately not having a child, now at age 43 she was going to be a mother again?

Her daughter Fiona, whom I'd lovingly raised as my own, had just moved away to college six months earlier, and now we were going to raise another child?! "Mother, where in God's name are you now?! And, if you *can* hear me, why don't you ask God why He hates me so much to put me through this!" I raged to myself in bitter silence.

The next day Megan began maliciously provoking me, saying

she had decided to move out and give birth to our child elsewhere. She wasn't sure where she would go; maybe she'd leave the area. Wherever she was going, she said she'd be raising our baby without me. I countered with the fact that I'd helped to raise her child, I most certainly was going to raise mine! I could see the fiendish calculations in her eyes as she spelled out exactly how she would make sure I would only see our child on weekends, alternate birthdays and holidays. She threatened me that any judge would grant her our home and she'd make sure that alimony and child support drained me financially for at least the next eighteen years.

Turning the tables was her most effective ploy yet. It sent my depression into a further tailspin. For a week I went into work in a clouded daze of anxiety. I was unwilling to let her raise my child without a set of parents. I conceded to the fact that I would have to bite the bullet and find a way to live with Megan, or at least nearby, for the next 18 years. She said she would only consider staying with me to raise our child on one condition, and for the second time in fifteen years, she insisted that I was messed up and required professional counseling.

The first time she'd suggested therapy, had been in the early second year of our relationship, one afternoon when she was talking marriage. I'd expressed doubts that I was ready to be a husband, as well as a father to her four year old daughter.

"I'm only twenty years old; I haven't decided what I want to do with my life yet." She promptly slapped me hard across the face, and said that *I obviously needed* professional help. We went together, once a week, for two weeks before she forbade me to go again, as soon as the therapist became aware of the origins of our relationship.

In June of 1971, armed with the emotional pretense of an unshakable fear of earthquakes, (in reality she was looking for a plausible lie to end her marriage) 26 year old Megan and her best friend Jean (an unwed mother) had taken two year old Fiona, along with Jean's infant daughter, from the Southern California home the four of them shared with Megan's husband Rex; to live "without him temporarily" in Oregon. Manipulated by Megan's false promises of staying out of California just for the summer, (earthquake season) unsuspecting Rex had moved the two women, children, and their belongings with the company van from Sir Georges's Smorgasbord, the restaurant he managed; where I'd been working since I was fifteen.

I'd just graduated from high school and Rex had become more than my boss, he'd become my best friend and mentor. In the past year I'd been to his and Megan's home socially on several occasions. There, Rex, Megan, Jean and I would drink beer, smoke pot, listen to music and talk. That's what young adults did in the seventies, and though at seventeen I was hardly an adult, I was accepted into their world as one.

Before Rex left town to move Megan and her tribe, he asked me if I would housesit for him while he was away. My home life had recently gotten worse due to my dad moving in with his mistress a few houses away from our own, and mom was on the verge of a nervous breakdown. I didn't know it at the time, but due to my dad's legal and illegal gambling debts, mom was facing foreclosure on the house and certain destitution, while dad was very comfortably secured by his divorcee's bankroll. I'd been oblivious to the full extent of dire straights mother was genuinely facing and jumped at the chance to stay *anywhere else* for a week!

My house sitting week passed quickly. On the day of Rex's expected return, I'd been out shopping; and as I rounded the corner back to his place, I saw Rex on a hospital gurney being hoisted into an ambulance! By the time I pulled in the driveway, the ambulance had started its siren and backed out of the driveway; I had no choice but to follow!

I sat alone in the hospital waiting room for two excruciatingly anxious hours. Because I was not a family member, no one would tell me what had happened, and I was left to imagine a menagerie of worst case scenarios.

It turned out that upon his return, Rex had decided to mow the lawn and a rock flew out from underneath the gas powered mower, breaking his leg. He had a cast from his ankle to mid thigh, and as I drove him home, he asked me if I would move in with him.

He'd known for years that my school and home life had been a physically and emotionally abusive environment, and since he was going to need assistance during his recovery, this would be a good solution for us both.

Earlier that day I'd confronted my dad about his flaunting debauchery. Not only was it an emotional embarrassment to myself and my siblings, I'd discovered that he was leaving mom with an avalanche of debt and no resources to pay for them. She'd been a stay at home mom for twenty years and now, without money, career training or any marketable skills, she was going to have to get a job to support herself and finish raising four kids alone.

I asked him how he could behave so selfishly irresponsible when he'd always been so quick to savagely choke, kick and beat us for even the most minor infractions, such as biting our nails or the way we polished our shoes!

His conscience and soul were sorely in need of polishing, but he couldn't see it, he was too immersed in his alcohol and gambling addictions to have any real concern of our family's fate.

Apparently he'd relayed the details of my visit with him to mom and when I drove out to the house to tell her I was moving in with Rex, I calmly rationalized to her that it would be one less mouth to feed. She was still very courageously holding her own, and thanked me for having a talk with him. "He will come to his senses." She said, holding back her tears. She clung firmly to the idea that he was just going through a mid-life crisis, he would eventually see the error of his ways and come home.

Unfortunately for her sanity, she still believed in a better future with him that would never happen.

I moved in with Rex, and helped him through his recovery. He missed Megan and their child Fiona immensely. I gladly assisted him as he buried himself in his work and managed to run the restaurant with his cast on. He called Megan every week, begging her to return. Her "earthquake" excuse was wearing thin, and she didn't have the guts to face the truth that she wasn't in love with him, so three months later she relented and agreed to come home.

I made the trip with Rex to Oregon to pick up his wife and child. Since Jean and her infant daughter were remaining in Oregon, Rex said I should continue living with him and Megan, and Megan wholeheartedly agreed.

One month after Megan's return, while Rex was at the restaurant and Megan and I were at home getting dinner ready for Rex's arrival, Megan started teasing me about a girl I'd been dating. The girl was calling me several times a day and Megan had just hung up the phone on her, telling her I wasn't home. Megan started jokingly jabbing me with her fingers, teasing me about how needy the girl was. She laughingly backed me up against the wall, while two year old Fiona was tugging on Megan's dress trying to get her attention. Megan continued teasing me about my "needy girlfriend" and as I jumped and squirmed with each jab and tickle of her fingers, my back rubbed against the light switch and accidentally turned the lights off. Instantly Megan began kissing me, and though I tried to push her off, she forcibly didn't stop until Fiona's whining cries of "mommy... mommy..." became so insistent that Megan was forced to release me and turn her attention to her child.

I switched the light on and stood in shocked silence. Megan took Fiona into the living room and sat her in front of the television. I knew I had to get out of there. As I made my way for the door, Megan intercepted me and ripped her blouse open exposing her bare breasts.

"Megan! What are you doing?!!" I freaked as I reached for the doorknob.

"I want you! I *need* you!" She demanded.

"No Megan! I'm just a kid and you're married to Rex! I have to go!"

She thrust herself up against me and tried to kiss me, I pushed her away and after a brief struggle, I managed to get out the door. I knew Rex would be home soon, I just had to stay away until he arrived, then I'd be safe.

I returned once I saw Rex's car in the driveway. The three of us had dinner together and Megan and I managed to act normal. I figured she'd gotten the message that I wasn't interested, and we could just bury the whole thing, no harm no foul.

Later that night, I awoke around three in the morning to find Megan performing oral sex on me while Rex and Fiona were asleep down the hall. I didn't stop her, I didn't have to; I climaxed as I groggily awoke to the situation.

"Megan what are you…" Before I could finish she interrupted me saying: "I'm in love with you, I've been in love with you since I came back." Then she slipped out of my room.

I sat up, stunned into alertness at what had just transpired. I'd been molested on five previous occasions by other adult men and women, since the age of fourteen, but none of them ever said they loved me. In fact, this was the first time I'd ever heard those words from any adult that I could recall. My inner torment, guilt, and confusion, began that night, and the days that followed brought on more bouts of Megan's sexual and emotional abuse.

With her neurotic, twisted rationalities, my teen confusion escalated as Megan, over the next year, with a host of malicious outright lies to Rex, and lies about Rex to me, cleverly severed both her and my connection to her husband. Megan decided that she, Fiona and I were moving to Seattle. Cunningly and successfully she'd "robbed the cradle" with no thoughts of guilt or remorse, and had since appointed herself the arbiter of my dreams, desires, ambitions, and emotions. She somehow managed to convince me that we were meant to be together. She decided that her nine year age advantage made her wise enough to chart the course of my life for the better, and since her profound love for me was sincere, I accepted her loving declarations as the first honest love I'd ever encountered. Someone who would love me unconditionally and help me nurture and build my dreams. Wasn't that what falling in love was all about? She seemed like the right candidate, she agreed with everything I idealized. I was too young to recognize the motivations for her agreeable "lip service" and for the first time in my life, I believed I was in love.

There was tremendous guilt about falling in love with my best friend's wife to be sure, but Megan knew all the right things to say in order for us to justify our relationship. Now that we lived two states away from Rex, and she'd obtained a divorce, we settled into a comfortable dynamic. We'd only been living together eight months before Megan decided that we needed to get married so that we could buy a house.

The Seattle therapist was sympathetic to my reluctance at getting married. She repeatedly pointed out ways that Megan was emotionally manipulating me in order to fulfill her self centered desires. The therapist told Megan that slapping me across the face for speaking the truth wasn't the way to enter a marriage, and getting married for the purpose of buying a home was not a valid reason either. This of course didn't go over well, and Megan made sure our sessions were quickly aborted. She didn't need a therapist to tell her she was controlling; it was an affront to her self described "intellectual dignity". Instead, Megan merely intensified and refined her mind games and I blindly allowed myself to be consumed. Back then, it was easier than fighting. I'd succumbed to my next incarceration with an emotionally abusive "Bomba!" Only this time, unlike my mother, my best interests were not considered, only Megan's insecurities and physical desires mattered.

Whip-smart "intellectual" that she considered herself to be, Megan also reminded me that her nine year age seniority over me made her wiser than any therapist. I deferred to her "wiser" dictums. In my eternally optimistic, naïve way, I actually believed that her age made her as intelligent as she claimed. What I didn't see then, nor in the ensuing years, was how completely full of guile her self proclaimed wisdom was.

But that had been fifteen years ago and many very different living locations in various states. Whenever she found out that I was starting an innocent friendship with another woman, a co-worker or anyone else, she'd decide it was time to move. She didn't want me to have friends or even acquaintances that might steer me away from her.

God forbid that I should pursue an acting or music career like I'd talked about, those professions required constant travel away from her as well as socialization, she wanted me all to herself. I was more than her husband, I was her obsessive possession.

Her most effective coup had been to convince me to co-desire isolation in this Oregon rural graveyard, this was her idea of paradise on earth but over time I discovered it certainly wasn't mine.

Finally, after eight long years of soul suffocation on Cemetery Hill Road, I'd swallowed enough. Now when she claimed to be the "wise" one, it was nothing but a four letter word. I didn't consider her the least bit wise anymore, merely desperate.

I'd always been adamant about not fathering a child of my own. I'd seen no sensible reason to extend the dysfunctional gene pool of my parents. But now Megan had found the ultimate way to trap me into continuing our dismal relationship, now she was going to make sure that my ideas of escaping from her would be banished forever.

This time, instead of a secular therapist, she insisted that I see a local Preacher. Evidently she felt that since I wanted to "go against the will of God" by getting a divorce, I was the screwed up one in need of some thorough demonic housecleaning. (Pretty rich coming from a woman whom I <u>never asked to marry me</u> and who also expressly forbade the mail order certified "cleric" who married us, to even mention the word God in the ceremony of the 1970's style circus atmosphere nuptials that she orchestrated.) But these days, Megan was a "born again" Christian. She'd allowed herself to re-accept her Christianity after I'd told her a few years ago that I couldn't live with someone who didn't believe in a Higher Power. Now she was using her faith to blackmail me into seeing things her way. Reluctantly I complied with her latest grand stand demands and went alone to the counseling session.

It turned out that the Reverend had devised an exorcism of sorts that he performed with the hopes of casting out whatever demons were contributing to my "rebellious spirit." But the Preacher, as loud and hard as he prayed, commanded and cajoled, could not coax or summon even the slightest appearance of evil or a fevered demonic shriek out of me.

"Perhaps they're just out lunching on someone else today." I reassured him.

I actually felt sorry for his pitiful failure to "fix" me. I calmly reported his frustrated "demon free" findings to Megan.

"There's nothing wrong with me except that I don't want to live with you anymore." I said sorrowfully.

Her face flushed red with anger as she picked up a Bible, raised it above her head, and as full of fevered wrath as Charelton Heston's portrayal of Moses with the 10 commandments, defiantly slammed the Bible to the floor and screamed: "It's not part of God's plan for us to get divorced!!!"

Shocked at her violent melodrama, I sternly replied; "And exactly just **who are you to decide** what God's plan for my life is?"

For the first time in our convoluted history, she had no answer. Now I no longer even cared what she had to say, needed, or wanted. I could only say: "I'm not in love with you. I can't do this anymore, but I *will be* a father to my child."

My outburst unfolded a wide map of fear, fury, panic, hatred, anxious hostility, and shrewdness across her face. The gauntlet of her shrieking threats, angry tears and emotional abuse came down with such force that I got in my truck and left her standing pissed off at me in the gravel driveway.

I didn't care where I went as long as it was away from her. I drove into the nearby town of Salem, simply because I knew the word; Salem, means Peace, and I unquestionably was in the market for some of that.

"No one can see me like you do"
From the song: No One Can See Me Like You Do by: Yoko Ono

As I drove aimlessly through the cold and raining, sleepy town, hopelessly distraught in the unhinged thoughts of my circumstances, I came upon a house with a small sign that read: Psychic Readings by Indira.

My New York Fifth Avenue Psychic had been a no show, and my teenage experience with the dog-food slinging haggard trailer witch had left a very bad impression.

I resisted the impulse momentarily before I pulled the truck into the driveway, thinking to myself; "Indira huh… I'm In-dire-a need of *some* direction that's for sure!"

I sat in the truck for a few minutes trying to decide if I even wanted to put myself through this. I was still quite skeptical of people who claimed to be psychic at will. My two previous experiences had been pretty much a bust. Only Mother had *proved* on more than one occasion to connect with me, and even when she did, I'd not seen her actions spelled out in cards, dreams, or clairvoyant visions. Instead, it always started as a quiet voice within me that I attributed as my own, until somewhere in the middle of whatever confusing proceedings followed, her vocal vibrations became more intense. Typical of my Leonine pride, that's when I'd begin fighting her intergalactic clues and prodding insistence, every step of the way! I'd always argue with her compelling instructions because they made no sense to me. I never realized during the early portions of the connections that she was trying to give me something amazing and beautiful, it was only after a miracle unfolded that I recognized her patient, loving, stern and playful, intercessions.

Psychic ability didn't seem for me at least, like something to be turned on and off by a deck of cards. For me it always involved an intense emotional saga, culminating in luminous and spine tingling nirvana, with physical artifacts of evidence thrown in, just in case I still questioned the veracity of the experience.

I sat in the truck and briefly pictured Indira as possibly Middle Eastern, dark, exotic and mysterious looking. The entire cliché seemed ignoble; did I really want to waste my money?

"What the hell, I'm here, might as well. Maybe Indira has a slice of Salem/peace for me today." I thought to myself as I turned off the truck, unlatched the seatbelt and stepped into the cold rain.

I cringed with regret the moment I knocked on the Cape Cod styled front door. I didn't want to be here. Before I could change my mind, the door opened and I was greeted by a mid-forty-something, blonde haired, pale skinned, slightly gap toothed smiling woman, wearing an embroidered 1970's fashioned linen caftan, with two loudly barking dogs at her side. My mind instantly squawked: "Paaa-perwawk!!! Paaa-perwawk!!!" I wanted to turn and run but it was too late.

Speaking in a thick Scottish brogue, the woman clasped my hand and said; "I'm Innn-dearrr-ahhh, come rrrright in!"

She led me to a large round oak kitchen table where bowls of multicolored crystals sat among various flickering candles and sticks of burning incense. There was a bright colored portrait of Jesus on the canary yellow wall bordering an oak china hutch. No signs of pendulums, Tarot cards, black cats, pentagrams, or Oliver Cromwell literature. This wasn't a rusting travel trailer or swanky Fifth Avenue office, it was just an ordinary home, and Indira seemed like an average garden variety housewife.

"Quiet now!" She commanded the still loudly barking dogs, and they immediately lay silently at her feet as she sat down. She then smilingly commanded me: "Sit!"

I did, and she looked at me with sparkling green eyes and said; "Sooooo, I see you'rrre he-rrre with verrrrey much confusion! Tell me young man, what is it that you wish to know?"

"I was hoping you'd tell me." I skeptically baited her.

"Well, I see that yourrrr confusion is caused by two women. One you love, but arrrre not in love with and one you have been trrrrying to get away frrrrom. Who is the woman that is lying to you dearrrr?"

I couldn't tell if her rolling r's were an affectation or genuine. I sat puzzled for a moment and replied; "Well I don't know because you said two women, and I can only think of one woman who I love, but am not in love with, and yes, I'm trying to get away from her, and she has lied a lot in the past. But you said two…"

"Yes, two. The one you are trrrrying to get away frrrrom is lying to you, she likes to bend yourrrr will to get herrrr way. The otherrrr woman, is someone you like being arrrround. You'rrre not "in love" with herrrr eitherrrr, but you love herrrrr."

The vagueness of her statements made me overly cautious, but I ventured to say; "The only other woman I can think of that I love, but am not "in love with" would be Yoko Ono. I told her I loved her, but I love her as an artist, nothing more."

"Yoo-ko Ooo-no??!!!!" She trilled her brogue higher. "How do you even know Yoo-ko Ooo-no?!!"

I relayed an abridged version of my New York experience with Yoko, saying only that I'd met her, how much I respected her as an artist, and that I'd written a story for her.

I questioned Indira at the end of my brief explanation. "Do you think Yoko read the story I gave her?"

"Well, I don't know if she rrrread it, but you will be seeing herrrr again, and the next time you see herrrrr, you will not be living herrrre, you will be living in New Yorrrk City."

"Wrong!" I thought to myself. She's full of it now, there's no way I'll be seeing Yoko again unless it's on television! Move to

New York? Not with a baby on the way!!! I gathered my thoughts and cleared my throat before speaking.

"I don't see how that's possible because my wife is having a baby and it doesn't look like I'm going anywhere for the next 18 years at least!"

"Have you spoken to yourrrr wife's docterrrr?"

"No, she just took one of those home pregnancy tests."

"Did she show you the test strrrrip rrrresults?"

"No. I never thought to ask her."

"Yourrrr wife is the one who is lying. She isn't prrrregnant, she is trrrrying to trrrrick you! She is the one you want to get away frrrom, but you arrre afraid to leave herrrrr!! She's verrry vindictive!"

"Well…yes. But she told me she was pregnant, I don't think she'd lie about that…what's the point?"

"She wants to contrrrrol yourrrr emotions; she wants you to love herrr. She is angrrry because she knows you don't, and now she is enjoying this game she has crrrreated, she wants to hurrrt you, because she is a vengeful perrrrson!"

"She's doing a fine job of hurting me already!" I tiredly lamented.

"You will see, she will not contrrrrol you much longerrrr, you will leave herrrr and move away."

"Yeah, right, whatever." I thought wistfully.

Anxious to get this farce over with, I came up with some more mundane questions, regarding my decision to purchase some expensive music equipment, whether or not I should buy it at this time or not. Indira advised me to wait; she said I would get better quality keyboards for less money once I moved to New York.

There was that impossible notion of moving to New York again. I figured I'd wasted enough time on Indira's "psychic predictions" obviously she was saying what she thought I wanted to hear. I thanked her for the reading and started to rise from my chair.

"You'rrre motherrrr passed away rrrrecently, and you've been hearrring frrrom herrrr."

It was a statement not a question. She said this like it was the most normal thing in the world. It took me by surprise because I hadn't mentioned mothers passing, and I froze in mid-stance, trying to quickly decide if I should even admit to her bold declaration.

"Well, yes…I did hear from her in April when I was in New York but since I've been back here…I really haven't felt her presence at all."

"The darrrrkness of yourrrr life has clouded yourrrr clearrrrr rrrrreception!" she snapped.

Feebly I concurred; "I…I…guess so…"

"Soon you will be clouded no morrrre! Is therrrre anything else you wish to know?"

"Well, I guess not, at least I can't think of anything else important to ask you…"

"All of the imporrrrtant questions have been answerrred." She said this with a tone of finality that instantly had me reaching for my wallet.

"You may leave whateverrrr donation you wish, on the table." She said, as she led the dogs to the back door, and disappeared with them into the backyard.

I'd been here perhaps thirty minutes. "What's the going rate for housewife psychics?" I wondered as I pulled some bills out of my wallet, and placed fifty dollars on the table.

"Is fifty dollars enough?" I questioned her as she swept back into the room.

"Most gene-rrrous sirrrr!"

Isn't it a pity, now isn't it a shame…"
From George Harrison's album: All Things Must Pass

My thoughts tumbled back and forth between belief and disbelief as I drove the twenty miles back home. "Is Megan lying about the baby? Would she stoop that low?" I knew she was cunning but I thought she was beyond this type of cruelty. Then I remembered many years ago when we were having an affair under her husbands nose.

Overwhelmed with guilt, I'd told her it was over. She had her best friend Jean call me at the restaurant to tell me Megan was so despondent that she'd swallowed rat poison in a suicide attempt. Of course, she hadn't, but I was a kid then, I believed her. That was the first time she'd tricked me with guilt into staying with her. She effectively played the recovering poison victim and begged me not to leave her; otherwise she would be successful the next time.

With all of the lies I'd seen Megan tell Rex, and all of the ones I'd subsequently discovered she'd told me, Indira had said she was lying, why should I be so surprised?

As far as leaving Megan and "moving to New York" I don't

think so! How could that be possible? I'd only stayed three weeks in the city and I'd quickly learned how expensive it was. Everything there cost five times the amount it did in Oregon, I'd have to save a lot of money to move there and we were strapped as it was. "See Yoko again"??? I doubt it! It had been miraculous that I'd run into her the three times that I had!

The only real peace I felt on the drive home was that more than a piece of my cash was wasted, fifty dollars worth! I was too skeptical and cautious to hope that Indira could be right, and too afraid of deluding my self about not having a child with Megan to believe otherwise. I wrestled with my thoughts all the way home, and as I pulled in the gravel driveway, the lyrics of George Harrison filled my truck with song; "Isn't it a pity/now isn't it a shame/how we break each others hearts/and cause each other pain…"

The following day, as pleasantly as I could, I asked Megan how far along her pregnancy was.

"About six weeks I guess but it's really none of your business, why should you care?" She snidely responded.

"I was just curious! You don't have to be a bitch about it!"

"So now I'm a bitch! You haven't seen the half of what a bitch I'm going to be!!!"

"Fine! Whatever! I hope it dies." I seethed back.

For the next two days she avoided me and I her. I didn't want to argue, I just wanted to quietly accept the fact that Indira had been wrong, Megan was sticking to her story, we were definitely having a baby.

Megan and I worked opposite shifts and purposely we hadn't seen each other for two days. On the third day we unavoidably met in the driveway as she was coming home from work and I was leaving.

"I'm going to look for an apartment later." She said with her head low, eyes averted.

Gently I replied; "Look, you don't have to move out, you keep the house and I'll move. You need space for the baby and you can't afford a two bedroom apartment on your own."

She looked down at the gravel, and softly said; "I won't be needing two bedrooms, you got your wish, I've miscarried."

She then looked up at me, her eyes welling with tears, and she reached out for me to embrace her.

"When? Where?" I asked as I took her into my arms.

"Yesterday; in the bathroom. You weren't here..."

She began rhythmically sobbing into my shoulder.

At first I felt true compassion for her, but as we stood together in the driveway, I couldn't help wondering if this was a new game. She hadn't looked at me when she told me, which gave her ample time to start her waterworks. Now she was hiding her face in my shoulder and I noticed her sobbing had a theatrical quality. Was she crying because she knew that I'd become suspicious and had to end the lie with another lie before I confronted her? Now she had the added advantage of blaming me for the miscarriage, (because I'd said "I hope it dies.") as well as my absent assistance when it "happened". She'd always been masterful at instilling guilt in me, but this time, I didn't believe her. I felt the crocodile tears were just her way of masking the pregnancy lie with the proper dramatic effect.

I thought to my self: "The only miscarriage going on here is one of the truth."

I decided to go with it. Two could play this game. I could put on the sad face too, even though I was overjoyed at the "sad news". I was willing to do anything that would foster civility between us, because I knew I could leave her now, even if it was just across town, and I wanted to do it as lovingly and as honorably as possible. I didn't want us to hate each other; we'd been through too much for that. Besides, I'd raised her and Rex's daughter Fiona, who still lovingly called me daddy, I didn't want that to change because Megan and I were at odds. I figured Megan and I could divorce amicably, we were adults, supposedly from a more enlightened generation, we could at the very least set a good example for Fiona by remaining friends.

We managed to be civil to each other again, even kind and loving, in a platonic sense. I went out of my way to make concessions for Megan as she accepted that we needed to separate. She made it clear that she expected the separation would bring us back together, eventually.

"Mamma Leone left a note on the door…"
From Billy Joel's song: Movin' Out (Anthony's Song)

"**M**amma Leone left a note on the door she said sonny move out…" I'd always loved this Billy Joel song (Megan hated it; for obvious reasons!) and while Megan was at work, I listened to the album that this song: **Movin' Out (Anthony's Song)** is on.

This *Marc Anthony* was definitely "movin' out!" and strangely enough, as Indira predicted, I was moving to New York City!

I'd been able to convince Megan that it was best for both of us. She managed to cling to her illusion that this would just be a temporary separation. I knew better, but if it would ease the blow of the reality for her, I was willing to play it her way.

She made three demands before I left: 1) I would tell my employers that I wasn't leaving her; I was just moving to New York City temporarily to see if she and I wanted to move there someday. (another "earthquake" lie) 2) That out of the $10,000 cash I'd recently received as inheritance from mom, Megan's car would be paid off, all of our bills would be paid in full, and I would pay to install central heating in our old farmhouse. (When we'd bought the house 9 years before, she'd been playing the role of "crunchy granola Earth Mother" and insisted on a wood stove to heat it. Apparently that had been fine as long as I was there to help chop the wood and feed the stove all those years…now she wasn't as willing to play the back to nature advocate she fancied her "intellectual" self to be.) and 3) Out of the remaining $3,000 I would leave $1,000 in the bank for any emergencies she might have, which left me $2,000 for moving expenses.

I was more than willing to comply. Mother's money was paying for my freedom, and if this was the cost, so be it. I should've known it was going to cost me far more in the long run, but I was too blinded by my impending "prison" release to concern myself with any future other than my imminent departure.

One of the last things Megan said to me, with a worried look on her face was: "I feel like I will never see you again."

I didn't know it then, but her fearful words held a universe of truth in them. We would see each other again two more times, but she never saw *me* again, she would only see new opportunities for more lies, manipulation, and malicious retaliation.

July 14, 1988 I felt like I was being born again as I stepped off the plane at La Guardia airport. As I gathered my luggage and raced to the street, I had the distinct feeling that *my* life was finally beginning! I hailed a cab and went to the South Bronx where I would be staying with my friend Bill. He'd moved to this location, known as Schwab Court, after Dan moved back to Pennsylvania, because the rents were much cheaper in The Bronx than in Manhattan. It was easy to see why. Tidal waves of trash littered the streets that were lined with fire scorched, graffiti tagged, crumbling, decrepit apartment buildings, that now served as crack houses and homeless squatters "shooting galleries". I'd not seen *this* slice of the "Big Apple" before! I felt as dazed and confused as Dorothy in <u>The Wizard of Oz</u> when the tornado finally dumps her in Munchkin Land except that this was not a place of beauty, and was a far cry from the sweeping green fields of Oregon or The Emerald City. I'd never before witnessed such slum conditions except on T.V. and as the cab drove through the grungy neighborhood I knew I wasn't "in Kansas anymore!"

Strangely enough I wasn't frightened in the least. I merely accepted the fact that evidently the "Schwab Court" that I was going to, had absolutely no relation whatsoever to the semi-sophisticated urban legend of actress Lana Turner, who supposedly, in the 1950's was "discovered" sipping on a soda at Schwab's drugstore. This neighborhood was a "drugstore" alright, South Bronx style! No future starlets were sipping sodas here!

As the taxi passed numerous seedy looking characters, menacingly meandering on the rundown sidewalks of the squalid streets, we finally pulled up to Schwab Court. I paid the East Indian cabbie who had been blaring Hindu ragas from his radio during his nervous drive, and I stepped out of the cab where the raucous sounds of Miami salsa music echoed through the crumbling canyons of empty buildings.

Two apparent gunshots rang out in the late afternoon sun from a block away, and to my own undisturbed surprise, it didn't seem strange, only different.

Oddly, Schwab Court appeared to be a very respectable looking building. The courtyard had some well tended semi-circle flower beds from the sidewalk to the front door, where the words Schwab Court in blue, green and white tile were embedded in brick above the entrance.

Bill buzzed the auto-locked door open and we carried my bags through the very clean and quite nice looking hallways and up the three flights of stairs to his apartment.

It was not a large apartment, but it was twice the size of the expensive tiny domain that he and Dan had shared at Columbus Circle in Manhattan.

At the moment, I didn't care where I was living; I simply knew that after my years of emotional incarceration with Megan, I could finally breathe.

I was reminded of that scene in the Wizard of Oz where the Wicked Witch has Dorothy captive in the castle, and Toto has just escaped over the drawbridge, whereupon Dorothy gleefully exclaims tearfully: "He got away!!! He got away!!!"

I easily settled in to my strange new surroundings, deciding I would not look for employment for the first month. I wanted to get to know Manhattan better, and now I was traveling back and forth from the mean streets and subway portals of The South Bronx, which required me to put on a seriously tough, street wise exterior, in order to safely survive.

As I've stated before, Leo is the sign of "The Actor" and I instinctively understood how to disguise my usually open hearted, jovial disposition, into an aura of brooding intensity. I had to look and behave with an air of impatient authority so that the blatant criminals who freely roamed my neighborhood, wouldn't sense my more playful, kitty cat in the jungle sensibilities.

This new persona was so unlike me, I certainly had seldom been intimidating, and I'd always complied for the most part with the governing authorities growing up. Between Megan and my parents "Do as I say or else!" admonitions, along with the 12 year guilt ridden scolding dictatorships of my various parochial school nuns and priests, I'd been bred to be a people pleaser. By the time Megan usurped my mind, body, and soul, I'd surrendered any concept of self assuredness I may have ever previously possessed. I'd always been too open and friendly, even to the point of being considered "an easy Marc." (Spelling pun not only intended but entirely appropriate!) I had to change my relaxed, laid back attitude, for survival.

I also had to learn the seemingly endless maze of subways to get around. For someone who was used to driving my self everywhere, this was a very monumental challenge. Many times in this first month I ended up on the wrong train, going in the wrong direction because the whole transit system seemed like a foreign language.

By mid-August, embroiled in the hot sticky humidity of the underground stations, I was neatly dressed and had my list of restaurants in Manhattan to apply for a job. Today was my birthday; maybe it would bring me good luck…

At 10am. as I stood on the platform at 125th street in Harlem, I was trying to figure out on the subway map whether I needed the A- train or the D-train to make it to my first appointment. I knew I needed to be at a bistro on 81st street by 11am. I was confused by

Italian Mothers Never Die

all of the blue, green, orange, red, and yellow numbered map lines that showed the various arterials and stops of all the trains.

In the stifling hot and oppressive humid air of the underground station, I stood fanning myself with a newspaper in one hand as I tried to read the map held by the other. I was already hot and sticky in my clothes and my day was just getting started!

I still hadn't decided which train I needed when the A-train pulled up on my left and the D-train pulled up on my right simultaneously. I had less than one minute to decide! At first I got on the A-train, fairly certain I'd made the right choice. Again I looked at the map and panic stared back at me as I realized I wasn't sure! "Take the D-train…" A tiny voice deep inside of me whispered. "No! I need the A-train don't I?" My brain responded. "The D-train, you need to take the D-train" the small voice grew a little clearer. "No! The D-train will take me to Mamma Leone's and they aren't accepting applications until 2 o'clock!" I argued resolutely in my thoughts.

The volume and vibration of the small voice increased, mixing in with the trains crackling loudspeakers just as the conductor instructed: "Watch the closing doors!" ***"Take the D-train!!!"*** overrode the voice. I quickly jammed my arm in-between the doors as they were closing and had to push them to a stop before I squeezed my way off the subway car and ran across the platform to the D-train where the conductor had just said "Watch the closing doors!" I barely made it onto the train and I stood there puzzled as it began its acceleration. The conductor's voice blared over the subway car speakers: "This train is express to 42nd street, there will be no local stops!" I knew immediately that I'd jumped on the wrong train. I instantly started berating myself. "What am I doing on this train! I'm supposed to go to 81st not 42nd! This frickin' train doesn't even stop at 81st street! What am I doing??!! I'm on the wrong damn train!" No hint of that other voice responded.

At the time, I didn't even consider that it had been mom's voice. It was simply my own errant sub-conscious. I hadn't heard from mother since my vacation in NYC 16 months ago.

When I'd returned to Oregon, I didn't bother to discuss mom's miraculous interventions with Megan; she wouldn't have believed me anyway. Also, the final year that Megan and I spent together had been so full of confusion, tension, and frustrated anger that I'd conceded to psychic Indira's statements regarding my "unclearrrr rrrreception!" I merely assumed mom had more than adequately performed her share of the Catholic Church required "3-miracles for Sainthood" during my last visit, and had moved on to some higher plane. Besides, the voice had started out as a whisper, and by the time it commanded: ***"Take the D-train!!!"*** it was mixed with the static filled loudspeaker blaring: "Watch the closing doors!" I was convinced the voice was just my imagination.

   I rode along on the crowded train mashed up against the other standing, heavily perspiring straphangers. The air was thick with moisture, and as the fast moving express train careened through the tunnels, at every track switch and turn, it rocked us all closer together like a load of laundry on the spin cycle. Unfortunately this produced an even hotter and stickier atmosphere and by the time I got off the train, my hair was plastered flat against my head, I was dripping with sweat and my clothes looked like I'd put them on wet. On top of my sorely disheveled appearance, I was completely pissed off at myself for taking the wrong train! It was too late to take another train to the 81st street bistro, and way too early to apply at Mamma Leone's Italian Restaurant whose green canopied, ochre yellow building, greeted me as I came out of the subway station. Besides, nobody was going to hire me in my "looks like I jumped fully clothed into a swimming pool" attire.

   I spotted the Majestic Theatre buttressed against Mamma Leone's. Surely the ticket office lobby had air-conditioning, I needed somewhere to cool off and dry my hair and clothes before I made another move.

   As I passed the entrance of Mamma Leone's there was a note taped to the door that read: Applications will be accepted at 2pm. It was only 10:30am.

   "Way to go Marc! Happy freakin' birthday! You took the wrong train dumb ass!" I hissed at myself under my breath as I headed for the door of The Majestic.

   The theatre marquee in bold letters read: The Phantom of the

Opera, and as I reached for the door I thought angrily to myself; "Well, you always wanted me to learn to appreciate Opera mom, I'd *really appreciate it* if it's air-conditioned right now!"

As I entered the lobby, the cool sweet scented air enveloped me as if I'd stepped into the soft petals of a lotus flower.

The ticket counter was set to open at 11am. and nobody else was in the quietly calm surroundings. I put my briefcase on a narrow counter that fortunately faced a mirrored wall. I set to work hastily reconstructing my hair and at the same time began billowing my shirt and tie away from my sweat drenched skin. For the next fifteen minutes I transformed myself from a sticky, hot wet mess, into a respectable looking arid coolness.

Finally satisfied at my calm regrouping, I wondered to myself; "Now what? Are there any other restaurants in this neighborhood that I could apply at?"

Looking through the theatre lobby window I spied the famous restaurant Sardis' across the street. I started thinking I should go there when the soft whisper returned: "Go to Mamma Leone's."

I registered it's appearance wearily, "Oh don't start again!" I whined silently to myself.

"Go to Mamma Leone's" the voice countered.

"No! I just saw a note on the door and it..." before I could finish, the voice grew more insistent.

"I know what the note says..."

"Well then what's the point!?" I vehemently argued.

"There's only one way to find out, go!"

I started to protest again: "But I..."

"But nothing! Go!"

Shaking my head in futile exasperation, I reluctantly grabbed my briefcase. I didn't want to leave this air conditioned cocoon. I'd have to walk quickly to Mamma Leone's because just a few moments on the sidewalk and I'd look like a sweaty slob again. I paused, ready to talk myself out of this...

"Go! No excuses!"

I knew it was my own Mamma Leone's (Mother Lion's) voice this time. *"No excuses!"* was one of her most often used expressions in life; apparently it was still on the menu.

I swung open the door of The Majestic and hastily scurried past The Phantom poster along the sidewalk as I made my way to Mamma Leone's entrance.

Upon entering I was surprised to see a crowd of about 50 people sitting in chairs, on bar stools, leaning against counters and sitting on stairs, all of them filling out employment applications.

I approached the Host desk and a very tall, swarthy and stern looking man in a dark shiny suit, scribbling furiously on a legal pad, ignored me as I said: "Excuse me…"

He held his large hand up without looking at me and barked: "We are taking no more applications until 2pm!!! Didn't you read ***the note on the door!?***"

I flushed with timid embarrassment and replied; "Yes, I saw it. Would it be alright to take an application with me?"

Without ever looking up at me, he ripped an application off a pad and thrust it at mc.

"Thank you, I'll come back at 2'oclock" I replied, shaken by his rude abruptness.

In a very agitated voice he responded: "Fill it out *now* and leave it on this desk on your way out!"

I found a tiny unoccupied space on one of the marbled steps and sat down with the application on my lap. As I filled it out I wondered if I wanted to work here at all! The "Host" had treated me like garbage, and the room was filled with obviously qualified and confident looking applicants. It was plain to see that they were well seasoned New York City restaurant servers, while I was coming from a very small mom and pop Hungarian establishment in Oregon. My rustic, small town restaurant server experience was certainly out of this big city league. I continued filling out the application with no false hopes of getting the job, but at least I was still in an air conditioned environment, best to take advantage of it before returning to the sizzling hot streets.

After 15 minutes had passed, I'd completed the form. I stood up and started to approach the rude host at his desk when a petite, attractive, wiry grey haired woman, came out of the adjacent restaurant bar. Snatching the application out of my hand she said; "Follow me."

I followed her through the kitchen and down a large winding staircase into a considerably sized banquet room.

"I'm Sandy, have a seat." She said.

"Thank you." I replied.

Sandy sat silently for a moment, looking over my application.

"You recently moved here from Oregon?"

"Yes."

"It says here that you worked in a Hungarian Restaurant, how big was it?"

"It seated about 40 or 50 people."

"This restaurant is three very large floors; we average about 600 people per night. Did you see the 2nd floor staircases?"

"Yes I did."

"The main kitchen is on the middle floor. Do you think you can handle a tray with say…14 to 16 dinners stacked on it, running up and down the staircases?"

"Sure!" I lied.

"Marc Anthony huh? You're familiar with Italian food I take it?"

"Yes, my mother was an excellent cook."

"Can you describe Fettuccini Alfredo for me?"

"Fettuccini with a parmesan and nutmeg cream sauce."

"How about Veal Parmesan?"

"Lightly breaded veal cutlets, sautéed and topped with marinara sauce and melted mozzarella cheese."

"The work shift here is ten to sixteen hours per day, 7 days a week from September until New Years Day. The season slows down after that and you'll only work part time until April, when business picks up again. Can you handle those long hours?"

Without hesitating I assured her: "No problem!"

"Can you start tomorrow at 4 o'clock?"

"Yes!"

"Welcome aboard then!" She smiled and reached out to shake my hand.

"I clasped her hand and said; "Thank you Sandy, thank you very much!"

"You're welcome! I'll see you tomorrow then! You know the way out?"

"Yes, thank you."

I quickly left the room before she had a chance to change her mind and bound up the winding staircase two steps at a time. Shocked that in less than 5 minutes with Sandy, I had a job! Not just any job, but a job at a world famous, and still thriving, more than half a century old New York City landmark! I made my way slowly through the applicant's crowd, still packed like sardines in the lobby, and past the brooding host, who looked up as I inched my way by and snarled: "Your application, here!"

"I've just met with Sandy and she has it."

"Fine then! Come back at 2!" he growled.

"Oh, perhaps you've misunderstood." I purred sweetly. "She asked me to come to work tomorrow at 4 o'clock."

"Well then, *be on time*!" He huffed and looked back down at his podium.

"I will be! Goodbye!" I sang with a smile.

Outside on the glaring hot sidewalk, I rushed to the shade of the awning that covered The Phantom of the Opera poster. I could see the lobby was full, and I wanted to be alone with my thoughts. I couldn't believe I'd gotten a job at the very first place I applied at! Leaning against the face of The Phantom on the wall, I was filled with happiness as I ripped off my tie, opened my shirt, and sang to myself in my head: "Happy birthday to me/ from Mamma Leone/ Happy birthday Marc Anthony/ happy birthday to me!" I laughed at my giddy childish lyric and then my thoughts segued from the traditional Happy Birthday melody, to Billy Joel: *"Mamma Leone left a note on the door…"* and then mom oscillated her words through me: *"Welcome home son…"* As the vibration of her voice gently quivered inside me, the hair stood up on my neck and arms, my entire spine pleasantly shivered and tingled, and a burst of jubilant tears began streaming down my face.

Way of the Peaceful Warrior
"A book that changes lives"

Fortunately the sneering Host at Mamma Leone's was fired a month after I'd started. On the day his termination was formally announced by Mr. Joseph Montalbano, the kind and affable "Directore" (or: "Mr. M" as he was affectionately known) it was further conveyed to the room full of about 60 employees, that we had just signed a contract with the local Culinary Union.

Among the cheers, handclaps and whistles, I heard mom's voice as it clearly entered and vibrated within me: ***"Marc, look around the room, it's like Noah's Ark, there are at least two of every Astrological sign here. Pay attention…"***

Her presence quickly left me as the wild cheers and applause of the crowd subsided. Then Mr. M. addressed me: "Alora Marco! You've been here a month now, how do you like working with us here at Mamma's?"

I felt a blush rush up to my face as I responded: "I love it here sir, it feels like I'm part of one big happy family."

Mr. M waved over the crowd and quickly bowed to my response. "Ah bravo!! Viva Famigilia!!!" He exclaimed, clapping.

The crowd applauded and cheered again, and as Mr. M. left the room, everyone dispersed to their individual departments.

As I made my way to the men's room to freshen up in this mid-shift break, I thought about mother's latest message. I'd only heard her mention astrology *once in her life*, and that was two months before she died.

In the spring of 1986, I'd just told Megan for the umpteenth time that I wanted a divorce. She argued with me all day using every excuse she could come up with why it wasn't the solution to my constant unhappiness.

I'd been depressed since September, ever since Fiona went away to college and it really hit me that now, and for the rest of my life, it was going to be just Megan and me, growing old in the middle of a cornfield, living on our Dead End street at the base of a Cemetery. I might as well walk up the hill and climb in a coffin because I was already dead. She was content with our lives as they were but I was drowning in foreboding regarding our future.

This was not the life I'd envisioned for myself, it was Megan's dreams we were living, the "hippie" "Mother Earth News magazine dream, and it bored me to tears!

Megan cried, begged, and argued with me the entire day, and that evening, I got a phone call from my older brother Jim, telling me that mom had been diagnosed with terminal cancer.

I left Megan for the next three months and stayed in Southern California with mom while she was undergoing chemotherapy.

One day as I was busy washing the dishes in her kitchen; she was on the phone with her best friend Judy. I could hear mom's voice loud and clear chatting gaily away but I wasn't paying any attention to the one sided conversation coming from the next room because I had the radio on.

Suddenly she clearly said something that made me nearly drop the dish I'd been rinsing; "Of course Judy!!! ***It's because we're both Leo's!!!***"

I stood frozen over the sink in disbelief, thinking to myself: "Did that just come out of *my* mother's mouth? The same mother whose only references to spiritual affairs of any kind were always solidly connected to her unwavering Catholicism!!? What's this? Did the Joia Barone who raised *me* just admit that she was open to the idea that our identities were influenced by the stars, which is entirely against the "Divinely infallible" rules, regulations and beliefs of her beloved church?"

I was decisively astonished at overhearing her Astrological acceptance so firmly invoked to her friend as factual.

I resumed doing the dishes and never said anything to her about it, there never seemed to be the right moment in what unexpectedly ended up being her last four months of life on this planet.

But here and now, less than two years later, in the middle of a crowded room at Mamma Leone's, she's talking Signs and Planets *again,* in the middle of our restaurant pre-shift meeting? Mamma mia!!!

The clear memory of that long ago overheard conversation flooded my head as I swung the door open to the men's room. I'd been stunned then and I was equally astounded to hear this new endorsement from her now, but somehow I knew *exactly* what she meant, and from that day forward I *really* started paying closer attention to how people of various Astrological signs interact with each another, and how they also behaved themselves.

I've come to understand this ancient science as a star mapped blueprint of humanity's **emotional** evolution, from the cradle to the grave. From the Firstborn Fire Sign, the infant Aries, who's motto is "I Am!" (As in The Light of God who is "The Great, I Am!") To the oldest sign Pisces, whose element is Water, baptized into rebirth through death, and whose motto is "I Believe." These first and last signs, along with all of the Fire, Earth, Air and Water signs in between, represent the full aging spectrum of human life, with all of it's emotional, physical and spiritual desires, and they are all contained, revealed, and explained in those twelve planetary "Apostles". Astrology seems to me like a giant celestial clock whose stellar influence moves with precision and order, and if we'd use it's knowledge and concepts as tools, not for fortunetelling, but for self awareness and human understanding, we could foster a world of genuine peace, hope, and vision, rather than one of self righteous political and spiritual mayhem.

Unfortunately the science and truths of Astrology have been bastardized by tabloid newspaper "psychics" of modern media, and reduced to the tired cliché's of "What's your sign?" and "Who am

I compatible with?" but it's roots in human behavioral awareness are centuries deeper than that. I know that my observance of it's finer details have brought me a greater sensitivity and clearer understanding of myself and of the world around me, and I'm a more patient, forgiving and loving person because of the invaluable emotional and behavioral insights "The Signs" have to offer.

I've heard that scientific proof has recently been established that human beings are in fact made up of the same substances as stars are. I'm fairly certain The Bible states that we are born of light, and I wonder if the Magi were referred to as "The Three Wise Men" because they were Astrologers who literally followed a star to The Light of The World! Certainly that was wise!

I don't believe that we are ***controlled*** by planetary influence, only that we are ***inclined*** towards various emotional and behavioral patterns, depending on the daily planetary transits. We always have the free will to ***choose*** our behavior, for as a wise saying goes: "The stars incline us but they do not *define* us."

I'm inclined towards my Leo feline sensibilities most of the time, but every once in a while, I have to shake off my leonine pussycat ways and become my bolder rising sign of Aries, the Ram. The roar of a lion can be sounded in a very calmly delivered sentence, and the Leo in me is usually content to issue a suitable verbal warning of displeasure when required. The Ram however is quick to race up the mountain and lock horns to defend his emotional turf because patience has not had a chance to fully develop in its infant sign.

I didn't know it yet but there was a battle of patience, literally *on a mountaintop*, looming in my future, and I'd all too soon realize that mom's admonition to ***"pay attention"*** to the ***signs***, was to become more beneficial than I otherwise would have ever have guessed.

I very happily lived at Schwab Court in the South Bronx, working at Mamma Leone's for nearly a year before moving into my own apartment in Manhattan. Understand that when I say apartment, I mean dump! For those of you who have seen the 1970's movie <u>Midnight Cowboy</u> and remember Dustin Hoffman's character "Rizzo" and the dumpy "railroad flat" he lived in, no description is necessary. However, please indulge me for a moment while I describe it for those who have no idea what a "railroad flat" is.

One dictionary describes it as "A long narrow set of rooms, without hallways or doors, leading from one room to the next." Mine was so much less than that! It was a very **short** set of three drafty rooms infested with and endless procession of mice. There was no shower, but there was a bathtub in the kitchen (with a rusting metal cover that fit over the tub and doubled as kitchen counter space) a 5'x7 foot "bedroom" that could barely contain a single mattress, and a tiny, paint peeling "living room" with several broken windows overlooking a courtyard riddled with trash. The decrepit, graffiti ridden building had a mural of a barbed wired head of The Statue of Liberty, with color cartoon faced people of various ethnicities clinging to Liberty's spiked crown, painted on it's outdoor walls. It was appropriate artwork aptly depicting its poor immigrant residents.

I was fortunate that the bathtub was directly across from the stove because there was scant water pressure, and the constantly cold water, flowed very slowly through a line in the claw footed tub, and even slower in the rusted 1930's sink nearby. In order to bathe, I had to get up each morning at least two hours early to fill pots of water and heat them on the stove in order to halfway fill the tub.

Twice daily I emptied the half dozen mousetraps and restocked them with peanut butter. Also, because it was a rent controlled apartment and I was secretly subletting it, I had to sneak in and out of the building so that the corporate owners who had an office next door wouldn't see me. All of this for the very real bargain price of $425.00 per. month! (I'd seen one apartment **much worse** for $600.00) I'd never lived in such squalor in my life!

In Oregon I could've easily rented a spacious two bedroom townhouse with a pool for less than half of that! I'd spent nearly nine years remodeling our house in Oregon which now stood as a palace compared to my new surroundings, and the mortgage for it, along with a sprawling portion of land was only $260.00 per. month. But this "railroad flat" was my own space, and despite its many very real shortcomings, I have to say that the two years I lived there were in retrospect, some of the happiest years of my life.

I was very happy working at Mamma Leone's and now I no longer had to commute from The South Bronx on the train, I easily walked the twelve blocks to work. Also, Mamma Leone's had a large group of employees, and there were several aspiring actresses, actors, writers, comedians, and a very gifted painter working there. I finally felt like I was in my element. A novice to be sure, but I quickly signed up for a music studio recording class, and before long I was doing something I never thought was even remotely possible, singing and recording my own songs!

The only musical training I'd previously had was for about a month, by a very violent Carmelite nun in the third grade, Sister Mary Mark, who screamed "Idiot!" and smacked my fingers with her walnut pointer during my lessons. My sessions ended when she told my mom that I was so stupid, I couldn't even spell my name properly because I ended it with a "**c** instead of a **k**"! Mom curtly informed Sister Mary Mark that it was on my birth certificate as Marc, and thankfully my lessons ended.

I tried lessons again in my mid-twenties for about two months, from a nervous man who talked to his mother on the phone during the entire length of each of my lessons, interrupting his phone calls only long enough to bark: "Wrong! Start over!"

Other than those two attempts, I'd taught myself how to play. I still didn't read music and I played piano solely by ear, but now I knew a talented music arranger who transcribed my home recorded compositions from cassette tapes and then played my songs professionally on his studio equipment. I was finally making strides in a direction that brought me true joy.

As Indira had predicted, I was able to buy some very fine keyboards in the city for much cheaper than I could have in Oregon. I was in the middle of recording my first studio album when Megan finally accepted that I had no plans of continuing our marriage. She called to tell me that she was willing to get a divorce, and in the same phone call informed me that Fiona was getting married in a few months. I responded with concern about Fiona not finishing college and getting married at 18. I knew from experience how having a family changed one's priorities and opportunities. Megan responded quite nastily saying: "Just because it didn't work for you doesn't mean it won't make her happy! Besides, I only called to invite you, I didn't ask for your opinion!" It was obvious she was trying to steer me into an argument. I could hear that Fiona was also in the room and Megan wanted to take this opportunity to discredit me in front of her. I'd seen Megan use this gambit before with her first husband Rex. (Fiona's biological father my ex-best friend.) I wasn't falling for it. "When and where is the wedding?" I calmly asked. She gave me the details and before she hung up, she took devilish spiteful delight in telling me that I would not be walking Fiona down the aisle. "Fiona and I have decided that it is nothing more than a barbaric tradition." Megan lied. (Translation: Self-serving Megan had cunningly manipulated Fiona into **believing** that it was a barbaric tradition in order to deprive me of the honor.)

The following morning, it was my day off and I was lazily strolling through Washington Square Park. Springtime in Manhattan is the most refreshing time of year. The air is delicately scented with clustered cherry tree blossoms and long narrow beds of fragrant hyacinths, dancing daffodils, and pastel colored tulips lining the sidewalks. There was a small crowd in the park and everyone wore a luminous glow of happiness shining on their faces as they stood around a large fountain, watching apples, pears, and bananas, being deftly juggled by one of a number of NYU students on spring break. There were lovers, intimately talking and tenderly caressing each other, bleaching in and out of the Botticelli blue skied sunlight, while rainbow tinted sprays of water shimmered behind them as they sat on the fountains edge. A trio of twenty-something rock musicians were softly rehearsing <u>Sweet Child</u>

O'Mine underlined on a park bench underneath a canopy of fresh new Hunter Green tree foliage, where flocks of birds seemed to be doing a fine job as backup singers.

I was taking in the wide spectrum of smiling and relaxed faces. The energy around me was perfumed by a spirit of jubilant renewal. Basking in the calm, unfettered vibrations of my personal rebirth, the harmonic rhythms of serenity pulsed within me as I closed my eyes with my face to the sky, and continued slowly walking. Absorbing the gentle spring warmth, I felt completely connected with God and nature. This connection was pleasantly flowing through me, mind, body and soul, when suddenly I stepped on a solid foreign object. I opened my eyes and looked down to discover that I'd just stepped on a book. I bent over to pick it up, reading its orange and blue bold lettered title: <u>Way of the Peaceful Warrior</u>.

I began looking around for someone who may have dropped it but I'd walked into a deserted area. I left the empty sidewalk and sat down on the grass underneath a giant Oak tree. Looking closer at the cover, I saw a vibrant color drawing of a gas station on a street corner, situated under a full moonlighted starry sky. The outline of a young man stands near the gas station. His face and body are filled in with portions of the street, the gas pumps, hillside homes and their surrounding scenery, along with an early morning rising sun. Underneath the title it reads: "A book that changes lives." I turned the book over and read the brief intriguing synopsis. I looked around again for someone to recognize their book in my hands, but no one was in the vicinity.

I remembered that the name Marc is derived from the word Mars, and that Mars (Astrologically speaking) is considered "The Warrior Planet". I opened the book and started reading.

For the next three hours I was enraptured by the story of the author Dan Millman and his spiritually awakening experiences. Dan is guided through some very miraculous events by his Zen like elderly gas station attendant and true life friend, whom he nicknames: "Socrates".

Some of the transformative events that Mr. Millman encounters are in so many ways similar to the ones I've experienced from mother. His vivid descriptions of these otherworldly communions read as though I could've written them myself.

Earnestly taking this all in, I burst out laughing as soon as the character "Joy" appears. It turns out that Joy seems to be a phantom of sorts, who brings Dan unbridled bliss, but then disappears for months on end. (Not only was Joy mother's nick name, this was also her same mode of operation…)

The message I derived from the book, in the most succinct terms is that, we are not to dwell on the past or the future, because *now* is all we have and thus it is called "the present" for the gift that it is. The book also ascribes that to be a warrior we must let a loving, generous and forgiving heart lead the way, for ultimately we are all intimately connected to the same Oneness of the universe, and indeed we, along with everything else, *are* that Oneness. The Oneness of creation, God in motion.

Since the word universe literally means "one song" this book, its message and its miraculous events, seemed tailor made for my psyche at this particular juncture of my life. As long as I remained removed from Megan and her selfish, destructive philosophies of what constitutes love, I was living in harmony with the "one song" for the first time in my life.

Pensively I went over the details and the lessons of my day as I made my way home, and my only lingering question, smiling and half-heartedly was, "Did mom toss this book out of the Heavens onto the sidewalk or merely tip it out of somebody's backpack…" Whatever the case, it seemed to be a sign I should *"pay attention"* to…

I could feel "The Ram" in me itching to lock horns with Megan every time she provoked me on the phone leading up to the wedding, instead I held back, clinging to the precepts of the Peaceful Warrior.

Unlike my own Father, who without conscience readily left our family destitute while mother was suffering from a nervous breakdown, I'd not left Megan in any clinical dire straights or without ample resources. I left her in a nicely modernized and redecorated farmhouse, situated on pastoral acreage with many overabundant fruit trees and endless vines overflowing with world famous Oregon blackberries, more than we were ever able to manually gather.

Through my brother Jim, I actually had a frozen food company who wanted to buy the fruit from Megan, but when I mentioned this to her, she spitefully declined saying that she didn't want any of my brother's or my friends at the house. I explained that it was a large Frozen Food company, business acquaintances not personal friends, and they would pay handsomely for the truckloads they would harvest. She'd have an added income without lifting a finger! Still she nastily declined, willing to stupidly cut off her own nose to spite *my* face.

I also left her with two very beautiful and fully paid vehicles, all other bills currently paid, and a bank account with a thousand dollars; in Oregon circa: 1988 that was a lot of money!

Of my own accord I'd faithfully sent her $400.00 per month since I'd been here. This amount in New York City didn't even cover the rent of my drafty, cold water railroad flat mouse nest, but in Oregon, it fully paid the mortgage and utilities with $50.00 leftover. Her only expenses were food and gasoline. This meant that Megan could spend the eight hundred dollars per month she made from her job, anyway she pleased.

I on the other hand, was living in the most expensive city in the United States. As any resident there can tell you, a hundred dollars a day is mere pocket change on the everyday streets of Manhattan.

Fortunately, as anyone who really knows me can verify, I've inherited mom's ability to live like a Prince on a paupers wage. I was more than happy to make things easier for Megan and sacrifice my own needs in order to foster civility between us, and hopefully an amicable divorce.

However, she was the raging epitome of: "Hell hath no fury like a woman scorned." She spitefully relished every new opportunity for vengeance whenever she spoke to me, while at the same time effectively playing the innocent martyred victim to her family, and our mutual friends. She definitely had her Libra balancing act fine tuned. I didn't have to be there to know this, the grapevine of our small town was able to extend across the country and keep me informed. I could certainly understand her hurt, what I couldn't figure out was her insatiable appetite for spite. It was an ugliness that I'd seen pieces of before but now it seemed to be multiplying in leaps and bounds!

She'd agreed to pick me up at the airport for the wedding, but she snippily informed me that I would have to get a hotel once I arrived as she'd taken out a restraining order barring me from the house. I was blindsided and stunned! What heinous crime had I committed? I'd been bending over backwards to be accommodating and pleasant to her during this separation. Due to her many requests over the years, I'd allowed several family and friends of hers to stay with us for extended periods, sometimes months on end and now she wasn't even going to allow me to sleep on my own couch for one weekend? It was utterly hypocritical to the kind and loving Christian life she was expounding to others, but I had to give her kudos for her Oscar worthy two-faced performances. I had no doubts she was pulling them off quite effectively to our future in-laws who evidently were rural Evangelical Ministers. A quote from Dana Carvey as the "Church Lady" on Church Chat, a skit from Saturday Night Live, seems appropriate here: "How con-vieeeeniant!" Megan had learned how to expertly play both Devil and Saint by doing "The Church Lady's" self-righteous "Superior" dance, and as Dana Carvey's character would sarcastically say; "Well isn't that *special*!"

Nonetheless, I was determined to continue behaving the way of the Peaceful Warrior; patient, calm, forgiving, loving. I'd been that way for most of my life anyway, I wasn't about to stop now. I hoped deeply in my heart that Megan and I could find a true, loving, enlightened way, to rise above our worsened situation, with equal dignity and grace, and to that end, on the night before I left the city to attend Fiona's nuptials, for both of them; I wrote the following song lyric.

When You Remember Me

You daydream of many things/movie stars/Kings and Queens/fancy clothes and limousines/the "good life" A to Z You fantasize of foreign skies/where Angels sing and the unicorn flies/ you speculate and theorize why life is such a mystery

Chorus: But when you remember me/remember that I
will always love you though we've said goodbye
When you remember me/remember the start
when we fell in love/not when we fell apart

Bridge: For I remember all the good times with pleasure
and all of our happy moments are still my
greatest treasure
as for the bad times well I've blown them all
away/my love for you still shines as it did on
that first day

Don't look back/with bitter regret/blocking out the past trying to forget/don't be angry and let yourself get into a state of high anxiety/Please don't decide that I didn't care and vanish our love into thin air/I'm at your side/though I'm not there/my love for you will always be

Chorus: So when you remember me/remember that I
will always love you though we've said goodbye
When you remember me/remember the start
when we fell in love/not when we fell apart

If you should feel like you need a friend/don't conceal disguise or pretend/don't let your pride win for in the end/we will always be family/I hope for you only the very best and pray your soul is peacefully blessed/and that new love puts your heart at rest and all your dreams become reality

Chorus: And when you remember me/remember that I
will always love you though we've said goodbye
When you remember me/remember the start
when we fell in love/not when we fell apart

I wrote the entire lyric in less than 30 minutes and was pleased with myself for verbalizing the spirit of the Peaceful Warrior in my heart. It was a carbon copy of my wish for Megan and Fiona, but I would soon realize that I'd apparently wished upon a dark star.

"It's a real long way to go to say goodbye…"
From the song: Long Way to Go by: Stevie Nicks

Megan picked me up at the Portland airport, and by the wan, phony smile, mixed with the knives sharpening in her eyes; I could see she was putting on her best Bette Davis imitation when she admonished me to buckle my seatbelt, dryly adding: "It's going to be a bumpy night!" It was meant to instill fear in me, but I had to turn away and look out the car window to clench my jaw closed before I started laughing in her face! Her performance had been both serious and flawless, but that she'd reduced her threats to such heights of camp was hilarious! She proceeded to be as bitchy as she could during the hour long drive, while I managed to remain calm and polite. I could tell the weekend was going to fiercely test my Peaceful Warrior skills and told myself that it was nothing I couldn't handle.

She was infuriatingly disappointed by my lack of petrified, submissive, or angry response. Clearly she'd only frustrated herself by the time she dropped me off at my lodgings in town.

I prayed that night that Megan would find some civility in her heart, if not for my sake, at least for the sake of Fiona's wedding.

The next day I went out to the house to get my truck in working order. On the ride from the airport, Megan informed me of a "minor detail" that she'd kept hidden until now. The wedding was taking place more than two hundred miles away, high on a *mountaintop* in the miniscule town of Saint Marie's (pronounced: Saint Mary's) Idaho. In the same breath she told me that my truck wasn't running and if I wanted to attend the wedding, I'd better get it fixed because she would *not allow* me to ride with her. (Of course the truck was no longer working because even though she'd never driven it in the 9 years I'd had it, since I'd been gone, she and her friends had obviously driven it into disrepair in the last year, and left it broken and rusting, in the ever present Oregon rain.)

I was working on the truck in the gravel driveway, going from hood to cab repeatedly, trying to get it started. It wasn't responding so after putting some gasoline in the bone dry carburetor, I got the engine started, and in the next moment there was a loud "pop" and the engine burst into flames! I raced out of the drivers cab, grabbing a filthy, molding towel someone had left on the seat months ago. I started trying to beat the flames out with the towel but it only fanned them higher! Megan saw from the kitchen window what was happening and along with a female friend of hers came running out of the house. Her friend shouted: "Megan move your car before the fire spreads from his truck to your car!"

The flames were reaching higher; black engine oil smoke began billowing into my face. I shouted: "Get the hose Megan! Get the hose!"

She ignored me and ran to her car. Her lady friend remained frozen, and the woman's young daughter joined her on the porch. They stood there watching the scene and I shouted again: "The hose!!! Will *somebody* get the hose!!!" as I continued beating back the flames.

The woman stood still but her approximately 9 year old child ran to the nearby hose and turned the water on. She then ran to me with it and I franticly started spraying.

Gravel spewed up and hit me like shrapnel as Megan in her haste to save her car, pealed out of the driveway with her drivers' side door wide open.

Amid the smoke and the sizzling truck engine, I heard a loud crack! I'd just gotten the fire out and I looked around the front end of my truck to see that Megan's open car door had just smashed into a fire hydrant positioned in our driveway! (Talk about instant karma!) She sat there with a horrified look on her face. I'd managed to subdue the smoke from the engine by closing the hood, and then went over to survey the damage of Megan's car.

"Look what you did to my car!" she screamed.

Startled, I paused before I angrily shouted back; "What *I* did?!! Look what *you* did in your hurry to save *"your"* car, the car ***my inheritance money paid for***, while you left me and my truck to burn!!!

She yelled back at me: "Well I can't drive it like this! How am I supposed to get to **I-da-ho now?!**"

I thought to myself; "You already ***are*-da-ho now**!" and gave her a look of pathetic disgust.

Forcing myself to remain calm, I went to the garage and got some nylon rope and returned to begin tying the crunched door closed. I managed to secure it but the indent was so deep that it pushed into the inside of the car. It was still drive-able, but Megan, who at age 43 had finally learned to drive in the last two and a half years, (I'd been her chauffer for the previous fifteen!) was now nervous about driving through the mountainous narrow roads of the Columbia Gorge. This made her rethink her decision to let me ride with her. I could see the selfish logic forming behind her angry, conciliatory eyes when she told me I could ride with her as long as I drove through the high mountains. Obviously she'd concluded that if anybody was going to fall out of her moving vehicle, it was going to be me!

The next day, Megan, (along with the young girl who'd brought me the hose) Christine, and myself, safely made our two hundred mile journey to the postage stamp sized town of Saint Marie's, Idaho. The little over one square mile town was at the top of a mountain, with barely any services at all and only one place for accommodations, a very old and run down motel. We went our separate ways to our rooms, mine was next door to hers, but I didn't see Megan or anyone else for the rest of the afternoon or evening.

The following morning I ran into Megan at 10 am. getting coffee at the only local "greasy spoon" and I asked her where and what time the wedding photographer was taking pictures. She told me it was being done at our future in-laws church, at 11am.

"You'd better go get dressed, you only have an hour." She said as she smiled shark like and sipped her coffee.

I got my coffee to go and went back to my room, showered, dressed, and was at the church down the street by 10:45. There was no one in the church or wandering the grounds, so I knocked on the vestry door.

"Come in!" A gruff male voice impatiently beckoned.

I opened the door to see a jet black dyed haired, middle aged, pudgy, stormy faced Reverend, wearing a dazzling white polyester suit and sporting a black patch over one eye.

"Reverend Fisher?" I inquired.

"Yes". He sniffed disdainfully.

"Hi! Nice to meet you! I'm Fiona's dad, Marc." I cheerfully said as I extended my hand.

My future Reverend In-Law recoiled in his chair, giving me a look like evil incarnate had just entered his chambers. He didn't offer his hand and said nothing. He didn't have to speak; his cold, one eyed glare, spoke volumes.

I cautiously hesitated before I spoke; "I'm sorry to bother you, but Megan told me the wedding photographer would be taking family pictures at 11 this morning. Do you know where everybody is?"

His voice thundered back at me: "The pictures were taken at 9 this morning! Your presence was *not* required nor missed! Now if you'll excuse me!"

He gave me the most hateful look possible with his one eye, and I was grateful the other one had a patch over it as I left the room. This was my first contact with my future in-laws and I was not favorably impressed!

"Got me again didn't you Megan!" I thought to myself as I walked back to the motel. I should have known by her frozen phony smile at the coffee shop that she'd done this on purpose. She'd never wanted me in the photographs, and she delighted herself with the opportunity to humiliate me.

The wedding was taking place at one o'clock and I got there at 12:30, praying this was not a continuation of Megan's cruel ruse. I was relieved to see people milling about the grounds and was startled by his appearance, but not surprised to see, my ex-best friend, Megan's first husband, Rex. We hadn't seen each other in more than a decade, and I was instantly relaxed when he greeted me warmly.

"Marc, how's it going?!" His smile was sincere and wide.

"Great! It's so good to see you Rex!" I replied as we shook hands.

We stood together exchanging pleasantries as other members of Megan's family and friends interrupted us for brief hellos. It was painfully obvious that members of Megan's large extended family were saying hello out of societal requirement and sheer curiosity, rather than genuine welcome, at least when speaking to me.

With Rex they chatted amiably, as they slyly looked me up and down with brooding contempt. They could accept Rex because Megan had left him. I however was the selfish bastard who had left Megan.

I understood their eyes of hostility. I was aware of Megan's well rehearsed Joan of Arc routines. She'd always known how to perfectly play the martyr, and now she was gloating in a corner of the vestibule, gleefully watching her family as they froze me out.

Finally she came up to us and said it was time to take our seats. She led Rex and I to the front pew on the left of the tiny chapel and then pointed each of us to our seats. Rex sat on my left and Megan on my right. I was in the middle of them again for the first time in sixteen years.

The black patch-eyed Reverend stood in front of the altar and I caught my first look at my future son-in-law. He looked like a child wearing adult clothes. He and his groomsmen looked like they'd just broken out of puberty.

The organ music started and Fiona walked up the aisle behind her pastel pink attired bridesmaids. I watched her avoiding my gaze as she approached. She smiled at various people but wouldn't look at me. I felt a knife in my heart, not because she wouldn't look at me, but because I knew at that moment, that Megan had irrevocably poisoned her against me.

Once all of the wedding party was stationed, I leaned towards Rex and whispered; "Is it just me, or do they all look like children?"

He whispered back: "At 18, aren't we all?"

I nodded my agreement and the booming voice of "Black Patched Bart" (Reverend Fisher hadn't told me his name and at this point, I hardly *revered* the Reverend) filled the room. I wasn't feeling even remotely "Dearly Beloved" as he began.

I concentrated on sending loving thoughts to Fiona and her beau as I sat through the rather stilted nuptials.

As they were pronounced man and wife, Megan had a line of tears trailing down her face, and I put my hand on hers as a sincere token of comfort. She froze with an icy stillness and removed her hand.

The ceremony ended and as we all filed outside, Megan informed me that the reception was taking place a mile away, further up on the mountain. She waited until nearly everyone had left before she let me know that she was riding there with Black Patch Bart and Mrs. Fisher. I asked for our car keys and she lied, saying she didn't have them on her. She told me I would have to find a ride with someone else or walk.

I'm innately a non-violent person, but at that moment I truly wanted to smack the supercilious smirk off her face, but my Peaceful Warrior paused, breathed, and in a calm and loving manner, replied: "Okay, its Fiona's day, whatever you want Megan."

She sneered in her reply; "You got that right, it *will be* whatever I want!" Abruptly she stormed off.

I began slowly walking up the steep dirt road in the direction the cars had gone. Black Patched Bart shot me a dirty look from his one eye through the open window of his car as he, his wife and Megan, sped past me up the hill, sending huge clouds of dirt wafting around me. I was trying to shield my eyes from the dusty folds of accumulating grit when suddenly Rex pulled up along side me.

"Want a ride?" He cordially offered.

I didn't want to breathe in the dirt so I nodded with my face buried in my sleeve, and walked around to the passenger side.

"Thanks Rex." I said as I closed the door.

He smiled kindly and replied; "Hey, no problem. Sure looks like the Reverend is in quite a hurry!"

Dusting off my tuxedo with a handkerchief I replied; "Yeah, so it seems. Rex; am I just being oversensitive or does the Reverend seem like…" I was searching for the right word when Rex filled in the blank.

"An asshole?!" Immediately Rex broke into his jovial guffaw and I choked on my own laughter throughout my reply: "Well I was going to say… he seemed a little stiff… but I think you captured him better!"

We were still laughing when Rex said; "Good luck at the reception man, everyone is being nice to me, but I can see you're in for a frosty time!"

"Frosty" would have been more than acceptable compared to the combustible stares and flame throwing vibes that assaulted me. I was obviously the leper in this colony and Black Patched Bart and his family made no attempt whatsoever to disguise their avoidance. I was quickly ushered to a table far away from theirs, and watched while The Bride and Groom were feted in the outdoor surroundings by the "Superior" dancing Reverend and his clan.

Megan's large family took turns tag team style, coming back and forth to chat with me in twenty minute increments; in an obvious attempt to "slyly" keep me away from the family table. They were about as sly and slick as chewing gum on sandpaper. They'd apparently forgotten that I'd seen every one of them play this exact game on many family occasions over the years, to their own Father, whom none of them could tolerate. However, one of my former brother in-laws was sincerely nice to me, and for that I'm eternally grateful. He probably didn't *want* to like me, (family solidarity was the theme of the day and I was certainly no longer considered part of the family) but I could tell by his kind words, that he still did. We'd always liked each other and he spoke admirably about me following my musical ambitions and encouraged my pursuits. Within earshot of his wife and Megan, he remarked; "At least you're following a dream that you love, unlike the rest of us." His comment stained a sour look on Megan's face, and it wasn't long before everyone else was surreptitiously herded away from me by Megan, or one of her family members, until finally, I sat alone at a distant picnic table.

The Reverend's wife Donna, to her Christian credit, came over and spoke nicely to me, asking what it was like to live in New York, and what my plans were for the future.

Donna was a good ten years younger than her husband, and much too pretty and sweet to be saddled with such a dark spirited "Man of The (appropriately polyester) Cloth" as he.

I could see pieces of Megan's and my relationship mirrored in Donna's life. The roles were reversed, she was subject to a brooding, controlling husband, and I to an obtrusive, manipulative wife.

Donna and I were both about the same age, both still easily wearing the early summer glow of youth, (while Black Patched Bart and Megan sported mid-winter frozen stone faces) and I wondered if Donna's once naive and innocent soul, had been emotionally ravaged and plundered in her youth by her husband, as mine had been by Megan.

Mrs. Fisher had a familiar spirit; at first I couldn't place it. I saw she was sincere in her attempts to include me in the late afternoon mountaintop garden party by introducing me to a swarm of babbling church members who managed to keep me occupied and pointedly away from the Bride and Grooms table. But was she being "Christian" or cunning? It was evident that Megan and B.P.B had formulated a fine plan to keep me excluded from where the real celebration was taking place, but I chose to believe that Donna was more than just doing her husbands bidding, and I'm pretty sure I recognized the familiar aura that at first had eluded me; the light of The Peacemaker Warrior. That was it, that's what else Donna and I had in common, we both were able to show loving compassion and tolerance, where Black Patched Bart and Megan could only behave with malicious contempt and self righteous "Church Lady" superiority.

Fiona managed to avoid me throughout the entire afternoon, but she did take a short moment to receive me when I approached her with a gift as she and her husband (who I still hadn't met!) prepared to leave.
I hugged her and wished her and her husband a lifetime of happiness. She mumbled: "Thanks." I told her I loved her and that I would always love her. She averted her eyes from me.
Fiona is a Scorpio, and though she didn't know it, she echoed the words of Scorpios Motto when she replied; "I know."
Only sad fact was that she didn't know what I knew; she'd been brainwashed to discard me by a litany of Megan's lies.

The Bride and Groom climbed into a horse drawn carriage and made their way down the mountain. The festivities were over and it was barely 5pm!
Rex gave me a ride back to the motel and invited me to his room to hang out and have a few beers. Considering my torturous afternoon at the liquor free reception, I was ready for a drink! We sat together talking, laughing, and catching up with each others lives. It didn't feel awkward at all, and since I'd married his wife and raised his child, I was surprised that we were getting on just like we used to, before Megan had played Master Puppeteer with our lives.
Rex expressed interest in hearing some of the songs I'd been recording so I went next door to get my Walkman. My room was in between his and Megan's and the irony was not lost on me; I was in the middle of them yet again. Only this time, Rex remained a true friend, and Megan was merely the common denominator of pain and misery for both of us. He and I had survived with our loving spirits intact. She on the other hand…

Rex and I were really having a wonderful time, enjoying our reunion, when around 7pm. Megan burst into the room, *acting* cheerful, inserting herself uninvited into Rex's and my private reconciliation.

She explained that she wanted to hang out with us because everyone else had gone to bed. Rex and I both knew that she was merely imposing her presence on us to break up any conversation we might be having about her. She needn't have wasted her efforts; we hadn't wasted one minute of our time together discussing her.

Megan grabbed a beer and started rambling on about her own interests. How she loved her new son-in-law and how well she got along with her newly extended family.

Rex and I could take her phony "we're all still friends" act for only fifteen minutes before he looked at me with eyes of unfortunate surrender at Megan's intrusion, and he suggested we call it a night.

Megan knew that neither Rex nor I wanted to hang out one on one with her, and as she unlocked the door to her room, the look of evil triumph on her face for sabotaging me at the wedding, as well as intentionally separating Rex and I just now, was clearly painted on her expression as she told me she was going to leave at 10 am. the next day and she expected me to be ready.

I told her I would be, and as I closed the door to my room, the words of a Stevie Nicks song about a trash talking ex-lover who goes to great lengths to make their former loved one as miserable as possible, reverberated in my head: "Well it's a real long way to go to say goodbye…"

There was a knock on my door the following morning at 8am. I opened it to find Rex standing next to his luggage, holding a six pack of beer.

"Hey Marc, I'm leaving now and I thought you might like to take this with you." He smiled as he thrust the six-pack at me.

"Thanks Rex but I don't drink very often, you keep it."

"Naw, take it with you, for old time sake." He said as he pushed it into my hands.

"Uh…okay, thanks. It was real good seeing you again Rex."

We shook hands and he replied; "Yeah, you too! Good luck with your music and have a safe trip home. See ya!"

"Yeah, best of everything to you too! Take care Rex."

I closed the door wondering if he and I would ever meet again. If yesterday was any indication of the future, I was never going to be invited to another family celebration. This invitation had been extended out of malice, a sheer golden opportunity for Megan to publicly emotionally flog and humiliate me.

I had no idea what mental torture she had planned for the drive home, but whatever it was, I was firmly committed to continue behaving as a Peaceful Warrior. I would only have to endure her for another few hours. Once we got back to Oregon, I was planning to spend a week with Bill, my former New York City friend, who now lived near Spokane, Washington. After spending the week with him I was flying back to New York for one day only, and then I was flying to Puerto Rico for two weeks, to stay with my very dear friends Jorge and Amanda Raigosa.

Thank God I'd extended my vacation to include a few more weeks; it was going to take me *at least that long* to recover from this weekend on a mountaintop in "Church Chat" hell. <u>On A Mountaintop In Church Chat Hell</u>; sounds like a country song don'tcha think?

The phone in my room didn't work so at 9am. I knocked on Megan's door to let her know I was packed and ready. She opened the door with a self satisfied smirk on her face. I could tell she was up to some kind of treachery but I sweetly and respectfully said to her: "I know it's earlier than you said, but I just wanted to let you know I'm ready to leave whenever you are."

And then, her evil fully manifested with the same demonic eyed, head twisting, satanic scowling face that actress Linda Blair as Regan; immortalized in <u>The Exorcist</u>, and Megan spewed her bile at me.

"*I'm not giving you a ride back*; you'll have to find some other way home!"

"*Excuse me?*" I said, stunned into derision. "How am I

supposed to get a ride off of this mountain? Everyone else has already left and there are no services of *any* kind here!"

Mega-Regan (pun apropos!) looking absolutely as horrifically possessed as Regan did in the movie, thrust her face inches from mine, and as virulently as she could spit the words out she seethed: ***"Well too fucking bad!*** I'm not giving you a ride! You can call a cab or something!"

The only thing missing was the split pea soup...
I steadied my voice. "You know as well as I there's no cab service here and it's going to take at least two hours for one to get up the mountain *if* I can get one to come at all!"

Her voice boomed from the depths of the damned as she spat back: ***"That's not my fucking problem!"***

I paused and took a deep breath... "Well the phone doesn't work in my room; can I *at least* use your phone to call someone?"

Her face twisted with malicious satisfaction; ***"No! Use the payphone in town!"***

"Megan, are you *serious?* I've been more than patient with all the crap you've dealt me this *entire* weekend, now you're stranding me on a mountaintop in the middle of *nowhere*, and you won't let me even use the *phone*?"

The hatred on her face demonically climaxed and if she could have sailed a piece of furniture at me I'm sure she would've. Instead; she recoiled with a toxic snarl and slammed the door.

Because it was Sunday, the whole scrappy village was closed and the motel office didn't open until noon. I walked from one end of the desolate main street to the other searching for a payphone.

Finally I spotted one, dangling from the side of a dirty clapboard excuse of a building. I picked up the receiver and found that there were people already talking on the line. They explained to me that they shared a common phone line in the town because it was so small, and I would have to wait until the line was open before I could place a call.

"Unbelievable! What Steven King novel have I landed in?!" I mused with disbelief as I made my way back to the motel.

I knew Megan was leaving soon. The thought of being stuck in this nightmare had me scrambling for the patience to ask her if she would at least give me a ride down the mountain so I could hitchhike on the interstate to a larger town.

I faced the dragon lady once again and petitioned politely for her assistance. She breathed more flames about not giving me a ride anywhere, but tersely she finally acquiesced to letting me use her phone.

I dialed Bill's number and when he answered I told him that I was in Megan's room in Idaho and that I had a major problem.

"What's the problem Bro?" He asked with mounting concern.

Mega-Regan was staring at me while tapping her nails on the table three feet away listening, her face hotly amused with her latest coup. I didn't want to inflame her further so, in a low voice, I cautiously said to Bill: "I'll give you three guesses."

"Megan, Megan, Megan!" He instantly answered. "Did I get all three guesses right?" He laughed knowingly.

"Yeah you did! Big surprise huh?"

The further pissed off look on Mega-Regan's face evidenced that she knew he'd guessed right too. I went on to tell him of my predicament and once he realized that I was among the <u>Children of the Corn</u>, he asked if he could call me back in a few minutes.

I hung up the phone and told Megan that Bill was going to call me right back. In the meantime, I very calmly said to Megan: "After all that you've put me through, not only during our fifteen years together, but especially after this weekend, I can't believe that you turned out to be such a phony raging bitch. I never told you this, but the very first time I saw you I was 15 years old bussing tables at Sir George's and you waltzed in one day acting all important and bossing everybody around. I asked Diana: "Who is that?" She said; "Oh, that's Rex's wife. She comes in and works once in a while." To which I replied; "She seems like a real bitch!" Diana laughed and agreed. Little did I know how much of a phony, lying bitch you'd *really* turn out to be!"

Megan struck back; "That's right! I *am* a bitch! Took you long enough to figure it out!"

"You're right about that! But now that I have, it isn't so much with shock as it is with sadness and pity that you find being a bitch to me is something to be proud of especially when you *act* so holy around everyone else. But go ahead Megan; be proud of being a bitch. Fiona and everyone else may buy your innocent martyr act but we both know the truth don't we? We *both* know that you're nothing more than a neurotic control freak! You have to live with that and I have to live with the fifteen years of my youth that were wasted on what you psychologically hog tied me into believing was love. You have *no idea* what love is. You only "loved" me as long as I complied with your neurotic emotional and sexual demands and lived my life by your standards and rules, but once I became aware of your manipulating bullshit and refused to play along, you couldn't stand it and the *real* you surfaced! So go ahead and play the self-righteous victim as you screw me over again, I've survived fifteen years of your abuse and I'll survive this!"

The phone rang before she could retaliate and I answered immediately. Bill didn't own a car but he'd asked a friend of his (whom I'd never met) to make the 6 hour round trip to pick me up, and he informed me that his friend was already on his way. I thanked him and hung up the phone.

Just as Megan was opening her mouth to speak I said; "Thank God for people who know what the word love *really* means Megan. For all your Christian posturing you seem to have managed to miss the whole concept of "What would Jesus do?" In fact, what *He would've done* is what a complete stranger is already on his way here to do, give me a ride. After all these years it's too bad that a total stranger is willing to extend a hand where you have only extended hatred. It seems you're the real stranger after all. And, lucky for you, this weekend I kept my mouth shut."

I turned and left the room. I hadn't yelled nor lost my cool; I'd merely spoken the truth.

In retrospect I'm extremely grateful that though my mom was unable to shield me from the weekend "crucifixion" I suffered on the mountaintop, (due to "unclearrr rrreception" amid the storm clouds of Megan) at least she seemed to have literally paved the way for my redemption by directing me to find <u>Way Of The Peaceful Warrior</u> on the sidewalk.

The pain from the "crown of thorns" I was made to wear, was certainly lessened by the secure knowledge that throughout the traumas Megan had put me through; I'd not struck back with hateful vengeance. Unlike the obviously "possessed" Megan, I left the weekend behind with my soul intact.

I spent a very pleasant week with Bill and then flew back to New York, eager for the next leg of my vacation in Puerto Rico. The plane was running six hours behind schedule and I didn't arrive in New York at La Guardia airport until 2am. I wanted to stop somewhere for dinner on the way home, but as I hailed a cab, I noticed the headline on a newspaper that read: "Zodiac Killer Looking for a Leo." (A copy-cat version of the San Francisco Zodiac Killer) Apparently the city was still under siege by a serial killer who was murdering in Astrological order.

"Great! It would be just my luck that I'll run into him, start discussing Astrology, he'll find out I'm a Leo and I'll never make it to Puerto Rico! I'd better go straight home." I thought to myself as I entered the cab.

On the ride home I suddenly had a very strong premonition that someone had broken into my apartment while I'd been away.

"Please, *please* God, don't let this be true! I don't want to deal with *that* right now! And Mother, you know I'm in no mood…"

I prayed to her all the way into Manhattan, and as I struggled with my luggage the five flights up to my railroad flat, my anxiety increased.

The moment I unlocked the door and entered, it was obvious there'd been an intruder. The six foot long iron grill that covered my fire escape window was lying on my bed. The lock was still on it so someone had kicked it in. Instantly I scanned the room to see what was missing. Gold jewelry I'd left on the table along with twenty dollars in laundry quarters, my computer, my keyboards, the television, everything remained untouched! Someone had been in here in the last 10 days and nothing was missing? Very strange!

Italian Mothers Never Die

Had the intruder seen the note that I'd left in the unlocked portable safe in my closet that snidely read: "Whoever you are rummaging through my personal belongings, remember, Karma can be a bitch!"

I'd put the note in the safe just before I left, not because I believed someone would break in, but just in case.

Indeed somebody had broken in and for whatever reason, they'd not taken anything. I didn't care why, I was just happy that I didn't have to deal with it at 3am. "Thanks Mom!" I gleefully said out loud as I leaned the fire escape grill against a wall and hastily prepared for some much needed rest.

As I climbed into bed I thought; "I'm glad I didn't run into the Zodiac killer on the way home... and I drifted into a peaceful sleep.

The next morning I nailed the fire escape back in place, with so many nails that King Kong wouldn't be able to kick it in! I'd made up my mind that I was going to Puerto Rico for the next two weeks and if someone was going to break in again, so be it; I wasn't going to worry about it.

I ended up staying a *month* in Puerto Rico at my friend's urgings. They didn't have to twist my arm either. I'd gone from my own private Idaho hell, to a beautiful and spiritually refreshing island paradise. The entire ugliness I'd experienced in Idaho began receding with the first warm waves of emerald sea that caressed my feet. This baptism of serenity continuously washed over me, and in the four weeks that I spent there, I'd written full lyrics to fifty-six songs. I only noticed how many I'd written when I counted them in my notebook on the plane ride home. This thought crossed my mind: "Fifty-six, one song for each year of mother's life". I smiled inside.

Let It Be
(Song by: Lennon/McCartney)

Back in the Manhattan, it wasn't long before the fall season of New York City tourists began and I was working fourteen hour shifts at Mamma Leone's.

I'd spoken to Megan on the phone regarding our divorce proceedings and she tearfully apologized for her behavior at Fiona's wedding. I should've smelled another trap but I've always been a forgiving person, and I wouldn't realize for another year that Megan was up to her old tricks again.

In the meantime, somehow in between my crazy work schedule, I managed to record enough songs for my very first album: <u>Love Is More Than A Four-Letter Word</u>. Because it is a love story, I decided to include the song I'd written for Megan and Fiona, <u>When You Remember Me</u>. I joked with my arranger Art Labriola that it was a good thing I'd written the song *before* the Idaho wedding fiasco because I'd never have been able to write it now. I was able to live my life as a Peaceful Warrior, but I wasn't willing to channel my muses into insincerity.

In April of 1991 I finished the first demo of my album, and while I could no longer write loving songs for Megan, I did sincerely thank her and Fiona for our lives together on the liner notes. After her sobbing apology, Megan had led me to believe that our divorce proceedings would continue amicably so I wanted to do my part to make that happen as well.

She'd been audited by the Internal Revenue Service for two years worth of back taxes to the tune of a few thousand dollars in taxes, penalties and fines. Though she'd taken on boarders in our home, supplementing her already more than comfortable income, she pleaded poverty and asked me to pay the bill. We weren't divorced yet so I was liable as well, and I told her to send me the papers and I would take care of it. She also asked me if I could give her our house in the divorce settlement, for Fiona's sake. She said she wanted to have something to leave Fiona as an inheritance in the event of her untimely death. She promised that if she ever sold the house before that happened; she would split the money with me.

I was fine with this arrangement. It seemed like a very loving thing to do for Fiona, as well as a logical plan. I know how much I appreciated the inheritance my mother had left me, and I knew the house would only increase in value. I too wanted to have something to leave Fiona, and so far in my life, the house that I'd spent nearly a decade renovating, was one of my proudest achievements and also my largest asset. I decided to give Megan the property on these mutual terms, because it was a loving thing to do for Fiona.

In August I flew out to Oregon to gather my belongings and move them to my brother's house for storage in Southern California.

I'd boxed up my clothes and my large record collection when I initially left Megan in mid 1988. They'd been stored in Fiona's empty room for the last two years and now that our lengthy interstate divorce was finalized, I had only to retrieve my belongings to settle what had been a long time coming.

Megan was very cordial during our phone conversation regarding my plans to come out to the house. I was staying at a nearby motel and I'd taken a fifty mile cab ride from the airport so as not to inconvenience her. Megan very sweetly told me I should've called, she wouldn't have minded picking me up, and she said I was also welcome to stay at our house if I wanted. She sounded sincere and I appreciated the offer, it meant that she was willing to be an adult about this. I thanked her but said I was fine at the motel, and we planned for me to come out to the house the following day, which coincidentally was my birthday. I took it as a good omen, another rebirth day. Megan and I could celebrate our new beginnings as friends, which seemed more in line with the Christian precepts she was expounding. Fiona, Megan and I were all adults who would forever be linked as family. There was no denying that though the origins and progressions of Megan's and my relationship was twisted, as a family we'd had many happy years together. It gave me a peaceful heart to think that we could also be the spiritually evolved people that I'd been envisioning we could be.

As things turned out, I suppose I should have been more cautious about my sunny optimism. Maybe it was because my last few birthdays in New York had been pleasant one's that made me forget my prior birthday anxieties.

I'd never been particularly fond of my birthday because my parents weren't big on celebrating their own. They always got us kids a cake and gifts, but they also gave us the impression that it was somewhat vain to celebrate yourself. Perhaps it was the Catholic beliefs of finding holiness and happiness in self denial that planted these ideals in our household, I'm not sure, but emotionally I accepted the "vanity" birthday creed for myself, though I always took great pleasure in buying gifts and celebrating anyone else's birthday. I just felt guilty celebrating my own.

As if to point fingers at proof of my vanity whenever I did celebrate, there always seemed to be something of a sad or momentous proportion that would happen on August 16th. In 1977 on that date, Elvis Presley died. His heyday was before my time and thus I was never a very connected Elvis fan, but there was a definite pall in the atmosphere of the nation that day that was inescapable. It was all over the news, rumors were flying, and people of all ethnicities and ages were gathered in the streets, mourning his passing. It did put a damper on the festivities at my house.

Another year, our home was broken into while Fiona, Megan and I were upstairs opening my gifts. The intruder had broken the kitchen window, stolen a radio, my car and house keys, and of all things, my birthday cake! Obviously this brought the birthday celebration to a screeching halt.

There were other birthday traumas in my years spent with Megan and this one was proving to be no exception.

As I went through my outdoor workshop, I realized that all of my power tools were missing as well as the camper shell to my truck. When I politely questioned Megan about this, she pleaded innocent ignorance at how they could've vanished.

Our house was in an area that never had crimes of any kind, and I knew these items had not been stolen, but I accepted that they could've been in order to keep the peace. I knew Megan had sold them or given them away and I was saddened by her newest batch of unflinching lies.

Listlessly I packed the boxes of records and clothes into my truck, that per our negotiations Megan had agreed to have fixed into running condition ahead of time. Megan and I'd agreed on certain items of antique furniture and household belongings that I would take but my heart was no longer invested in the memories they held, so I left them behind.

Fiona and her husband were living with Megan; and Fiona was several months pregnant. She baked me a birthday cake that I'm sure was Megan's suggestion because Megan knew how much I hated celebrating my birthday. I knew this was Megan's manipulative way of making me feel worse, under the guise of being "thoughtful" and she had no reservations about using Fiona as her unsuspecting pawn.

I continued to cling to my Peaceful Warrior honor, and I played the song I wrote for them: <u>When You Remember Me</u> on the stereo for Megan and Fiona before I left.

Fiona offered me some cake, but I was in too sad of a mood over Megan's new batch of transparent lies for celebrating, so I asked her to pack me a slice to go. Before I left, I said to Fiona: "No matter what, remember that I will always love you." Megan and I exchanged goodbyes in a civil and loving manner. That should've put my "Mega-Regan" radar on higher alert, but I didn't discover Megan's ultimate betrayal until I made it to my brother's house in Southern California the next day and began unpacking my boxes.

All of the many boxes of my clothes were completely ruined due to Megan's tribe of cats, who'd apparently been encouraged to use my cartons as their litter boxes, before Megan resealed them. I was distressed, but I could handle it. What clued me into the fact that Megan was never going to stop her abuse as long as we remained connected was that my vast collection of valuable and rare Beatle records was missing. Megan knew they were the only physical thing I truly treasured, not for their monetary value, but for the music. I'd grown up listening to them and their music had provided me with the only renewable source of happiness in the midst of my turbulent childhood.

I'd purchased unavailable Beatle rarities in Europe when I'd been there. I owned a mint copy of "The Butcher Block" album, now worth thousands. An original and very rare <u>Two Virgins</u> album with the fully nude John and Yoko covered by its brown paper sleeve, an original copy of <u>Love Me Do</u> (The Beatles first record) and many other collectibles.

Everything was gone. I called Megan to see if she knew what happened to them. Again she feigned immaculate ignorance but I could tell by the tone of her voice that she was lying, and enjoying it. That's when I knew, *finally*, that I could no longer allow her to abuse me. She had every intention of doing so until I got the message loud and clear that she hated me, and she was making sure that Fiona and I would no longer be connected.

It ultimately dawned on me that Megan was unwilling to remain friends because she'd never been my friend, she'd been my dictator. She'd only loved me as long as I was willing to deny myself and live my life according to her needs. She was fully aware that by destroying everything I treasured, including my relationship with Fiona, she was destroying another part of my heart, my childhood, my adulthood, and my soul. She hoped to sever our connections once and for all with her latest acts of malice, and at that moment I granted her wish. I realized that I had to stop giving her the opportunities for further abuse, or it would never end.

From that day forward, I haven't spoken to Megan or Fiona, nor have they tried to contact me. I found out from a mutual friend that a year after our divorce, Megan sold the house. She never bothered to let me know, let alone split the proceeds. She'd known all along that her "inheritance for Fiona" story was a hoax, and frankly, looking back, I deserved to lose my portion of our joint investment, for being foolish enough to believe her. The same friend of ours has since asked me why I don't contact Fiona, and I've explained all of my reasons; first and foremost, I don't like the conniving and phony person Megan is, and I'm unwilling to suffer any more first hand emotional crap from her. I'd have to wade through another trough of her barbs and lies in order to see or speak to Fiona. Also, I'm certain that Megan has spun all sorts of denigrating tales about me and as such, Fiona thinks I'm a horrible person. I recall how Megan trashed Rex to me when she was lying her way out of her marriage to him, so for her to spin lies about me to Fiona and everyone else we knew, comes as no real surprise. Lastly, Fiona must be aware by now that I can't tolerate her mother, and if I were in Fiona's shoes, for that reason alone, I wouldn't want to speak with me either. I'm not so foolish to think that blood isn't thicker than water, and I don't blame Fiona in the least. As usual it's Megan's gospel that must be adhered to and Fiona should remain her mother's biggest supporter.

I'm aware that Megan thinks she's "won" but it's a melodrama she created and stars in, in order to whitewash for Fiona, the ugly truths behind the genesis and corruptness of our relationship.

Since Megan is determined to portray herself as the innocent victim, I've granted her that empty, untruthful victory. As my Peaceful Warrior implores, and The Beatle song says, I've decided to simply, "Let it be." Megan has to live with herself and her lies, while at least I have a clear conscience.

Nothing Can Change The Shape Of Things To Come
(Song written by: The Ramones)

Upon returning to New York, I resumed my happy life. Within a few weeks I moved into a rodent free apartment, with plenty of hot water, a shower, and most important, no bathtub in the kitchen!

I continued working at Mamma Leone's which was within an even shorter walking distance than my previous "railroad flat" commute had been.

For the most part, things were going smoothly in my life. I had a wide circle of friends who encouraged, delighted, and stimulated my creativity.

Unfortunately I wasn't making much headway in the music business as I was discovering that "ageism" is a very real factor. The general consensus being that if you hadn't "made it" by the time you were 30; you didn't stand a ghost of a chance.

I hadn't even entered the fray of the Joni Mitchell penned "star maker machinery" until I was 34, now nearly forty, what chance did I have? Also, House, Grunge, Hip-Hop and Rap were the up and coming popular genres, and my musical style couldn't have been further removed. Peace, love, and forgiveness were "out"

Italian Mothers Never Die

while; anger, bigotry, and vengeance were "in".

Remaining a Peaceful Warrior is an everyday challenge in any environment, in the music business it's a moment by moment affair.

Still I was happier than I'd ever been with Megan and my dreams remained optimistic.

In January of 1992, I was invited to attend a Super Bowl party at my friend Finley's house in Queens. I've never been much of a sports fan, and I still have extremely limited interest and knowledge of sports, especially football, but I'm always open to new experiences and knew Finley would throw a great party. She'd invited me to spend the night along with her boyfriend Luca and a few other friends on the evening before the game so that we could have a mini pre-Super Bowl gathering before the main event the following day.

I spent the morning shopping for supplies, and the afternoon making mom's shrimp and macaroni salad, guacamole dip, and an assortment of other snack foods. I noticed the microwave clock at 3:45 as I picked up the phone to call Finley and let her know that I would be arriving around 7pm. I finished cleaning up the kitchen, showered and dressed, and by the time the microwave clock blinked 5:30 I'd packed up the food and was ready to leave when all of a sudden, a strong feeling of dread washed over me and a small voice entered into my head saying: *"You're not going anywhere."* I stood stunned in my kitchen, holding the food laden boxes. "Excuse me?" I quizzically said out loud to my own surprise.

The tiny voice gained some volume: **"You're not going anywhere."**

An unexplainable fear seized me tighter as I answered back defiantly: "I'm *going* to a Super Bowl party!"

Patiently the voice replied; *"No you're not. Call Finley and tell her you're not coming."*

My shock and fear spread into angered panic. "What the hell is this?!" I cried. There was no response. Immediately my mind raced to a story I'd recently seen on the program Dateline about people who'd developed some disease that made them afraid to leave their homes. There was no rational explanation for their fear, and none for my own. Had I just developed this malady in the last few minutes? This was ridiculous! I put the boxes down and sat at the table, arguing with myself that I was in fact *going* to the party, I was not about to become a prisoner of some irrational paranoia! The more I argued, the more the terror increased.

I decided to go out for a short walk in order to prove to myself that I was not afraid to leave my house.

I started to walk along 42nd street which at that time had not been renovated by The Disney Corporation. It was littered with drug dealers, hookers, pimps, drunks and other sordid characters that stood in the shadows of the various run down porno movie theatres, boarded up storefronts and crumbling hotels. I figured if I could face this plethora of dangerous malcontents, then I wasn't really fearful at all.

As I walked, no "small voice" interfered, but I was still gripped with terror. I wasn't afraid of any of the strangers milling along the sidewalk, I was petrified about being away from my apartment.

Suddenly a loud voice cried out from a passing car: "Hey you fucking faggot; how much for a blowjob?!!" Weather or not the chilling jibe was directed at me was unclear but the hateful yell stung my soul quickly like a scorpion.

"Okay, *that* was pretty scary! Is that what I was trying to avoid?" I questioned myself.

The voice returned and this time there was no doubt it was mom: ***"No, that's not it. You need to get home and stay there! You're on restriction until further notice!"***

I'd heard the last sentence verbatim from her during most of my adolescence and by the tone of its delivery, I knew it was her.

I bitched at her all the way home: "Why are you doing this to me? Why can't I go to the party?!! What am I going to do with all the food I made and what am I going to tell Finley?!! My *"mommy"* says I can't come to the party???!!! She'll think I've lost my freakin' mind!!!"

I continued my rant as I angrily raced my way home. No

response. By the time I closed the door to my apartment I was so worked up with fever pitched anxiety that I began pacing the floor with the phone in my hand, trying to come up with a plausible explanation to tell Finley why I wasn't coming. Mother had tuned out so I was getting no assistance from her.

I called Finley and said that I couldn't explain it, but there was a voice inside me telling me not to leave the house. Finley had witnessed my E.S.P. on a previous occasion, but I'd not fessed up to the depths of my mom's communications before this, and I wasn't ready to do so now.

Finley could tell I was upset by my inexplicable fear, but she said that she completely understood, and that if my inner voice was warning me, I'd better listen. I told her I would call her the next day, maybe my paranoid siege would be over and I could attend the football party after all.

I hung up the phone and spiraled into depression. What the hell was going on with me? I couldn't shake the wall of bitter resentment, and paranoia.

I put all the food away. I was hungry but too upset to eat. I thought maybe a cocktail would calm me down, so I poured myself a vodka gimlet (mom's favorite) and sat staring out the window at the heavily falling snow. The wind fiercely picked up and started howling which only made me feel like I was captive in a horror movie, waiting for some demented murderer to burst through the door.

I sat there for a long time, sinking further into my restless panic and depression until finally I couldn't take thinking about it any more.

"Maybe I can sleep this feeling, this anger, this disease or whatever the hell this is away, and I'll be better in the morning." I disgustedly reprimanded myself for my cowardice and foolishness as I flung myself on the bed in despair.

I awoke the following morning and noticed the dread in my spirit as vibrant as it'd been the night before. I couldn't believe that I'd been taken over by some incomprehensible state of fear.

What was there to be afraid of? I frustrated myself with this question over and over and couldn't find one iota of evidence to support my emotional train wreck. There were no voices or signals of any kind this morning from mother and I seriously began thinking that I'd *actually caught* the mental illness I'd seen portrayed on <u>Dateline</u>.

I'd always been on the lookout for signs of mental illness in my own life because of its hereditary factor and my irrational fear certainly seemed to be a qualification.

I tried watching television to escape the grip of tormenting uneasiness, but couldn't concentrate. I tried listening to music, it wasn't soothing. Finally I decided that I'd have to face my fear again by leaving the apartment but I was so petrified of doing so, that I put my coat on and took it off again three times, bitterly and fiercely arguing with myself in between, before I defiantly found myself running down the stairs and stepping out onto the snow covered sidewalk.

"I'll just go to the post office and the vegetable market, it won't take long." I reassured myself as I tried to force some sense of normalcy on my spirit.

Mom's ethereal voice returned and started nagging me a block from my apartment. To every argument I threw back at her she overrode it with the same phrase: **"You're on restriction until further notice!"**

I tried to suppress it and turned up my walkman but her voice invaded my thoughts incessantly. By the time I'd walked the nineteen short blocks to the post office, I was brimming with panic. I grabbed the mail out of my P.O. Box and decided to skip the market; I absolutely had to get home!

My anger returned as I forcefully stomped my way back uptown. I was especially pissed off that, not only was I going to miss the party today, but apparently I was never going to leave my apartment again without the poltergeist of terror on my back!

"What the hell is going on?! What are you doing to me?!" I raged silently to mother and myself as I rushed past everyone on the sidewalk.

By the time I finally reached my apartment, I was so sick of the senseless fear invading every pore of my being that I crawled into bed, pleading in desperation; "What the hell is wrong with me?! What have I done to deserve this!? Do I need to call a doctor or what!!??" My whining questions echoed end over end of each other until I eventually fell into a fitful sleep.

I awoke several hours later to the jarring sound of someone loudly knocking on my door. The building couldn't be accessed from the street unless the visitor was buzzed in by the tenants. I assumed it had to be Mr. Lyons, the building superintendent from upstairs. The building only housed three units and I knew that my downstairs neighbor was out of town.

I was in no mood to talk to Mr. Lyons so I just lay there, hoping he would leave. The insistent knock came again and I continued laying on the bed thinking; "Go away." A moment later I heard a jiggling of the doorknob and I figured Mr. Lyons was going to enter at any moment. He was of a somewhat suspicious character and had the keys to my apartment. I surmised that he was going to take this opportunity of my absence to enter and nose around.

I sprang out of the bed in my thermal socks and underwear and tip-toed to a chair facing the door. I sat there, getting angrier as I heard him trying to insert his key in the lock. I couldn't wait to see the look on his face as I surprised him with my presence.

As I sat there waiting, I impatiently wondered; "What's taking him so damn long to get in the door?" He only needed three keys to the units, what was taking him so long to find the right one?

I got up and tiptoed to the door. As I looked through the peephole my impatience turned into wide eyed terror! There were two large, scary looking strangers on the other side, trying to pick the lock! I could see their faces clearly; they looked strung out on drugs.

I raced to the kitchen, picked up the phone and dialed 911. Rummaging through a drawer I grabbed a hammer for a weapon. The 911 female operator's nasal voice answered; "What's your emergency?"

Tethered to the wall phone, in a low controlled voice I replied: "Two men are trying to break into my apartment!"

"Why are you keeping your voice so low sir?"
"They don't know I'm in the apartment!"
"They're trying to break in?"
"Yes! They could be coming through the door at any moment!"
"What's your address sir?"
I gave her the information, adding; "I have to go now!"
"Sir, please stay on the line. Do you know these men?"
"No! I've never seen them before! I have to go stand by the door so I can be ready for them! Please send the police now!"
"Sir; please stay on …"

I put the phone down on the counter before she could finish and sprinted quietly to the door. If they were going to get in I'd have to be ready to fight and I wanted to take them by surprise!

They were still fussing with the lock; I grabbed a pair of jeans and jumped into them as I ran to the window. The police station was a short half-block away, within view. I would be able to see them coming. I fiercely flung open the window and looked out to see if they were on their way.

The snow had stopped but the howling wind and traffic deafened me to the sounds of the criminals at my door, so I kept sprinting from the window to the door quietly in my stocking feet as I waited for the cops. There was no sign of them coming and when I'd go back to the door, the lock was still jiggling.

I thought that I might need to flee down the fire escape if the crazed intruders had guns so I jammed my feet into a pair of boots near the window. Still no police! I ran back to the door, trying to be quiet in my boots, the men were still maniacally trying to get the lock to give. I ran back to the window, no police!

I debated with myself about abandoning the apartment down the fire escape. What good was a hammer going to do me against two scary large men? I ran as quietly as I could back to the door, the floor trembled with the vibrations from my boots. The jimmying of the lock had stopped. Holding my breath, I looked through the peephole, the men were gone! I ran to the phone, the 911 operator had hung up. I dialed Mr. Lyons number. No answer. Crashing the receiver onto the phone, I ran to the window looking for the police, no sign of them. Wondering if the intruders were still in the building, cautiously I opened my door and stepped into the hall. It was a small building and I could hear if someone was on one of the other two floors. Calm silence. The building's door buzzer sounded and my heart pounded faster as I ran into my apartment and anxiously answered; "Yes?"

"Police! Open up!"

I buzzed the entrance to let them in and ran downstairs to greet them. Three burly policemen were coming up the stairs where I met them half way.

With winded breath I informed them: "The intruders may still be in the building but they've left my door!"

Two of the policemen put their hands on their guns, the other one wielding a nightstick, gave me a stern look and said; "How many intruders are there?"

As I led them upstairs I answered; "Two men."

"Can you describe them?"

"Two large white men, one with long red hair, one balding blond, they looked strung out on drugs and... I only saw them through the peephole for a second or two but they were trying to break into my apartment for the last ten minutes!"

"What were they wearing?"

"I don't remember!" I answered as we approached the landing of my floor.

"Which apartment is yours?"

I opened the door to my unit for them. They swept quickly through the three rooms. The leader of the men motioned for the other cops to follow him as he said; "Let's check the next floor."

The four of us went upstairs to Mr. Lyons unit and the lead cop pounded on the door yelling; "Police! Open up!"

Mr. Lyons partially opened the door, his wife beside him. They were both squinting, they'd obviously been napping.

"Is there anyone else in there with you?" The lead cop gruffly demanded.

Confused, Mr. Lyons replied; "No sir, is there a problem?"

Excitedly I interjected: "There were two men trying to break into my apartment, you didn't hear anything?"

Drowsily Mrs. Lyons offered: "We were both sleeping."

The lead cop said; "Sorry to bother you, lets check the roof guys."

As we started towards the rooftop door five feet away, Mr. Lyons spoke; "The door to the roof is always locked."

One cop checked the door, still locked. There was nowhere else in the hallways to check; apparently the intruders had left the building seconds before the police arrived.

As the four of us started back downstairs, the lead policeman questioned me.

"Are you *sure* two men were trying to break into your apartment sir?"

"Am I *sure?!* Yes I'm sure! I saw them through the peephole in the door and they were trying to pick the lock for at least ten minutes!!!"

"They were at your door for ten minutes and you can't give us a better description of them?"

I could tell by his suspicious tone that he thought I was making the whole thing up!

"I only saw them for two seconds! I didn't have time to stand at the door looking through the damn peephole! I had to call 911 and get ready to defend myself! I kept running from my door to the window to see if you were coming! The whole time they were jimmying the lock on my door! And by the way, what took you so damn long? You're only half a block away!"

As we reached my apartment door, my eyes met his and his formerly stern face relaxed. He knew by my outburst that I wasn't fabricating this.

"Well, they don't seem to be in the building now, so if you don't need our assistance, we'll be going."

Emotionally exhausted, but with genuine sincerity I said; "Sorry to bother you officers. Thanks for coming."

The leader looked at me compassionately and with honest empathy said; "No bother sir, that's what we're here for. Sorry you had to go through this. Call us if they return."

I could tell by his assurance that he meant it. He may have not understood what had transpired at my door, but his words and the look on his face told me he believed my story now. The cops

Italian Mothers Never Die

continued down the stairs, I locked the front door, and mentally drained; I went and sat down on a stool in the kitchen, facing the microwave. The clock blinked: 5:30 and at that moment I realized it had been exactly 24 hours *to the minute* since the terror began the night before. I felt all the tension release from my body and mind like air releasing from a balloon. I suddenly recognized that mother had been warning me the whole time, 24 hours in advance!

Humbled and embarrassed at my angry resistance against her, I thanked her. I then wondered why the criminals had so abruptly given up. They'd worked so furiously…what made them change their minds? My boots! They must've heard my boots on the floor or felt the floor vibrate, and realized that someone actually was *in* the apartment! That's why they'd knocked first, to see if anyone was home! If I'd stayed at Finley's the night before, I wouldn't have returned home yet and the thieves would have certainly gotten in!

I breathed a sigh of great relief and gratitude. I felt normal again. No trace of nervousness or fear of any kind. I hadn't lost my mind nor gotten the <u>Dateline</u> paranoia disease.

I may have missed the football party, but I'd won *this* "super bowl" and the refrain from a song written by The Ramones echoed in my head: "Let the old world make believe it's blind and deaf and dumb/but nothing can change the shape of things/nothing can change the shape of things/nothing can change the shape of things to come…"

Sheepishly I began apologizing for my angry and stubborn twenty-four hour tirade against mom. I couldn't believe I still fought against her prodding's after all these years! I should be used to them by now considering everything she'd done before, but each time she got involved, I didn't concede her interventions were making sense until, whatever the miraculous event, like a blossoming flower, had completely unfolded. Only then would I fully recognize the essence and messages of her divine intercessions. Only *after* her "incoming details" had played themselves out, were my heart, mind, and soul, infused with awareness.

In A New York Minute
(Song by: Don Henley)

Before I ever moved to the city, I never wholly grasped the significance of the phrase: "In a New York minute" but as my fifth year here year raced by, I came to fully appreciate the authenticity of that expression.

Walking the endless maze of streets in Manhattan on a daily basis, with it's kaleidoscopic view of diverse world cultures up front and personal, condensed on this relatively small, concrete, sky scraped island, one's entire life could change from placid to panic with one wrong turn of a corner.

I'd been on the streets running errands all day. My never ending list of chores had me covering the sidewalks of a six-plus mile radius according to the pedometer snapped onto my baggy nylon gym pants. It was an unseasonably hot and humid early May afternoon.

My stomach rumbled noisily with insatiable hunger as I searched for a casual place along Eighth Avenue to have a very late lunch. I wasn't in the mood to wait in line at any of the many open air seating pizza joints that were already fully occupied with patrons.

"Too hot for pizza anyway, I want something cold and filling but… what?" I thought to myself as I briskly made my way further up the block.

Stripping my thin cotton work out jacket off down to my perspiration dampened tee-shirt; I mopped my wet forehead with the jacket. I was walking extremely fast, propelled by famished thoughts of finding somewhere air-conditioned where I could cool off and eat something relatively healthy. Unfortunately, I knew I was in an area of town where the only places with decent food that were also air conditioned, were too upscale for my casual, gym attired appearance. My bulky wallet in the front pocket of my loose fitting nylon pants was bouncing and slapping against my thigh as I continued racing along the sidewalk. I knew the wallet was fully visible bouncing inside the sagging pocket, and ordinarily I would have zipped it inside the pouch of the gym jacket I'd tied around my waist, but I was at that frenzied stage of hunger, the stage where it didn't matter what I ate right now as long as it's *food!!!* For once I didn't care that my wallet was in full view of anyone who bothered to notice.

I spied the familiar yellow and green lettered sign of a <u>Subway</u> sandwich shop half a block away.

Propelled by the prospect of imminent food I excitedly thought: "Yeah, I could go for an Italian sub right now...and there's air-conditioned seating!" I salivated over thoughts of salami and cheese as I sped up my pace.

By the time I swung the door open, I was as hot and sweaty as if I'd been jogging. My gasping for breath, disheveled appearance, went unnoticed by the few people sitting in the orange plastic booths. As soon as I stepped up to the glass sandwich ingredients counter, a far away voice echoed into my head: *"Trouble! There's trouble in here!!!"*

As I waited for the lone employee to notice me, I angrily responded silently to the voice: "Not now! I don't need this crap right now!"

I surveyed the room impatiently. Three nicely tailored middle aged business women were sitting a few feet away, heatedly discussing office politics over their sodas and sandwiches; across from an elderly single man sipping coffee and reading a newspaper. A tall, chubby, uniformed Afro-American security guard leaned lazily against the yellow wall in the back of the narrow shop, and I saw two other "brothers" one of medium height and slightly framed, (like myself) the other, much taller, with a solid linebackers build. Both men stood at the stainless steel soda machine about thirty feet away.

The voice grew louder and I recognized moms inflection: ***"Those two! Watch out! Trouble! "***

I barely glanced at the two men before I impatiently said to the sandwich maker: "Excuse me…"

The rail thin, dark circle eyed thirty-something male, raised his head from the stupor of his slow and aimless counter wiping. His dark red eyes were glazed over and I saw immediately that he was completely stoned.

He stared vacantly at me as I continued: "Can I please have a number five combo on whole wheat?"

He looked at me as if I'd just told him there was no more valium left on the planet.

"You… wanna… num…ber… fi…" He slurred.

I hurriedly finished his sentence; "Five…yes, an Italian sub combo on whole wheat."

Clumsily he slouched against his prep board and responded; "Duh ya… wan that on… white …or whole …wheeee…?"

I could see I was going to have to walk him through this. I pointed to the whole wheat rolls on his bread rack: "*That one.*"

In slow motion he moved towards the rack, and mom's voice returned: ***"Watch it son! Those two men…trouble!"***

I blithely looked over again at the two black men standing and talking at the drink machine. I was far too consumed with hunger to feel threatened by them, and the security guard was standing nearby.

"Not now ma! What's the big deal?" I wearily argued.

She instantly shot back: ***"Your wallet!"***

Impatiently I mentally replied: "Yeah, so? What are they gonna do walk up and take it out of my *front* pocket?!"

My argument in our telepathic connection was interrupted by the drugged out employee who looked like he might pass out at any moment.

Italian Mothers Never Die

"Duh ya wan…um…six…inch… or…um…"

Irritated, I cut him off: "A six inch Italian combo!"

At a snails pace he sliced the roll, opened it and froze in a blank stare. I started to instruct him: "Oil and vinegar…"

He numbly grabbed the cruets and splashed the liquids all over the roll and his prep board.

I continued to instruct him: "Now, put on the lettuce…"

Waving my hand I motioned him towards the sandwich ingredient bay. Mesmerized, he spread a handful of lettuce on the soaked bread…

"Yes, now provolone cheese…" I cooed to him encouragingly as he mechanically surveyed his assortment of items. Sluggishly he began reaching for the cheese. I was overwhelmingly starved by this point and I reached over the counter as he laid the cheese on the lettuce and I grabbed several slices of pepperoni, salami, and tomatoes and handed them to him. He barely registered what I'd just done as he continued to assemble the sub.

I took my wallet out of my pocket, pulled out seven dollars and slapped it on the green Formica counter top next to the cash register. I grabbed a drink cup and a bag of Lays potato chips as he fumbled with the tomato slices.

Mom loudly came through again: ***Trouble with a capital T!!!***

Exasperated, I mentally responded: "Puhhh-leeez ma! Can't I just get something to eat!?"

The sandwich maker cut the sub in half, picked it up and stood holding it with a dazed expression. I slid a tray under his hands and on auto-pilot, he dropped the sandwich.

"Money's on the counter!" I said as I rushed to the drink center where the two men paid me no mind. The ice noisily clunked into my cup and I pressed it up against the root beer nozzle. Sipping the foam off the soda, I grabbed a lid, a straw, and some napkins.

I quickly passed the two men and the armed security guard, and sat with my back to them on the edge of the seat of an orange plastic booth.

Greedily I bit into the sandwich and tore open the bag of chips. The vinegar and oil doused lettuce dripped in clumps onto the paper as I ravenously began devouring the sub, simultaneously stuffing the salty chips into my mouth two at a time.

I was completely lost in the reverie of my wildly animalistic consumption, right in the middle of a slug off my soda when all of a sudden, the very tall and pumped-up "brother" walking hesitantly by, fake tripped and slammed into me. The moment his hefty body collapsed onto me on the edge of my seat, my vision was obscured by my soda cup and face buried into his chest.

"Oh…excuse me!" He said as he pressed against me harder, falsely flailing his arms over my shoulders in an effort to pin me in the booth. At that moment I felt my wallet slide out of my pocket. Forcefully I freed the cup from in between us and slammed it on the table as he continued pressing against me.

Enraged, my adrenaline kicked my normally placid hormones into overdrive as my swimmers body suddenly morphed into "The Terminator" and I pinned the tall mans thick muscled arms to his sides. Violently pushing him off I stood up and threw him aside shouting: ***"NO! Excuse me!"***

He clumsily stumbled backwards with a shocked expression on his face, his wide open palms at his shoulders. "Hey man it was an accident…" He said with a false look of innocence spreading across his face.

"Bullshit!" I thundered back as I looked kitty-cornered behind me at his smaller accomplice who wore a frightened and anxious look in his eyes while sitting on the edge of a plastic booth, his faded brown leather jacket bundled on his lap.

I reached over and yanked his jacket from him with a snap. My wallet flew into midair and landed at my feet. I picked it up, furiously annoyed, and using mother's most earth shattering tone, I sarcastically shouted one of her most frequently used direct quotes: ***"Now you may be excused!!!"***

The two stunned and perplexed men looked at me as if they'd just seen a ghost and one of the three business women empathetically called across the room to me: "I saw what just happened are you alright?"

I looked at her gratefully and said; "Thank you, I'm fine! I knew these two jokers were trouble the minute I walked in here!"

Turning to the Security Guard who now pretended to be waking

Italian Mothers Never Die

up from his standing napping position against the wall, I realized that he'd been in on this. I'd seen him nodding to the two men out of the corner of my eyes just before I'd sat down.

Further enraged I yelled at him: *"And **thank you** for absolutely nothing!!!"*

His guilt ridden eyes widened as he slunk up against a windowed swinging door and disappeared.

The two assailants hurriedly made their way to the exit and I resumed eating calmly, as if nothing at all had happened. Inwardly my head and heart were overflowing with silent gratitude to mom for her "heads up" and there were also a few timid apologies; "For not listening, for arguing, for bitching…" thrown in.

The heightened drama of my lunch made me slow down my eating as I thoughtfully re-lived the whole thing over again in my head. I leisurely finished my meal, sat back and lit a cigarette. I chuckled over the ridiculousness of the men's lame and faulty ploy. I wondered: "Who bumps into someone while they're sitting in a booth anyway?!" Smiling, I shook my head at the stupidity of that move. Just then, the shop entrance door swung open and the same two men entered. They stopped dead in their tracks, surprised to see I was still sitting there nearly an hour after their exit. I guessed they were returning for their next victim and I fixed them a venomous, steely eyed stare. Both of them instantly froze with terrified expressions on their faces, turned around and left. I completely understood at that moment the lyrics of the Don Henley song lyric: "In a New York minute everything can change…"

Though I still resisted whenever she intervened, I'd certainly honed my "listening to mother" skills to a sharper degree now, more than I had when I first moved here; perhaps that was the reason for my "Auh-nald Schwarzenegger" bravado at this most recent attempted mugging.

I hadn't picked up any details of "up coming mugging clues" from mom the first time I was attacked several years ago, in my early city days when I still lived in the South Bronx with Bill.

At that time, a waitress I worked with at Mamma Leone's was staying in Paris from April until June and she'd asked me to house sit in her Manhattan apartment while she was away. Beverly had a beautiful, spacious; art filled two bedroom brown stone on the Upper West Side, only eight blocks from Strawberry Fields. Her neighborhood was the West Side epitome of "New York chic" and made my South Bronx digs look like Beirut! I hadn't been to Central Park much my first year here because I was too busy starting my life over and still dealing with Megan.

It was my first afternoon at Beverly's, and after unpacking my bags I decided to go for a leisurely Central Park stroll.

Beverly's place was a two minute walk from the 81st park entrance. I'd recently purchased a very expensive designer leather jacket. This was the perfect opportunity to wear it along with the brand new Nike's I'd been saving for any special occasion. This was certainly a special occasion; I was off from work for the week so I could "vacation" among the obviously moneyed residents of the Upper West side. I could live like a real Manhattanite for a change.

I'd never entered the park at this entrance before, the surroundings were completely foreign. I was intently listening to a tape on my Walkman of music I'd played the night before, a piece that I just sat down, turned on the recorder and composed on the spot. I was in the deepest throes of inspiration when I'd effortlessly played the eight minute piece on my keyboards and had no idea how I'd done it. I liked it a lot, and now I was trying to memorize it so I could try to play it again at a later date.

Absorbed in the music as I walked along on the path in this unfamiliar section of the park, I noticed the scenery wasn't quite up to par for this upscale "chi-chi" neighborhood. There were large patches of grass balding acreage, an absence of benches, sculptures, fountains, or anything that would make this slippery, muddy path interesting to look at. Only a large thicket of trees that lined the path showed any signs of beauty, and only because they'd recently blossomed and were glistening with wetness from a light rain that had begun.

It had rained the day before; I cursed myself for not checking the unpredictable weather and for wearing the new white Nike's, they were being splattered with dirty raindrops and picking up mud on the treads.

There weren't very many people in this area and it was easy to understand why. Apparently this portion of the park attracted the more disenfranchised residents of the neighborhood; the people that passed me as I walked by appeared to be homeless rather than yuppie "home-ies." Maybe it was the just the combination of strange and aimlessly wandering faces, along with the eerily quiet, dreary grey skies, and the rain falling on me without an umbrella, that was beginning to make me feel some kind of threatened as I continued my walk.

I pulled my jacket up onto my head, hooding myself from the now hard driving rain as I tried to concentrate on the music.

Suddenly someone tapped me on the back. I hadn't heard anyone come up behind me because my headphones were loud. I stopped and turned around, reading the man's lips as he said; "Can I get a light?"

The tall, sweatshirt hooded, muscular man, motioned his cigarette towards me. I pulled the jacket off my head and unzipped the pocket to get my lighter.

He moved in closer to shield the flame from the rain as I clicked the lighter.

The next thing I was aware of, I was returning to consciousness, gasping for breath as someone from behind was choking me, lifting me off the ground with his forearm as I thrashed.

I'd been dragged into the heavily wooded thicket of trees and the sweatshirt hooded man who'd asked for a light, now had a large hunting knife pointed at me as he yanked off my shoes and sox. "Stop looking at me!" He viciously ordered as he thrust the blade at my face. I turned away, still defiantly struggling with whoever was strangling me, locked into the crook of his arm and shoulder as he covered my mouth with his other hand.

I felt my Walkman holder nylon waist pack unclick, and the knife wielding thug unlatched my belt, ripped open my pants and pulled them off. Terrified, I looked at him again.

"Stop looking or you're dead!" He menacingly hissed, as he ripped open my shirt and started to pull it, along with my jacket, off of me.

I had no idea what they were going to do next, but I knew whatever it was, they were definitely in control. In that moment of clarity, I let myself go completely limp in my captor's strangling arms. I needed desperately to breathe and as long as I continued feverishly struggling, I knew he'd keep applying pressure.

As the other thug pushed the flat of the blade against my face, the strangler felt me go limp, and lightly released my mouth as I gasped for air.

"I don't think this guy's gonna give us any trouble, but hurry up!" The strangler said with a note of agitated concern to the other attacker.

I kept my face turned away from the other guy who was still violently trying to get my jacket and shirt off as I remained pressed up against his accomplice.

The strangler kept lightly taking his hand barely off of my nose and mouth to occasionally let me breathe. I'd quit wrestling, he knew I'd surrendered to my captivity.

Refilled with air, I spoke as calmly as I could beneath his hand as my arm was being pulled out of my jacket sleeve.

"Please leave the cassette tape, take the Walkman, but leave the tape. I only want the tape...please."

Here I was, being stripped nearly naked, choked and threatened with murder, and I'm asking my attacker to leave me the cassette tape because I realize I can never re-compose that melody again, I didn't know it well enough yet!

Upon later reconsideration, even I'm bewildered by my hugely distorted priority of retaining the tape, but at the time, I couldn't have been more serious in my request.

Even though the entire monetary value of everything on my person had totaled more than two thousand dollars, not to mention the very imminent threat of murder, in the face of danger I was more concerned about my new composition.

My plea was of no avail. The knife wielder put the point up to my throat as the strangler pulled my arms behind me. The crazed look in his hate filled eyes said he was itching to stab me as he spat these words into my face: "Stay right here and count to a hundred facing this tree or you're dead! If you turn around to look we'll come right back and *kill you! Understand?!!!*"

I nodded, and the strangler pushed me up against the tree. He waited for his friend to get a running head start and just before he released me he said; "Don't leave this tree until you know we're completely gone 'coz my friend *will come back and stab you!!!*"

I could tell by the way he said it that he was trying to protect me from getting seriously hurt, I nodded again.

I could hear them both running through the muddy thicket as I numbly stood there in emotionally shattered annihilation. Shivering in my shorts as the cold rain began pounding harder; I was mortified at my near nakedness, desperate to have some clothing.

Without waiting for them to entirely get away, I began haphazardly walking, dazed and disoriented, slipping and sliding among rough muddy branches, rocks and leaves as I made my way in the direction they'd run. The rain pelted me like paint bullets and my cold wet legs and feet felt every sharp slice of my flesh as I scraped against the debris of the muck raked terrain.

Suddenly elated at the sight of my crumpled wet pants in the misty, muddy distance, I rushed to them and pulled them on; looking around for anything else the thugs might have left behind. Virtually no traces of any of my personal effects were visible as I desperately searched in vain for the music tape among the sludge.

Unfamiliar with the surroundings, without shoes, sox, jacket or shirt, I eventually found my way to the park exit, grateful to be back on solid ground.

My muddy rain splattered eyes barely recognized whatever section of Central Park West I was on. As I anxiously charged along the slippery bustling sidewalks in manic search of a phone booth, I felt like I was a participating "extra" in some strange, distorted, nightmare of a movie. Seeing the coldly disgusted, disapproving stares and side glances of the well heeled passersby was like watching a parade of Ingmar Bergman characters in close up. I couldn't have cared less about their perceptions of my mud spattered, rain soaked half nakedness as I raced from one phone booth to another trying to find one that worked!

I finally got a dial tone at a phone on the corner of 72nd Street.

My scraped and bloodied muddy hand held the cold slippery receiver to my face as I gave the operator instructions for a collect call to Bill in The Bronx. I prayed fervently that he was home as the ringing began.

My first shred of hope flickered the moment he picked up. The Operator put us through and I briefly explained my circumstances. I told him to bring me some sox, shoes, a shirt and jacket, and to meet me in front of The Dakota which was right next to the 72nd Street subway station.

As I leaned against the black painted, lion faced iron railing bordering The Dakota, I settled into a hollow state of shock. People were passing back and forth in front of me, glaring like I was some dirty, rabid wild animal, and I didn't care what they saw, I was too focused on my detached emotional displacement and growing despair.

I kept re-enacting the entire mugging in my head over and over and over. From my instant blackout, apparently from the strangler who had choked me so hard at first that I'd lost consciousness as I was dragged into the muddy thicket of trees, along with terrifying flashes of the knife threatening mans angry, hate filled face as he violently ripped off of my clothing. The echo's of his murderous threats reverberated incessantly until, for some strange reason I remembered that at the age of ten, I'd seen the word "rape" in bold letters on the front page of the newspaper as my dad was reading it and I asked him what it meant. For the very first time he didn't peevishly admonish me to "Look it up in the dictionary!" Instead, his eyes softened with a mild uncertainty as he looked at me over the top of his paper. Wanting to explain without telling me the whole truth he replied; "To take something by force."

I'd contented myself with his innocuous explanation at the time, and of course I eventually learned the definition without "looking it up" but its full, sick, hideous meaning washed over me now.

I'd certainly been raped on numerous occasions in my teens, but they were non-violent sexual molestations by adults who calmly calculated their actions before hand. Also, some of them had required involved emotional seductions of trustworthiness before they touched me, not viscous, life threatening abuse.

While there'd been no sexual activity in this attack, it was a rape that was far worse than any of the others. I'd never felt more violated and the only thing I could think as I waited for Bill to arrive was: "What am I going to do?"

How could I ever find a way to live in peace with this atrocity to my spirit? All of my youthful traumatic events I'd learned to get over, but this, its darkness was just *too* much. I'd never be able to walk in Central Park or on these streets again without anxious lethal anger and suspicion. How could I ever possibly learn to cope with this?

"What am I going to do?!" I wasn't asking anyone but myself that vacuous question, and I wasn't finding any answers, only an increasingly resentful acidic rage and an all too consuming mire of depressed confusion.

In was then, in my abject surrender to emotional hopelessness that she came through loud and clear: **"Son, it's like falling off a horse, the only thing you <u>can</u> do is dust yourself off and get back on."**

I sat onto the cold and wet railing, profoundly depressed and utterly disillusioned, absorbing what she'd just said, and clichéd as it was, it was simple and to the point and I grudgingly knew she was right. I wasn't sure I could accomplish it, but I had no other viable choice and realized I'd have to at least find a way to try.

I wasn't consoled by her message, not even close, but she had answered my question of "What am I going to do?" and that was the only question I'd asked.

There was no point in asking *why* it had happened. It happened, and I was lucky to be alive. I remained in shock sitting among the iron lions, and the rain fell on my face in place of my non-existent tears. It seemed like the sky was doing the crying for me and I was too emotionally drained to bother, but I'm certain my emotional anguish was visible to the blurs of people passing by.

I hadn't seen Yoko again since I'd moved to the city, and for once I wouldn't have even noticed if she were to walk right past me now, I was far too buried intensely in a haze. Talk about <u>Walking On Thin Ice</u>! I'd barely made it "across the lake" with my life. In the rushing torment of my tortured mind, body, and soul, I couldn't help but be reminded of the flip side of that 45rpm. recording, a verse Yoko had written in 1963 that was set to music and video shortly before John Lennon was murdered. The song is aptly titled: <u>It Happened</u>.

<u>It Happened</u>

"It happened at a time of my life when I least expected/It happened at a time of my life when I least expected/I don't even remember how it happened/I don't even remember the day it happened/but it happened/yes it happened/oh it happened/and I know/there's no return/no way."

It's short on lyrics but epic in it's emotional intensity and I knew every note and nuance so well that I kept replaying it note for note in my head as I continued waiting for Bill to arrive with some clothes and a subway token so I could just get home to shower and scrub away the filthy hands of the muggers.

As the sad song replayed itself over and over in my brain I wanted desperately to cry, my spirit ached for some form of release. Instead the song became a repetitive mantra in my mind, and slowly, just as I felt a slight surge of a tear begin to well up, abruptly my trance-disconnect from the world was invaded by the voice of a man who stopped directly in front of me.

He stood alone, and I could tell he was a Japanese tourist by his well dressed appearance, the Nikon camera strapped around his neck, and the very polite way he haltingly said: "Excuse ah...me. I don't mean to ah...bot'tha you ah... but... do you know if this... is the ah ...building whe'ah ... John Lennon was shot?"'

At first I was confused, unsettled by the sounds of his words penetrating my numbness, forcing my focus to return to the consciousness of the present moment.

No one else had spoken to me in the past hour; I'd only garnered fearful furtive glances or cold and contemptible stares. Now here was a man who approached me without trepidation or judgment. Evidently his love for Lennon overrode any fear my grubby, dazed and crazed appearance had instilled among the other passersby.

Blinking back the small swell of tears that were just on the brink of spilling over, blank faced, I raggedly nodded to his question, and weakly managed to respond; "Yes."

His face lit up with gratitude and anticipation when he continued: "I'm ah...so saw-we to ah...bo'tha you ah... again, but ah... could you please take a pic-chaw of me ah...in front of this ah... building?"

Deep in the throes of the thunderstorm that had been raging in my grief stricken soul, I looked at his excited face and I recognized myself in his warm Japanese eyes as I said; "Yes."

He hurriedly removed the camera from around his neck and handed it to me. He jumped up onto the raised portion of the sidewalk next to the entrance, the exact spot where Yoko had stood for me on my first N.Y.C. tourist encounter with her.

I stood shivering, shirtless and barefoot, on the icily wet pavement looking through the lens. He smiled the ecstatic smile that countless fans must have smiled over the years, mine included. I forced my involuntary quivering to be still, and snapped the shot.

He thanked me profusely, nodding his head in a continuous ecstatic bow, as backwards he excitedly walked away.

I returned to my seat on the railing, and in my still mournful state, I realized that I'd only said two words to the tourist, and they were one and the same: "Yes".

I remembered that John had first met Yoko at The Indica Gallery in London in 1966 at one of her art shows. He'd climbed up a tall ladder to look through a magnifying glass dangling from a string attached to the ceiling, where he read a small note with the word "Yes" printed on it.

I remembered how graciously Yoko had said "Yes" to my request when I'd asked her for a photo.

I'd been metaphorically climbing a tall ladder of pain until the tourist interrupted me, and to his request I'd also said; "Yes".

A small muffled chuckle escaped from my mouth as I thought to myself: "*Only me*, in my devastated, angry, fragile state of mind, could still understand the man's devotion enough to put aside my agony and take his picture."

I imagined John and Yoko would be proud, they must have granted a photo for fans many times when they didn't feel like it, in the midst of some pain of their own.

I shook my head at the ironic statement my action on the tourist's behalf had made, taking his picture where Yoko had patiently posed for me, and I realized that I'd just married one of my life's happiest memories with now, one of my futures most painful and sorrowful ones.

I wondered if Yoko and her son Sean felt the same Yin/Yang wholeness of joy and pain, whenever they walked along this sidewalk where John was shot.

And the sky continued to rain torrents of tears that I still, could not.

Bill finally arrived with a bag of clothes and I dressed openly on the sidewalk. He tried asking me what had happened but I was too overcome with distraught emotions to answer. I glared at every man on the subway with anger and suspicion, hoping to see among them the faces of the assailants who'd so viscously raped me of my serenity. The knife brandishing muggers threatening face was indelibly etched in my memory, and I searched the features of every similar looking man at every stop, getting on or off, with venomous fire blazing from my eyes.

Once Bill and I got back to The Bronx, I showered for close to an hour. I scrubbed every pore of my body five times over before I went to my bedroom, turned on the tape recorder, sat at the keyboard and composed the most harrowing piece of music I've ever created. The impromptu composition ran its course through me like unrelenting lightening. I played non stop for nearly forty-five minutes before the hostile piece, suitably christened afterwards as: Central Park Mudslide, sorrowfully ended, and I felt I'd purged at least a remnant of the living nightmare from my spirit. I still hadn't cried, but the tears were evident in portions of the tragic symphony I'd just performed. The notes were the only tears I could cry.

Getting ***"back on the horse"*** hadn't come easy, but by the grace of God I managed to resume my normal, cheerful disposition, a couple of weeks later. I'd also learned a valuable lesson about being aware of my surroundings, and now several years later, that knowledge had paid off.

There would be no more scary "New York minutes" for me as long as I was in control of the situation, and this latest attempted mugging at the sandwich shop had proved that. I had *taken* control, and: "<u>It Happened</u>" alright, only this time I'd played the flip side of that record and my attackers had been the ones left mentally crippled and: <u>Walking On Thin Ice</u>.

"Mrs. Lennon"
(From the song: Mrs. Lennon by: Yoko Ono)

Since we've entered the Yoko zone here for the third time, you're probably wondering if she and I ever met again since I moved to the city.

True to psychic Indira's prediction, I did see Yoko again. It was on April 21st 1989, exactly two years *to the day* of our very first encounter.

I had the day off so I went to Strawberry Fields to enjoy the springtime afternoon. I sprawled out on the freshly cut grass with a blanket and a deli container of fresh fruits and a blueberry bagel, lazily leafing through a book Yoko had written decades ago titled: Grapefruit.

I'd been lounging contentedly for a few hours, enjoying the peaceful serenity of the surroundings and doing some of the avant-garde suggestions in the book.

Placidly I dozed among the sounds of chirping birds and children playing soccer in the distance. Out of no real sense of hunger I suddenly had a mad craving for pizza.

I'd just left the park and was crossing the street towards the Dakota. Briefly I wondered if I'd run in to Yoko today, seeing as how it was the third anniversary of our first meeting, but in my heart I knew it was just wish full thinking. No sooner had those thoughts crossed my mind, when a cab pulled up to the curb and I had to walk around it to reach the sidewalk. As I rounded the back of the yellow car, Yoko and her tabloid conjectured boyfriend, Sam Havadtoy, were getting out of the cab.

Yoko's eyes met mine and I instantly held up the yellow book. She smiled knowingly as she and Sam approached me.

I looked quite different from how I'd looked in the spring of 1987 when we'd last met. In the past two years I'd allowed my formerly blow dried straight, short hair, to grow shoulder length and into its naturally curly state. Gone were the faded denim and flannel traces of my former J.C. Penney "country couture". People often stopped me on the streets to ask if I was Michael Bolton, Kenny G, Peter Frampton, or some other musicians from other bands.

I didn't think Yoko recognized me but I saw a glimmer of familiarity come upon her face as she took the book and pen from me and very pleasantly asked: "What's your name?"

"Marc, M-a-r-c" I rapidly spelled it for her so she wouldn't misspell it as Mark. As she signed, I wished my name was anything *but* Marc, since it was an overzealous fan named Mark that had murdered John. I hoped she didn't think I was *her* star struck stalker, her Mark David Chapman. I wondered if she was making the same name comparison as she signed. I was too self conscious about it to say anything else to her. Besides, she was with Sam, I felt like I might start gushing about how much I loved her and I didn't want to embarrass myself. On the inside I was vibrating with excitement, but very calmly I looked her in the eyes and said; "Thank you so much" as she returned the book to me.

"You're welcome." She replied warmly and smiled. I backed away from them, and they continued to walk towards The Dakota entrance. The entire scene had taken hardly more than a minute.

I stayed where I was on the corner until they entered the building. I needed to walk in the same direction to go to the pizza joint up the street but I didn't want to make them nervous by walking behind them.

Once I knew they were in the building, I walked alongside of

The Dakota and said a short silent prayer of thanks to mom. "I love you Mother" I said with a smile under my breath as I began passing the entrance. And then I grinned a little wider as I remembered that John used to call Yoko, "Mother." This left me wondering if it was possible that John had also just said; "I love you Mother" to Yoko, through me.

Three years very quickly flew by, and though I'd walked past The Dakota countless times, I hadn't run into Yoko again. I wasn't the least bit surprised, or disappointed. She was a very busy woman, with a lifestyle I could scarcely imagine, not to mention, various other residences world wide.

My chance meetings with her had been magic enough to satisfy my fervor, and had equally fulfilled the Salem Oregon's psychic prophecy. Indira had been right about everything else, Megan, my move to the city, mom's communications, etc…and I was certainly much happier than I'd ever been, or dreamed possible. What more could I ask for?

I did become excited when I noticed in the Village Voice that Yoko was presenting an exhibition of her sculptures at the Mary Boone Gallery in April of 1992. I had no expectations or illusions of meeting her at the gallery; I just wanted to see the exhibit.

I was working a fourteen hour shift at Mamma Leone's and had a two hour break between the lunch and dinner crowd. With just enough time to get downtown and spend an hour at the exhibit, I changed out of my uniform and took the subway to West Broadway.

It was 2:30 pm. when I entered the near empty church like stillness of the gallery. Only one other person was looking around, a tall brunette with a canvas bag slung over her shoulder. She was very quietly moving from one object to the next. In silent communion across the room from her, I began doing the same.

Wishfully my spirit ingested the utopian message of Yoko's all white pieces chess set, displayed on a white chessboard, in a glass box, titled: <u>Play It by Trust</u>.

My heart ached over the sadness of isolation, and somber

Italian Mothers Never Die

reality, of her life sized bronze sculpture of a modern family, appropriately labeled: <u>Endangered Species</u>.

I continued pacing leisurely through the pin dropping silence of the gallery, taking in the eloquent and often times amusing pieces, such as her set of four bronze cast keys designated as: <u>Keys to Open the Skies</u>.

I was right in the middle of contemplating another piece when the tall young woman, toting her canvas bag, and wearing a camera strapped around her neck, approached me.

"Are you very familiar with Yoko's works?" She asked with sincere interest.

Smiling, I turned from the glass case, faced the woman and replied; "I'm more familiar with her music and films, but I love her sculptures too. I saw an exhibition of them at The Whitney Museum in 1989 and enjoyed it very much so I thought I'd check this show out. What about you?"

"Actually, I'm not familiar with her work at all, though it is rather interesting. Hi, my name is Marion."

"Pleased to meet you Marion, I'm Marc."

We shook hands and she said; "Would you mind walking me through the show? Enlighten me a bit more?"

I smiled doubtfully, saying; "I don't know if I qualified enough to enlighten you, but I can explain them as I see them."

For the next forty-five minutes we took in the art show, and I explained to Marion what I thought each piece represented. Other than the few curators who were in the middle of lunching in an adjacent room, Marion and I seemed to be the only people in the building. I was glad that we had the exhibition to ourselves, the silence made the sculptures more thought provoking and poignant.

We'd thoroughly discussed and made our tour of all the pieces before Marion said to me; "You know, Yoko's coming to the gallery today."

Surprised that she, a Yoko neophyte would know this, I responded; "Really? How do you know that?"

"I'm a freelance photographer on a photo assignment and I'm here to photograph her. Would you be interested in being my assistant? I could use some help switching cameras and lugging this equipment around." She said, tugging on the large canvas bag slung over her shoulder.

"Yeah! That would be great! When is she coming?"

"She should be here in the next half-hour or so."

Thrilled by Marion's invitation I replied; "Oh, this will be fun! But I have to go call my job and let them know I'm going to be a little late returning from my lunch break, I'll be right back!"

I was trembling with excitement as I left the gallery to find a payphone and make the call.

When I was a child, I always loved the cartoon character; Felix the Cat. (No stretch for a Leo I guess...) When I was thirteen years old, I was told that I had to choose a Saint's name for the Catholic ritual of Confirmation. I looked on the church's list of "approved" names and was delighted to find Saint Felix. Mother was less than enthusiastic and ordered me to choose something else. At her suggestion, I settled on Saint Patrick. She was very pleased with "my choice".

Anyway, Felix the Cat had a sidekick known as The Professor, and The Prof. always carried a "magic bag" that got Felix out of whatever trouble the curious cat might find himself in.

Since the 1970's I've always toted some form of "magic bag" of my own. Friends and family joked that in any emergency, they'd like to be with me because they knew that somewhere in my "magic bag" I'd have the necessary implements for filling any need, or surviving whatever catastrophe presented it self. (I possessed McGyver skills long before that television show was written!)

I opened my latest incarnation of a magic bag, hoping there would be something magical in it for Yoko, and was thrilled to find that I had a beautiful blank verse greeting card, and two copies of: Love is **More** than a Four Letter Word, my first studio album demo that in it's liner notes expressly thanked many people, including Yoko. She'd definitely inspired one of the songs on it.

I wrote a thank you note on the card for Yoko, telling her how much I loved the exhibition and that: "The echoes of its visions were still reverberating in my soul." Hopefully I could give it to

Italian Mothers Never Die

her along with a copy of my album, and ask her to sign my own copy, for good luck.

I'd been gone for about twenty minutes. By the time I got back to the building, the whole place was swarming with people. Marion said that Yoko was already in the office, and she would be coming out for photos soon.

It was only a few minutes before Yoko appeared, looking twenty years younger than her age and absolutely radiant! Her hair was cropped short, and styled in a tousled slight bouffant. Along with her trademark large rimmed glasses, she wore black shoes, black slacks and a black blazer over a thin black cashmere sweater, with a tear dropped shaped crystal necklace.

Her petite frame stood on a high platform that overlooked the crowd, and she began to announce that she would be walking through the exhibit for the photographers. As she was speaking, looking over the crowd, she spotted me. I saw a slightly nervous look flash across her face, and then she said that instead of giving media interviews in the gallery as she'd planned, she would give them in the back room and the reporters would be led back one at a time.

I couldn't help but think that maybe this time; she did suspect I was her Mark David Chapman. It was nearly three years *to the day* that she was seeing me again! Apparently we were on some sort of cosmic springtime cycle; this had happened three times now, and each time in the third week of April.

Given her tragic history, and the escalation of celebrity stalkers in the 90's, in her shoes I certainly would've been skittish at public appearances too! Too many assassins bask in their notoriety, and if I was an obsessively twisted fan, this would be the perfect opportunity. The security was minimal, there were no personal searches or scanners, and the media was already on the scene. What more could any fifteen minutes of fame seeking stalker hope for! I immediately felt bad that my presence may have caused her undue anxiety at her opening, but I completely understood, and resolved I would have to find some way to make her feel at ease.

Flanked by the gallery employees, Yoko casually walked out into the main gallery and stood for pictures, as various photographers were led to her.

Wearing a photographer's pass, Marion and I waited on the sidelines of the crowd in the reception area until we were ushered into the gallery by Yoko's assistant.

As we stepped up to meet her, Marion in a very businesslike manner, shook Yoko's hand as she calmly introduced her self and then revealed the magazine she was on assignment for, finishing with: "This is my assistant, Marc."

Yoko extended her hand to me and in a most beguiling manner she said, "We've met before haven't we Marc?"

I could tell by the way she said it, and by the look on her face, she already knew the answer.

I was very calm and collected as I took her hand and gently responded, "Yes we have. Actually we've met briefly on a several occasions, and you're looking absolutely fantastic by the way!"

I saw her eyes twinkle through her light tinted shades as she replied with a sincere and smiling: "Thank you!"

Marion positioned her camera and when Yoko nodded at her assistant, he waved permission for Marion to start shooting.

As Marion was clicking away, I watched Yoko slowly move from one sculpture to the next, explaining the time and place each was created, I could see that she was tranquil with my presence.

I played the perfect professional assistant to Marion as she rapidly switched from one camera to another. Each photographer was allotted several minutes before another one was called forward.

When our time was up, I handed Yoko a cassette of my album, along with the Thank You card I'd written. She thanked me and as she handed them to her assistant, I asked her to sign my own copy. Thoughtfully she wished me good luck with its success as she signed. Marion and I politely thanked her and then returned to the sidelines of the gallery spectators.

Yoko posed for a few more photographers, then excused herself and left the room. Our moment with her was over. Marion and I were not officially among the group of network T.V. newsmagazine interviewers being called to the back room. I was grateful I'd been able to give her my Thank You card because in it

I'd been able to express how much I loved the show. I hoped she would listen to my songs and enjoy hearing echoes of her and John's influence, as well as read my special thanks to them both in the liner notes.

About ten minutes later, Marion and I were talking about our moments with Yoko and the ever growing crowd, when suddenly we were approached by Yoko's assistant and led to the back room. We inched our way into the small area that was wall to wall with media reporters, photographers, television crews, and a bank of microphones were placed around Yoko as she sat in front of a canvas backdrop, surrounded by a slew of white umbrella shaded lights.

Marion and I stood among the front lines of the reporters as cameras rolled, questions were politely asked and answered, and Marion and all of the other media photographers, bended and stretched from different angles, with the fluttering sounds of their shutters rapidly changing among the explosion of popping flashes.

As I stood there listening and watching Yoko thoughtfully answer a string of questions, she appeared to be completely at ease. I was standing only a few feet from her and if she'd previously been wary of my presence, she exhibited no trace of nervousness now.

Once the interviews were over, Yoko thanked everyone for coming and left the room. Marion and I returned to the still crowded reception area. I assumed that was the end of it and Yoko would be slipping out the back door. Marion and I chatted momentarily about our fortuitous invitation into the "inner sanctum" before I realized I was more than an hour late for work and told Marion I'd better be getting back; I certainly hadn't expected to be here *this* long. She said she was going to stay a while longer and suggested I do the same adding: "Maybe she'll come out and mingle a bit and I can get a picture of you and her together." The possibility of *that* happening seemed entirely remote; absolutely more than I should begin to hope for. Besides, I was more than blissful with my enchanting afternoon.

A few moments later, we were still in the middle of discussing the dubious possibility of getting another picture, I was arguing that Yoko certainly must've left by now, when suddenly from six feet away, she appeared from behind a burlap covered wall that bore paintings of another artist, and walked right up to Marion and me. The three of us stood inches apart.

Yoko looked directly at me, smiled and very sweetly said; "Did you enjoy the show?"

Completely surprised I quickly answered: "*Yes*! Everything was really great!"

Marion shook her head in agreement, saying; "Yes, it was very insightful, I enjoyed it very much! Would it be possible for me to get a picture of the two of you together?"

Yoko smiled wider at me and said; "Yes."

This time I didn't have a noisy, cumbersome Polaroid, or need the assistance of Yoko's bodyguard to take our picture. This time "Felix/aka/Patrick the Cat" was partnered with a professional photographer who carried her own magic bag!

Marion winked and gave me a sly smile as she prepared to do the honors.

As I did at our first meeting, I asked Yoko if I could put my arm around her.

Smiling coyly she nodded as she replied, "Yes."

Marion took the photograph and the three of us chatted for the next fifteen minutes or so, about the show, its themes, and the large enthusiastic crowd. I was having the time of my life. Our intimately comfortable tableau was completely relaxed and at the same time, almost <u>Alice In Wonderland</u> surreal, when suddenly I realized, like the Mad Hatter; "I'm late! I'm late! For a very important date!"

It was already well after 5pm. and the dinner service at Mamma Leone's had begun. My waiter friends could only cover for me for so long before they would be swamped! It was the very last thing I wanted, but I had to leave, now!

Very hastily I made my regretful apologies to Yoko explaining that I hated to leave, but I was due back at work over an hour ago.

She looked me squarely in the eyes and seemed genuinely disappointed when she responded, "Oh, it's really too bad you have to go."

Reluctantly I agreed: "Yes. I know. I would much rather stay here, but I'm already late...thank you so much for everything, you are such a great inspiration to me."

She extended her hand, as I clasped it she smiled and said, "Thank you for coming, I'm so glad you did."

In the bright overhead lights of the gallery, her eyes were clearly visible through her light tinted glasses, and when I replied, "Yes. I'm very glad I did too." I saw her eyes sparkle like starlight, and I felt in her hand at that moment like she'd graciously given me my own set of: *"Keys to Open the Skies."*

Marion thanked Yoko, and then excused herself also, saying she wanted to take pictures of the gallery spectators. The three of us exchanged quick goodbyes again and dispersed.

As Marion and I began slowly elbowing our way through the massive crowd, we paused in the center of the room and were making plans to get together the following week. While we were busy exchanging phone numbers, I looked up from my pad and pencil and saw Yoko standing closely behind Marion, talking with another woman. Over the constant buzzing conversations in the room, I couldn't quite hear what they were saying, but I saw Yoko notice me looking at her, and then I heard her raise her voice and distinctly say; "Let me give you my phone number." I assumed she meant she'd give the woman her number at a later date. I couldn't believe it when she looked at me over the woman's shoulder and started to recite the digits clearly enough for me to hear! Instantly, because I knew *I would call her*, I forced my brain **not to listen** and turned away from them so she wouldn't think I was intentionally paying attention to her conversation. With great willpower I allowed the digits Yoko recited to bounce off my brain intentionally. She had just given me so much courteous consideration, I didn't want to be greedy, and I respected her too much to violate her privacy. I was so caught up in the excitement of the last three hours, and now this? I had to leave now, before I changed my mind!

I quickly expressed my thanks and said goodbye to Marion. I rushed out the door into the street, jumped in a cab and began a slow crawl in rush hour traffic back to Mamma Leone's. I sat in the cab in utter disbelief at my good fortune. These past few hours were something I never could've imagined, and yet every detail replayed itself over and over in my heart and mind as I blankly looked out the taxi widows at the people scurrying along the sidewalks.

It was after six when I arrived at Mamma's and the place was already jumpin'. I knew I was already behind before I even got started.

I ran downstairs to my locker and threw the clothes I'd been wearing inside, exchanging them for my uniform. Charging up the back stairs two by two, buttoning up my shirt and jacket as I ran, I was delirious with joy due to the seemingly miraculous afternoon's events. As I fumbled to get my red tie on, an energy of a total oneness with the universe coursed and pulsed through my body like blue static electric currents, buzzing, snapping and crackling inside a glass laboratory globe. Electrified in bliss, I slipped, fell, and slammed my knee on the bare concrete steps, but I sprang right back up laughing through my "Ouch!" and continued running, even the newly isolated pain of my throbbing knee couldn't slow down my ascent on cloud nine!

It didn't even occur to me until nearly a decade after that incident, that maybe, just maybe, Yoko had wanted me to "overhear" her phone number! Did she usually give out her private number so clearly and casually in a crowd, or had she staged this setting with her friend, for my benefit? Had I been *so* respectful of her privacy (by intentionally ignoring her phone number) that an opportunity to become genuine friends had been wasted? Looking back, it is certainly possible. We had become very comfortable with each other, she knew I was more than a "run of the mill fan" and I'm sure she recognized that I didn't have a stalkers bone in my body. I was just an honest admirer who knew her entire catalogue of music and found joy and inspiration in all genre's of her work. I'd been listening and learning from her for more than half of my life, and by the way I behaved and the things I said, she knew it at the gallery that day.

Italian Mothers Never Die

I'm still in love with Johns music, and always will be, but I am equally indebted to the wisdom and pleasure I derive from Yoko's many talents, she has so much more to offer than what the media has ever given her credit for.

For instance, no other recording artist I can think of has had a Number One record on the dance charts *twenty one years after its initial release*. Talk about ahead of the times!

John once published a short book in his early "Beatle" days titled: In His Own Write. I'm sure he would be the first to agree that *in her own right,* Yoko's artistic genius is far superior to her status as "Mrs. Lennon."

I can feel mother telling me at this very moment that as much as she's enjoyed this review of her Yoko magic, it's time to get off of my Onobox and get on with her next miracle, it's one of her favorites, and one of mine as well. She knows I'm more than willing to do this, but not before we've both slipped in that last reference to Yoko's collection of CD's titled: Onobox. Cheeky lad that I am, I'll slip in *one more* before the other of the two *"Mother"(s)* gets the floor, and now that I have mom, it's all yours…

Angels For Christmas

My very dear friend Bonnie "had it all" as far as beauty, brains, talent and financial security were concerned. She was a young and beautiful aspiring actress in New York City who also possessed an angelic singing voice, delightfully enchanting those who had the pleasure of seeing her one woman off Broadway show.

When one gazed at her beauty, you couldn't help but notice she recalled a classic look from another era, in the vein of the young Andrew Sisters, Lauren Bacall, and more recently, Nicole Kidman.

Her lithe dancers body was graced with glowing translucent skin, and her face was a sirens song of sensuality, alluringly innocent, yet sultry.

Bonnie Rivers, even her name evoked sounds of melodic harmony. Her disposition and demeanor were gentle and sweet, almost saintly.

She lived in a small high rise apartment in a very fashionable and expensive section of Manhattan's Upper West Side. She belonged there. She'd been born and bred in a very wealthy family from New Hampshire. Her parents were primarily sponsoring her financially, but she worked part time at Mamma Leone's as a hostess, to pay her incidental bills.

Like me, she was astrologically a Leo with starry eyed

ambitions. We very quickly connected as friends and supporters of each others art shortly after we met.

Bonnie was only 24, but with her looks, talents and other resources, I was certain her artistic dreams would come true long before mine, and mine were long overdue.

About the only thing she lacked, (and she didn't even know it was missing) was any firm belief in a "Higher Power". It was not part of her upbringing to believe in any power other than her own, and while I had to admit she seemed very happy in her perfectly secured world, we would sometimes find ourselves at odds during our discussions of a Supreme Beings' presence in her life.

I contended that God was obvious just by looking at the endless multitudes of blessings in her life. She quite casually chalked them up to heredity, genetics, her family's wealth and her own efforts, clearly dismissing the notion of God and Angels as nothing more than religious folklore.

I respected her views, and was even somewhat awed by her self esteem; she had everything going for her, while I, "The Believer", possessed a few cupfuls of worldly abundance, compared to her oceans.

My lack of comparable good fortune only reinforced the weakness of my arguments, for if I believed in such a loving and generous Divine Energy, why had my life thus far been a very rocky road, while hers was nothing but smooth sailing. If anything our belief systems should have been reversed!

We were both able to argue about it good naturedly, and in a special way, it was a bond like no other, one that brought our friendship warmly closer when we allowed ourselves to be caught up in the seemingly irresolvable discussion.

Snow spellbound Manhattan three days before Christmas, and as usual, I'd postponed my shopping until the last minute.

It was still snowing outside and I could barely see a few feet ahead of me as I trundled through the three foot high snow drifts of 8th Avenue toward Chelsea and Greenwich Village, where the shops catered to the young and hip. I figured I'd easily find a beautiful gift for Bonnie in this neighborhood.

"What should I look for?" I wondered, as I cautiously maneuvered myself along the icy streets and snow banked sidewalks. "What kind of gift can I get for someone who truly does have "everything"?

I knew she harbored a special affinity for dolphins. In my head I was telling myself to look for dolphin jewelry, maybe a dolphin sculpture. Perhaps a gorgeous vase filled with dolphin shaped Godiva chocolates? Playful, artistic, or serious, which way should I go…? Suddenly a distinctly different voice inside me whispered: *"Why not get her an Angel?"*

I felt a look of annoyance stretch over my face. "Ohh-Puh-leeeez!" I shot back, of all things an Angel!? Right! ***Insult*** her for Christmas, *that's* the gift that keeps on giving! The last thing I want to do is come across like some religious zealot pushing my beliefs on her…"

I was in the middle of scolding the idea when the small voice overrode my thoughts again, a bit louder this time: *"Marc, you're jumping the gun! Nobody's asking you to <u>convert</u> her, just consider an Angel instead of a mammal; you might be surprised at her reaction."*

I pondered the responding message briefly and quickly dismissed it in favor of a line from a Beatle song that started running through my head: "Mother Superior jumped the gu-u-un/Mother Superior jumped the gu-uh-uh-un/ Happiness is … "

I continued singing the song in my thoughts, drowning out the inner intrusive voice as I slid and struggled awkwardly across the street. I finally landed safely at one of the fashionable storefronts I'd been seeking.

Stomping the fresh powder off of my boots, I opened the door and entered the first of many shops I would be entering, on this snow storming afternoon.

For the next several hours I went in and empty handedly out, of every gift shop from 23rd Street in Chelsea to Christopher Street in The West Village, combing all the windows, walls, racks, bins, cases and shelves of all the "hip" establishments.

"Hip establishments"? I believe that phrase must be an

oxymoron. I always thought that the "establishment" was considered by the young and "hip" to be decisively: "un-hip"!

Perhaps these days, one doesn't cancel out the other anymore, but the merchandise certainly seemed to have "sold out".

Dolphins were displayed in all sizes, mediums and textures. Some were crystal, marble, sleek stainless steel or brass, but none were original or beautiful enough to justify the exorbitant prices. Others were carved on smooth varnished driftwood, but seemed entirely lifeless. Brightly colored velvet dolphin paintings were laughably awful, and I didn't see many pieces of dolphin jewelry, but the ones I did see were obviously tacky leftovers for the last minute shoppers.

I cursed myself for procrastinating. I noticed there weren't many Angels on display either, and the ones that were left, were desolate faced, cliché ridden plasters, boring sun burnt orange terra cottas, or vacant eyed, ghastly gold flecked Cupids. They were hardly inspirational; they merely validated my distaste for the memory of even considering an Angel for Bonnie.

I sifted through books, clothes, candles, food and bath luxury baskets, music, various crafts, and the latest techno gadgets but nothing seemed interesting, unique, or beautiful enough to own, let alone purchase.

The sun had set hours ago; I had nothing to show for my efforts except a couple rolls of wrapping paper. I was cold and hungry and wanted to stop somewhere to eat, but time was short. If I didn't get back uptown before 8pm, I wouldn't be able to visit my favorite greeting card store

I'd already covered every shop on this side of town to no avail. I was absolutely determined to, at the very least, find a box of Christmas cards and fill them out so that I could salvage my wasted day.

Shivering, hungry and frustrated, I shuffled on to the subway with the rest of the huddled masses. It didn't seem like we were all getting ready to celebrate "Christ's Birthday", far from it! The exasperation and angst were visible on the faces of those around me; the air of the crowded subway car was scented with anything but "peace on earth" and "goodwill towards men". Everyone looked anxious, tired and irritated. No one wore a look of holiday cheer as they tightly gripped the various bags and boxes of their shopping excursions. At least they *had* bags and boxes! Knowing that I'd only wasted my day made me instantly sink into a case of the Christmas blues. Chewing over my empty handed, last minute, rushing to shop routine, only made me angrier at myself.

Dusting the snow off my freezing clothes, I rattled along on the screeching subway to my neighborhood, known locally as: Hells Kitchen.

By the time I squeezed my way off the train at my stop, I was in full frustration mode. Crunching my boots through the frozen snow, racing impatiently past all the other last minute shoppers on the busy sidewalk, I ran upstairs to my apartment. My self reprimands had shortened, to mid air visible breaths of freezing curses as I hurried to turn up the heat after slamming my front door.

I made a very quick dinner and regrouped my emotions. I was still far from being in "the holiday spirit" but I was determined not to let the evening slip away without getting a box of cards.

It was 7pm. I still had plenty of time to walk the short distance to the card shop. I re-bundled myself head to toe and stepped out into the night.

The Full Moon light gave the snow covered sidewalk a light tint of Virgin Mary blue. The sky was completely clear and the stars shimmered with such clarity that it was hard to believe I was in the middle of New York City. The wind and snow had stopped; all was "calm" and "bright" on this suddenly "silent night". The sidewalks were no longer bustling with people; in fact there was an organically peaceful silence as I began to walk.

The temperature had warmed to a comfortable cold and I pulled the goose down hood off of my head. After a few short blocks I found myself feeling strangely enough "in the holiday spirit" when I happened to glance in a store window. I slid to a stop and backed up on the icy sidewalk to take a second look.

I'd walked this stretch of 8th Avenue countless times before and had never noticed this antique store. I'm sure I would have passed it by again had it not been for the still photographs of The Beatles from their motion picture: <u>HELP!</u>

I thought of my youngest brother Tony, who still carried the torch of my long since abandoned frenzy of Beatlemania. I still loved the music of course, but he was now the obsessive collector. I wondered if I should go in for a closer look…

Glancing at my watch I realized that the card shop would be closing in less than an hour. No time for this I reasoned, besides I'm sure the photographs were probably too expensive and I needed the kind of <u>HELP!</u> that The Beatles couldn't provide right now.

I picked up my pace as I approached 52nd Street and thought to myself: "Wasn't there a movie about a miracle on 52nd Street with Jimmy Stewart or Fred McMurray, or someone else of that era, and what exactly was "the miracle"? Also, "Why haven't I ever seen the movie?" I silently asked myself as I rounded the corner onto 52nd Street.

Just as I was correcting myself that it was a Billy Joel album titled <u>*52ndStreet*</u> and the movie I'd never seen was <u>*Miracle On 48th Street*</u>, I glanced up to see that the card shop I'd just been to at Thanksgiving, had suddenly been transformed into ***The Gap***. I was stunned and perplexed! Aside from the fact that ***The Gap*** stores had sprouted up like weeds all over Manhattan recently, I couldn't believe they had taken over the largest card shop in Mid-Town!

"Well this ain't the miracle I'm looking for!" I angrily said out loud in a low growl.

My maddening frustration quickly returned with a vengeance as my boots angrily stomped through the frozen snowdrifts back towards 8th Avenue.

I spied an open drugstore and ducked in hoping to at least purchase a box of cards. I was looking at a picked over limited selection of cheaply made, boring boxed cards, while a *most annoying* computerized rendition of <u>*Joy To The World!*</u> blasted over a microphone that had been placed next to a card with the offending micro-chip. The monotone melody was techno-dead, as for joyous? Ha! That was it! Enough is enough! I can't take another minute of this noise!

I thought of my mom, calling out to her in my mind with frustrated sarcasm: "Joy to the world indeed! Earth to Joy! Earth to Joy! Come in Joy! Can you hear me mom?! I could sure use a little *joy* right about now!"

I slid back onto the sidewalk in a grumbling huff. I was bitching and cursing to myself like Scrooge on a triple espresso as I made it to 48th Street and saw The Beatles in the antique store window again.

As I stood before the store entrance I hissed under my breath: "I could certainly use some *HELP!* alright!" Condescendingly I thought to myself: "How about a *real* "*Miracle on 48th Street*"! as I swung the door open and entered.

Immediately a sense of calm enveloped me as the door to *Jonah's Whale* closed with a cowbells clank, behind me. I hadn't noticed the name until now. "Strange name for a store." I mused silently.

My eyes adjusted to the hazy blue fluorescence of the lighting in the vast room, and the eclectic menageries of dizzying merchandise taking up every available inch of wall and floor space. The countertops, shelves, bins, racks and islands were overflowing with all sorts of dated things. There was very little aisle room; even the ceiling was claustrophobically dripping with objects.

Three people were in the store, all probably in their mid-60's, a man and two women.

"Good evening" said a white haired, bearded man, sitting behind a fenced cage, at a dimly lit desk next to the door; "Can I help you?"

"No thanks, it looks like I might need at least a week just to look at all the stuff in here!" I replied.

"Yeah, a week ought to about do it." he said as he adjusted a pair of magnifying goggles on his face and bent over to inspect a piece of jewelry.

Intrepidly I slowly started to peruse the many overabundant shelves that threatened to crash down upon me with one false move. I decided to take my time. In order to see everything, I had no other choice. I was determined with new resolve to find *something* for Bonnie. I began to feel as if I might have a real chance here.

Antique jewelry splashed against black velvet in rows of glass cases, but no sign of dolphins or Angels. Stained glass lamps illuminated row upon row of shelves bulging with cut crystal animals, Carnival glass vases and wine stems, Blue Delft patterned casserole dishes, Milk Glass serving platters, gravy boats and bowls, tarnished silver tea and coffee services, various kitchen utensils, and antique toys. Hand painted porcelain Hummel's crowded several shelves. Woodcarvings, sculptures, ceramics and brass figurines competed for space in bins and floor crates. Pictures, drawings and paintings covered the walls, many too tall to reach without a ladder, but nothing I saw was even mildly interesting enough to inspect closer.

I approached the center of the store where the two sisterly looking, middle aged women, were having a conversation, in a familiar Brooklyn accent.

"Da yas need hep wit sahhm-ting?" said one of the women wearing a red sweater with the word *JOY!* emblazoned in white brocade on the front.

"No thanks, I'll know it when I see it." I replied with an unconvinced smile.

For the next hour my eyes scanned and searched through every item available among the avalanche of merchandise. The room became silent as the two women wandered down a dark hallway. I saw many things I would've liked for myself, but nothing stood out as the right thing for Bonnie.

"How is it with all of these things, decades of someone else's former treasures, I can't find *one* item interesting or original enough for Bonnie?" I thought sullenly.

That Brooklyn accent suddenly pierced the store silence as one of the ladies, the one wearing the *JOY!* sweater, emerged from the dark shadows of a dimly lit hallway.

"Deahs lots mo-ah stuff dahhn-staeahs." She nasally whined, as she smiled and pointed to a very narrow staircase.

With waning interest, I descended the well worn wooden staircase that was lined with racks and shelves. Vintage clothing brushed against me and shelved objects rattled slightly as I hesitantly stepped down. I made it to the bottom and found a cavernous room filled floor to ceiling with thousands of old National Geographic, Life, The New Yorker and Post magazines, and a huge wall of Readers Digests towered precariously over my head.

Shelves and islands overrun with old percolators, toasters, pots, pans, dishes, bread bins, rusting cheese graters, and other kitchen items that I hadn't the slightest idea what their uses were for.

I started to sift through a box of old vinyl records before I realized that I was absentmindedly shopping for myself, and that was not my objective.

I'd spent at least 45 minutes downstairs before I realized that I simply wasn't going to find anything for Bonnie in this store, it was time to go.

Now I faced a new dilemma, I'd been in the store for nearly two hours and was completely embarrassed that I was going to leave without buying anything!

No one else had shopped in the store the whole time I'd been here and I felt sorry for the obviously family owned business that wasn't racking up any last minute Christmas sales.

I inched my way slowly towards the door, staring blankly at items I'd already rejected, *acting* like there was still some hope that I might make a purchase, before I conceded defeat and made a hasty exit.

Now I completely understood the stores name; *Jonah's Whale*. I had just rummaged through several decades of accumulated dusty memorabilia and long ago forsaken treasures, and "the whale" was ready to spit me back out onto the frozen sidewalk, empty handed again.

As I stood before a shelf lined with threadbare tapestries that I'd already seen and rejected, I couldn't help overhearing the middle-aged sisters behind me.

"Nat deah Syl-vee-uh, to da left! High-ya! Nah, hiiigh-ya!!"

"Whadda-ya mean high-ya Dee?!! Deahs na ma room fa dis high-ya!! I can only go so high befoah I fall ovah!!!

I glanced over my shoulder, past the islands and narrow aisles, the women were about 15 feet away. I saw Sylvia teetering on a step ladder against the wall, holding a small picture frame and a hammer. The picture dangled from her hand against her leg as she pointed to a space on the wall with the hammer. I couldn't see the front of the picture, only the back of the picture frame.

I don't know why, and I don't recall *flying* across the room, but it seemed like that's exactly what I did, and suddenly I found myself standing next to Sylvia, gently turning her hand to look at the front of the picture she was holding.

"That's it!!! That's *exactly* what I've been looking for!!!" I shrieked with delight.

Startled by my presence, puzzled by my outburst, Sylvia said; "Whaaat?! Dis?!"

"Yeah! That!! I've been looking for dolphins or Angels, and that's it!!!"

"Whaaa-lll, we hasn't got nahh daahh-fins, but we have an Angel up deah..." She pointed to a plaster, gold trimmed monstrosity that nobody could love.

"No! Not that ugly thing! I want this!!!" I said as I tried to take the small picture from her.

Sylvia backed against the ladder and stammered; "But dis..dis just came in da stoah nat fi-vah min-aahts agah!!"

"Five minutes ago ten minutes ago, whatever!!! I've been searching for this all day!!!" I yelped as I tried to take it from her again. I got a grip on it but she didn't let go.

"Ahhh, dis is ratheh nice isn't it..." she said as she slowly descended the stepladder and began to *really* look at the picture for the first time.

It was an antique painting, probably watercolor, on parchment, about 8"x12inches, in a leaded glass frame. It had to be at least fifty to seventy years old.

In what looked to be a Venetian style, it depicted a young woman, in a periwinkle blue dressing gown, stretched out on a scrolled, satin covered chaise, peacefully asleep.

The chaise was positioned in front of a large window that opened up to a beautiful arched terrace, overlooking an emerald bay lined with swaying palm trees, under a star blanketed sky with a full moon.

Surrounding the young woman, who appeared to be a Princess, were seven delicately detailed cherubs. One hovered mid-air with a bouquet of flowers, while another, holding a crown of light, was getting ready to place the halo headdress upon the sleeping beauty.

The other cherubs, draped in golden gossamer, surrounded the Princess with imploring gazes. The expressions on their faces seemed to say; "Wake up Princess! Wake up! We have so many gifts we wish to give you! Please wake up!"

"Look at dat moon!" Sylvia squealed. "And dat Princess! So fincly detailed!"

"It's perfect! It's just what I've been looking for! I'll take it!" I exclaimed excitedly as I tried to pry it from Sylvia's grasp.

"But dis..dis *just* came in da stoah! Ah daahn't even knah hahhs much ta cha-a-a-ghe yahs!" she whined wearily.

We were both holding on to it tightly now, both mesmerized by its exquisite beauty. I could feel Sylvia tugging it closer to her, unsure if she wanted to part with it or let me have it.

Dee had moved in closer to assess the situation, and she reached out and touched an Angel as she said, "Dis really is quite be-ootiful isn't it! Such a peaceful scene! Lov-ahly Angels!!!"

My Cheshire cat grin turned into laughter as I felt the goose bumps rise all over my body. "Thanks mom!" I blurted out loud amid my laughter.

Puzzled, Sylvia gave me a strange look and said, "Whadda yas tankin ya ma foah?"

My laughter turned into uncontrollable howls as I spied Dee in her ***JOY!*** sweater. Tears flooded my eyes, gasping for breath, I tried to explain:"My mom's name was Joia, the Italian word for Joy! She passed away in 1986, but she did this! From Heaven she made sure I found this! She's done my Christmas shopping for me! I know it's her, she's done things like this before!" I was quivering from the energy running through me.

Placing her hand over the **JOY!** on her sweater, Dee said with a beatific smile: "Ya must have good Kha-ma, a mir-ah-cal just happened ta yahs!"

I could see plainly on her face that she was indeed convinced a miracle had just occurred.

I looked into Dee's eyes and replied; "Oh, believe me; I *know* a miracle has just happened! You have no *idea* what I've been through today! Obviously I was meant to be here tonight, at this exact moment, to find this perfect gift. This isn't the first time I've been aware of my mother's otherworldly involvement. And every time it feels just like this, ecstatic goose bumps tingle all over my body, and there's always, *always*, joyous tears and laughter. There's no other feeling like it in this world! It feels like I'm bursting with light! She's the one who had this special delivered from Heaven, as Sylvia said, *five* minutes ago, while I was still downstairs! Wrap it up! It's going home with *me* now!"

A look of terror shot across Sylvia's face. She yanked the painting from our "tug of war" and started running up the aisle towards the man at the front desk.

"Nee-al! Nee-aaahhlll!!!" She shouted as she ran.

I was immediately behind her. I was afraid she wasn't going to let me have it. She obviously fell in love with it while we'd been looking it over. We both reached the desk in time to see Neil putting on his wire rimmed glasses, and suddenly his face had an uncanny resemblance to Santa Claus...

"Nee-ahhlll!!! Wheah did dis picksha come frahhm!!! Dis guy tinks his dead mutha dropped dis off heah, by some mira-cahhll or sahm-tink!!!"

Sylvia thrust the painting inches from Neil's face, he delicately took hold of the frame, but Sylvia didn't let go.

The only light at Neil's desk was his jewelry spotlight and a row of blinking Christmas lights that surrounded the counter of his dark shadowed cage.

As he pointed the spotlight at the painting, he was instantly transfixed by what he saw, and the light from his lamp illuminated his face with a soft white glow as he began to explain, with wonderment filling his eyes: "About 10 minutes ago a woman opened the door; she didn't come all the way in, just halfway. She leaned on my desk with this and asked me to buy it. I barely looked at it because I was going over this batch of estate gems. At first, I told her no, nobody would be interested in that here. But she started to insist that *somebody* would be, and… well…because it's Christmas, and I figured she needed the money, I told her I'd give her 10 bucks…I handed her the ten and she said, "Thank you so much! God bless you for this!" She grabbed the cash and was gone. I didn't see her more than a minute or two… and then I asked Dee to find a spot for it. I barely saw it until now…"

My wallet was wide open and I grabbed a hand full of bills, ready to pay whatever he asked, which I assumed would be at least five times what he'd paid, it was obviously worth that and more.

"How much do you want for it?" I asked.

He vacantly replied, "Oh… I dunno…how 'bout twelve bucks."

Neil, still transfixed by the painting, was speaking absentmindedly, trancelike, with his 20% profit margin mindset, but the radiance on his face was priceless. He knew the painting was worth a lot more, but profit didn't matter at the moment, only beauty and wonder. His gaze was infused with tender admiration as the twinkling Christmas lights of green, red, blue and gold danced across his delightfully captivated boyish smile.

"Sold!!!" I barked. And the serene spell of our magical tableau was broken.

Sylvia shot me a horrified look as I thrust the money at Neil. He let go of the painting and took the money, at the same time he handed Sylvia several sheets of Christmas tissue paper and said, "Wrap it up Syl, obviously this is meant to go home with this man."

Sylvia gave me a sad puppy dog look of defeat as she whimpered: "Oh-awww-raaght". She looked longingly at the antique painting, she knew it was the last time she would ever see

Italian Mothers Never Die

it. I could see her trying to memorize every detail, with a tender, loving, sadness.

I had seen that look before, on my mother's face, the last time we'd seen each other in this lifetime. She knew she was dying, and I had no clue.

I found out later from her best friend that mother knew the cancer had returned, and though she'd secretly started chemo again, a blood clot formed and went to her heart, killing her instantly.

I felt sorry for Sylvia at that moment. I now knew the anguish of my mother's last look at me, to its fullest. Still, the minute Sylvia started to wrap the painting, the exuberance in my spirit returned. I could scarcely believe she was going to hand it over, and the anticipation was running through me like volts of electricity.

"I think it's great that you can feel your mother's presence!" Neil said as he sat back and relaxed in his chair. Only then did I notice with quiet amusement that he was wearing a well worn and fading Santa jacket ... He continued; "*I know* what a wonderful feeling that is because my mother passed away many years ago, but on several occasions I've…"

Suddenly Neil was interrupted by the ringing of his telephone.

"Excuse me a moment…" He said as he picked up the receiver and answered; "Jonahs Whale". He paused; "Well, I guess we'll be open another hour or so… yeah… mmm… okay, bye.

Neil looked at me and said; "Mmm…okay…now where was I…?"

"So, can you tell me Neil, what the woman who brought this painting in looked like?"

No sooner had I spoken those words, the phone rang again and Neil said to me before he answered; "Hang on a minute, don't leave, I want to talk to you about this!"

I nodded yes to him and Sylvia handed me the bag.

"Tank-ya saah, yaahs have a Mehh-ry Christ-maaasss nah ya heah."

She forced a resigned smile and suddenly, with a cowbells clank the front door swung open. In the narrow entry I stepped back against the wall as several people entered the store. Sylvia was blocking the aisle and was forced to back her way towards the middle of the store where Dee stood.

I sat down on a folding chair by the door, beaming with happiness! I couldn't wait to get more details of the mysterious woman from Neil.

As I sat there waiting, reveling in my ecstasy, the door swung open again and more people entered. I noticed as they passed that Neil was saying goodbye to the caller and then punched an extension button on his phone and answered; "Jonah's Whale" as he gave me the "one minute finger" and I nodded yes.

Again the cowbell clanking door swung open and more people entered the store.

The whole time I'd been shopping, not a single soul had come in, except for the mysterious woman with the painting, and according to Neil even she'd only leaned half-way through the door.

Now the store was building a *crowd* and I could see that the whole row of red extension lights were impatiently blinking on Neil's phone, as he hurriedly tried to keep up with the callers.

It was as if an army of Angels had just flown in with all the sudden activity and I heard one of them excitingly whispering in my ear: *"Time to go! Time to go! We don't need anyone analyzing this situation; you got what you came here for, now it's time to go!"*

I struggled to stay in the chair as the constantly mounting goose bumps tickled my body. I didn't want to leave, I wanted to hear what Neil had to say about the mystery woman, but it became apparent that things were getting purposely stirred up to distract that from happening.

I *understood*. I looked at Neil; we smiled at each other warmly, knowingly. He *understood* too.

As I stood up to leave, I looked over the heads of the people crowding the store and saw Sylvia and Dee in the distance. They both looked at me and in unison they shouted over the lively crowd: "Mehh-rry Christmaaasss!!!"

I shouted back and waved: "Thank you!!! Merry Christmas to

you too!!!"

The insistent cowbell clanked again as the door swung open and more people entered, after they'd passed I made my exit.

I walked across the street and sat on a bench outside of *The Symphony Café*. I wanted to open the package and look at the painting again, but I was so gratefully overwhelmed by what had just happened, all I could do was smile as the tears started to flow.

The energy coursing through me was electrifying! I lifted my face towards the heavens, in the crystal clear skies, the shimmering lights from the moon and stars mingled with my tears, and they became like diamonds, with rainbows of colors arcing from them as they streamed down my face.

"Thank you Father of the Universe!" I said aloud. "Thank you, thank you, thank you!!!" And then; "Thanks Mom!!!" I cried out loud with joyous abandon.

I could *see and feel* the light energy emanating from every pore of my body, soaring towards the heavens, interfacing with the symphony of the universe.

Again out loud, I began to softly chant: "Thank you!" over and over and over...and I didn't care if the passersby thought me strange, I couldn't see them anyway, through my diamond tears of *Joy*.

The next night at work, I gave Bonnie her gift. I'd written a story of the string of events that led me to find her present, without revealing what I'd found for her. I made her promise that she would read the short story before opening the package. She also gave me a present, but we were too busy dealing with the customers to open them. It had been a very busy Christmas Eve, another fourteen hour day; we didn't leave the restaurant until 11:30pm.

When I got home from work, I poured a glass of wine, and sat down with the package Bonnie had given me. Before opening it, I raised a toast to my mom and thanked her for leading me to find the perfect gift for Bonnie on time.

It was 12:03am. Christmas Day. Bonnie was probably opening

her gift right now I thought, as I tugged on the gold ribbon of the box she'd given me.

Immediately I started laughing the minute I lifted the lid of the box when I saw a beautiful Angel looking back at me. Bonnie had given me an exquisite Day Planner with an Angel on the cover, and various antique paintings of Angels throughout the book. I was leafing through it, chuckling to myself over the fact that Bonnie had given me Angels, when the phone rang.

Trying to hold back my laughter, I picked up the receiver giggling; "Hello?"

"***Marc!***" Bonnie sounded ecstatic! "I know it's late but I just *had* to call and tell you, this is the *most beautiful* gift I've *ever* received!"

"Oh, I'm so glad you like it sweet heart." I replied. "I absolutely love the gorgeous date book you gave me! I can't believe we got each other Angels!" I laughed.

"Me either!!!" She was laughing too, and then she said, "Marc, ***that story***!!!"

"I *know!!!* I can still hardly believe it myself, and I was ***there!!!***" I shouted.

We continued laughing together until Bonnie interrupted, coyly asking me: "Marc, did you notice anything *special* about the Princess reclining on the lounge chair?"

I knew what she was thinking, but I wanted to hear *her* say it. "Special?" I replied evasively, "In what way?"

"Marc, the Princess looks ***exactly like me!!!***"
I felt the shiver rush through my spine and replied; "*I know!* Maybe you posed for it in another lifetime!!!" I laughed louder.

Bonnie was giggling deliriously as she said, "I've had goose bumps all over my body ever since I opened your gift Marc! And they're even stronger right now!!!" Her uncontrollable laughing escalated, as did mine, and I shouted; "Me too!!"

And the crescendo's of our laughter rose like a symphony, climbing towards the heavens, as the circuits of light raced through us over the telephone lines, raising the dancing goose bumps on our flesh in continuous ecstasy, until our hearts, finally spent and contented, rested into a peaceful, loving sigh, and we both sat silent, knowing that we had just experienced the remainder of the miracle, together.

Between New York Rock...and a hard place

Hopefully, an angelic afterglow from mom's <u>Angels for Christmas</u> surrounds you with the same unconditional love that I feel, every time I re-live it.

If that story were a <u>*Hallmark Hall Of Fame*</u> Christmas Eve. movie (Starring: Nicole Kidman as Bonnie, Mark Ruffalo as me, Valerie Harper as Sylvia, Betty White as Dee and Ernest Borgnine as "Nee-aallll!!!" in his Santa jacket…) it would be over now and we'd all be getting ready for bed, to "sleep in heavenly peace".

Please forgive me then for bringing on a blizzard instead, but as *this chapter title* indicates, the roller-coaster of my life is teetering at the pinnacle of an imminent drop. And so, in this brief moment of hesitation, the *choice* to hold on to that afterglow of Divine energy for a while longer…or free-fall with me… is entirely yours. Take a moment to decide. Ready…? Set…?

Pre-<u>Angels for Christmas</u>, in November of 1993, the local Culinary Union formed a picket line outside of Mamma Leone's. Our staff was neither asked, nor recruited, to participate. Everyone was allowed to work their normal shifts because our Union rep's said the Union was merely sidewalk marching for a wage hike in our new contract. The picketing ended a week later and nothing was related to us by the Union regarding the outcome. Our staff didn't press for further details because we knew we'd find out soon enough if the "pudding" was in the paycheck!

Our check stubs did not reflect a raise in December but in the first week of January the Union assured us there were regular bi-annual wage increases in the next four years of our new contract, which they were on the verge of approving.

On January 11th everyone came to work as usual and to our utter shock and dismay; the entire décor of the restaurant was in shambles and almost everything was gone. We were informed that Mamma Leone's was permanently closed. I don't know whether it was due to pressures from our Union "Mafioso" or if Mamma's Corporate "Familigia" pulled the plug, but either way the lioness's reign over this terrain was over. Or, to use one of mom's expressions: "It was the end of an era."

We were given a months worth of wages as severance and were allowed to take a few small items (plates, tablecloths etc...) for souvenirs from this landmark institution that had opened its doors several decades before I was even born. Many of the elderly *original* waiters had worked there longer than I'd been alive, and the grieving, lost looks in the eyes of the dying "Pride" were haunted with desolate fear.

The closing of Mamma's doors in winter left the large staff with little hope of finding work in the city until April when the restaurant season picked up again. That was everyone's first concern, our second was even more disconcerting, we knew the family bond we'd shared for years was being scattered into the wind.

Winter truly was "Going out like a lion" and the lions' heart in me felt the reverberating echoes of the anguished roar. I'd spent enough time living in Manhattan to know that most of the restaurant jobs that might possibly be available in the spring, were non-union, offered no medical or dental benefits, and many were quickly opened and just as suddenly closed with alarming regularity, due to the capricious nature of the dining public. Even with a decent paying job at Mamma Leone's, after nearly seven years I was still struggling with monthly expenses.

Aside from the everyday basics, (rent, utilities, food, car fare etc...) I was constantly spending money on studio recording and mixing fees, cassette duplications, photos, bios, business cards, lyric sheets, bubble wrap mailers, postage, and a wide array of other music business paraphernalia that quite literally was being *thrown away without ever being opened*, by music executives who, at numerous and expensive Music Business symposiums, lectured the large crowds about out how next to impossible it is to get our parcels noticed, let alone listened to.

They received hundreds of artists' demo tapes weekly and didn't have time to listen to them all, and if by some remote chance they miraculously happened to open *your* submission, they decided within the first thirty seconds of a song whether or not it was a "hit".

At one of these three hundred dollars a ticket seminars, I met a Music Executive who approached me and said that I definitely had: "The right rock star look..." but then he listened to *less* than thirty seconds of only one of my songs before he said, "No one listens to Cat Stevens anymore."

At first I was puzzled by his two fisted flattery; that he was even comparing me to Cat Stevens was a huge compliment and the sucker punch hit when I realized the song he'd scarcely listened to: <u>Lost In Your Eyes</u> did have a Cat Steven's feel to it, I was pleased. But as the Music Executive quickly made other one note assessments among the head phone thrusting throngs, I stood in the middle of the crowd and thought: "That was barely twenty seconds, of *one* song among a dozen others on my tape, others that don't sound the least bit like one of Cat's tunes..." The Music Executive just happened to listen to one that did and discarded his interest on that basis alone.

Well, I (and countless other Cat Stevens fans I'm sure...) would certainly *love* to buy a brand new Cat Stevens album, but he'd stopped recording more than twenty years ago!

(Note: The preceding incident happened in 1994. Just last week, in the May 2006 issue of <u>Rolling Stone Magazine</u>, I read that Cat Stevens is releasing a brand new album soon. Evidently *some* Music Executives out there must think Cat is still relevant or he wouldn't have gotten a contract! And while we're on the subject of Cat, have any of you astute popular music listeners noticed that the Number One album of this summer: <u>Back to Bedlam</u> by James Blunt is vocally, lyrically, and musically, nearly a twin brother to a Cat Stevens album? Obviously *somebody else* is still listening to Cat!)

The definition of "starving artist" used to mean that the artist was too busy plying his craft for very little money until he got noticed, instead of working at a *real* job. Those idealistic days of the penniless, halcyon troubadour, are extinct if you want to make it in today's music biz. Now "starving artist" includes being a business man eighty percent of the time, with very high overhead expenses, while somehow getting in a few hours to create and practice, and for me at least, working fourteen hours a day at one of *the most real jobs* out there, feeding the multitudes. An artist must make enough money to support everyday living as well as artistic production costs, legal fees, travel, self-promotion and related networking expenses. Pursuing my elusive dreams was more of a full time job, than my full time job! (And now I was jobless!)

As for the emotional and financial expenses of a love life in the past seven years, who had time? Certainly I didn't. I was too busy trying to make up for the fact that in the music business, my youth had long since passed its expiration date.

Recently turned forty and barely six years in: "The Business" I was still a beginner; it was far too late to *start* paying my musical dues. I'd spent that youthful time, energy, and money already, on Megan and Fiona's needs.

There was no room for me to seriously *develop* a music career in my youth; I'd been too busy being a physical, financial, and emotional slave to a neurotic control freak, while at the same time, trying to be the father I never had, to her child.

I'd used up at least six of my Leo "nine lives" in many different rural areas and cities with Megan and Fiona, starting over wherever Megan's gypsy spirit decreed we should be living. In the first seven years of our relationship we'd changed our address more than a dozen times. Whenever her irrational fears, boredom, or insecurities flared, it was time to move.

I'd become an expert at being thrown into the air and landing on my feet but by the time I'd gained my freedom from Megan and actually began building *my* dreams, in the business and performance world of popular music, I was more than a generation behind.

Now that Mamma Leone had rolled a stone in front of the lair, I had to focus on starting over, *again.* I just wasn't sure I wanted to start over in this city. I'd never had to work this hard in my life just to maintain a substandard style of living. Certainly my apartment in Manhattans "Hells Kitchen" was a step up from my former "railroad flat" digs, but it was still small living quarters for the $800.00 monthly rent.

I was also tired of hearing the traffic noise of Ninth Avenue echoing non-stop inside of my second floor apartment. Emergency sirens, car alarms, grinding trucks, honking horns, and especially annoying were the raised slurring voices from sidewalk drunkards who bellowed unintelligible diatribes at nobody in particular.

There were many occasions were I was forced to eject some stray drunk, hooker or drug dealer who'd squirmed their way into the lobby of my building, looking for a place to do business. I'd actually made and posted a sign in the buildings lobby that read: "No mas prostitutes aqui!" to discourage the late night ringing of my buzzer by many Puerto Rican, Dominican, Columbian, and Mexican "Johns" who apparently frequented this former red light district where my building had previously been a brothel.

From my Crack infested neighborhood in The Bronx, to my mouse nested railroad flat, and presently in this prior whorehouse, my living conditions were light years away from the comforts of *any* place I'd ever lived in on The West Coast.

My spirit longed for the serene, tree lined streets of a suburb, where the only noise would be birds chirping, kids playing, and the sound of an occasional car passing by.

I believe the reason New York City is "the city that never sleeps" isn't just because there's always someplace open, it's also because it's *too damn noisy* for most people to get a quiet nights rest!

Glumly I sat down at my electronic keyboards. The lyric and melody of a Carole King song, from her mid-1970's album: Fantasy began playing in my mind; "All I want/is a quiet place to live..."

As I slowly began to physically play the song, a taxicabs crackling radio frequency from the street below, infused it self with my playing through the same electronic lines of my keyboard speakers. I struggled to continue playing over the unrecognizable dialect of a cab driver feverishly babbling to his dispatcher *through my speakers*, loudly making snap, crackle and pop noises as their radio conversation invaded my apartment. I became worried that the electrical interference might blow out my speakers and the distraction was more than I could take! I gave up playing in an angry frustrated huff. At that moment I realized that finding a "quiet place to live" didn't have to remain just a song from Fantasy, if that's what I truly wanted, there must be some way I could make it a reality. I needed to seriously think through my options, so I went to a place in the city where I always felt connected to my higher energy.

I'd discovered several years back, while sitting on the steps of Saint Patrick's Cathedral, that this portion of Fifth Avenue had an interesting spiritual feel to it. It's a very well traveled section of the city and the area is often shown on television because directly across the street, facing Saint Patrick's is the NBC building at Rockefeller Center.

Sitting in the middle of the cathedral's concrete steps, one can't help but notice the gargantuan bronze statue of Atlas (shown weekly in the opening credits of <u>Saturday Night Live</u>) holding the world on his arched shoulders, as his well muscled legs appear to be walking from the NBC building towards the cathedral.

Is he coming to do battle? Or is he going to lay the world down on the church steps and leave it in God's hands?

As I looked closer at the bands of bronze that sculpt the shape of the Earth Atlas carries, I noticed that all of the Zodiac signs of mankind are also represented. As if the juxtaposition of the world, its inhabitants, and the media, facing the cathedral wasn't enough, as I looked to my right, further up the avenue, the blazing red numbers (666) from what is referred to as The Triple Six Building, stared back at me.

The ironic triangle of these three man made buildings, each representing their forces of energy (666 darkness, media hypnosis, and Divine Oneness) literally incarnated into concrete matter, while Atlas shoulders the world in the center of the triad, blended innocuously into the urban landscape along with the bumper to bumper belching traffic, the endless streams of people passing by, and the sounds of a live music performance, coming from <u>The Today Show</u> soundstage.

I always sat on the steps of the cathedral out of a sense of spiritual protection. It wasn't my former Catholic faith reassuring me of a safe connection, but rather my inner creed of *One Divine Energy* who created us all, The One who *is* unconditional Love.

Nonetheless, I wasn't averse to a few sprinkles of celestial support from Saint Patrick; after all, I had changed my Saint Felix (evidently a Saintly "cat") Confirmation name in favor of Saint Patrick's, Irish snake driving sainthood.

Whenever I had a pressing decision to make I'd always come to this location. And tonight as I sat on the steps, allowing my consciousness to expand in the midst of the incessant business of living, I noticed a picture of The Sphinx of Luxor gracing the cover of an abandoned copy of The Village Voice, three steps down from where I was sitting.

I didn't really feel like reading but I leaned down, picked it up, and looking closer at the photograph, thought to myself; "Never mind solving the riddle of The Sphinx, how about solving the riddles of my life…" I randomly opened up to a long and detailed article about the enormous growth the city of Las Vegas was experiencing.

Starting Over
(From: Double Fantasy by: John Lennon and Yoko Ono)

I'd lived alone in Las Vegas for nine days in 1972, when I moved there in my first attempt to escape Megan's clutches. I had just turned 19 years-old and the previous 14 months of Megan's constant barrage of physical and emotional seduction was taking its toll on my soul.

At the time, Megan was still playing Rex for a fool as she focused on consuming me. I couldn't take the intrigue and guilt of what we were doing behind Rex's back, so I moved out of their house in Southern California, and got a busboy job at The Four Queens Hotel and Casino in downtown Las Vegas.

I remember telling my mom on the phone: "It feels like the safest city I've ever been in." Her reply was sincere and immediate: "Well of course it's safe, The Mob doesn't stand for any nonsense! You either behave or they'll make you behave!"

Can't honestly say I was behaving, but apparently I was able to slip through the cracks unnoticed by the authorities when I'd be out for an evening of drinking and gambling. In those days, underage revelers were not carded unless you were drunk and boisterously out of control.

Inconspicuous with my pork chop side burns, and cowboy hat, I was confident that I looked older than my nineteen years. Freely I moved undisturbed from casino to casino, walking with a cocktail in my hand along Fremont Street without a care in the world.

For the first time in my life I felt emotionally free and independent, from every confusing thing that formerly bound me. My illicit affair with Megan along with the host of lies it entailed, my violent and alcohol abusing dad, sniping priests and nuns, and the stinging memories of growing up in a town where I experienced far too many traumas from other physically violent authority figures, sexual molesters, and emotional tormenters.

The low self esteem struggles of my youth began to pleasantly fade away, as I began *my life*, on my own terms. How could I ever have known it was all going to be too good to last?

Nine days after moving to Vegas, mother called and told me that my number had come up for the draft and in order to avoid going to war in Vietnam, I must come home and enlist so that I could choose where I would be stationed.

As a committed pacifist; I'd protested the war. I didn't want to murder anyone let alone fight a war that our own nation was against. Admittedly I'd become a lapsed Catholic, but I still believed in the commandment: "Thou shall not kill!"

Rex had done his Army tour of duty in Vietnam and Megan said his horrors were so horrendous that he wouldn't discuss it. The war was winding down but U.S. involvement and the threat of new draftee's being sent to battle was still very real. I couldn't risk the chance that being drafted might put me on the front lines of unspeakable crimes. If I enlisted I could *choose* where I'd be stationed; if I waited to be drafted, I'd have to go wherever Uncle Sam dictated.

My number had come up and Lady Luck had rolled me a pair of snake eyes, so I regretfully quit my job at The Four Queens, said a wistful goodbye to my newfound freedom, and immediately went home to enlist.

I hadn't been away from Megan for ten days and she

immediately resumed her obsession. She didn't have a drivers' license (too afraid to drive...) so she'd call Rex at the restaurant and ask him to send me with his car to take her shopping. She was very cunning at finding new ways to isolate us from our friends and families so that she could force herself upon me. Sometimes she'd be so bold as to molest me while others were in the next room, or covertly in a public place while two year old Fiona played close by. In those stolen moments, she'd tell me how much she loved and needed me as she proceeded to grope her way into sexual situations. As much as I knew it was wrong, it was also pretty heady stuff for a nineteen year old virgin. To think that I was satisfying an older woman (when the only other experiences I'd previously had were teenage crushes and frightening child molestations) was an encouraging impetus to my emerging sexuality. Her daily unyielding lust and declarations of love became a huge boost to my ego and at the same time, an avalanche of guilt.

My formal military induction was three months away and in the interim Megan made Rex move out, saying she needed a trial separation for "a while." Rex moved in with his mother on the other side of town and Megan managed to persuade me that because she and Rex were separated, our affair wasn't wrong; although she suggested we should still hide it from him and everyone else. I shuttled myself and my uncertain emotions back and forth between "Mrs. Robinson" and my unsuspecting best friend, trying to please them both. By the time my entrance into the Army came around, I was more than ready to leave all of the subterfuge behind.

My military training was performed at Fort Ord in Northern California. The blatantly chauvinistic mentality and robotic rigors of military life were even more repressive to my artistic sensibilities than my Catholic school interment had been. I adjusted to this new form of barking dictatorship with bored resignation. The Army officers now in control of my life who shouted orders telling me who and what I should be, were no different than my parents or the priests and nuns, except that they didn't beat me, and wore different uniforms. They trained my body to be a killing machine, but the mentality they tried to foist upon me was a lost cause. I was squarely entrenched in my anti-war sentiments, an all out "make love not war" devotee. How could I *not* be when all we were saying was: *"give peace a chance"*? Still, I was more than adept at following orders and was an exemplary soldier, outperforming many of the more macho grunts in my platoon.

After graduating boot camp with honors, I went home on leave for some much needed R & R, only to find that mom was smack in the middle of an indisputable nervous breakdown, freely exhibiting frighteningly schizophrenic behavior, and living with my siblings in absolute squalor on the outskirts of town. I could see she had to be hospitalized; her words were full of manic paranoia. "California has been declared a police state! No one can enter or leave because the military is guarding all the borders!!! Ronald Reagan has stationed the National Guard at the grocery stores!!!" She told me she was going to seek sanctuary in the church because that's the only place that Governor Reagan couldn't arrest her. My siblings informed me that she would go out to lunch with friends and insist on buying plates and coffee mugs from the waitress. She was living off Welfare and received scant child support from my dad. She most certainly had no extra funds to buy useless dinnerware. She'd spend hours burning cigarette holes in her maple coffee table saying she liked the "antique look" the burn holes created. I noticed at least twenty cartons of various brands of cigarettes in her kitchen cupboards, but scarcely any food in the house. When I questioned her about the quantities of cigarettes she said they were for her friends, in case they dropped by. Obviously no one had been dropping by, and her "friends" were amused by her eccentricities in public, but blindly didn't see her condition as problematic. My siblings were fending for themselves the best they knew how, and I could tell by mother's behavior that she was a danger to herself and the entire household.

I was well aware that mother had shock treatments in the late 1950's (for what most likely was post-partum depression) and I called the local hospital to have her committed for whatever mental health treatment they could avail themselves of. They told me that I was too young to have any legal rights for committing her, and that only she or my dad had the authority. I tried to talk her in to letting me take her to the hospital, but she got very angry with me. With scorching red eyes she bared her teeth in the most menacing way as she screamed; "Just wait until the lights go out tonight in this house!!! You'll see!!! Just wait!!!" This statement made me fear for the safety of my brothers and sister, and I called my dad on the phone to explain the situation. He was cruising on his usual river of denial and urged me to: "Give her an hour or so and see if she calms down." I didn't think that was sound advice so I called Megan and asked her what I should do. She told me to pick her up and we would go to my old neighborhood to convince my dad to call the hospital in order to have mom committed.

The more I thought about my dad, living in his secure and comfortable surroundings on the same block where we used to live, while my family was living in poverty and dangerous mayhem, the angrier I got as I pulled into his driveway. Wildly enraged, I pounded on his mistresses' front door. He swung open the door and in his angry drunken stupor said; "Who the hell do you think you are pounding on my door and who is this bitch?!!" This incensed me further and I screamed at him: "Never mind her! What are you going to do to help mom! She's out of her mind and the kids are in danger!" He glared hotly at me and said, "Just what the hell do you expect me to do?!!!" I couldn't believe his lack of concern and I yelled at him: "You just have to pick up the damn phone and call the hospital!" His face flushed red with murderous anger and his voice was filled with sarcasm when he bellowed, "Oh that's all I have to do huh? Call the hospital!? Why don't you and your whore just get the fuck out of here!!!" I was beside myself with angered frustration and I shouted at him: "Fine you fucking asshole!" He lunged at me and as I was fighting him off I yelled for Megan to get in the car. Kicking and swinging he cursed at me to: "Get the goddamn fuck outta here!" He was much larger than me and I'd had a lifetime of his insane violence, I already knew he had the power, strength, and madness to send me to the hospital. I made it to the car as he was still trying to take me out, and tried to slam the car door on his leg as he continued kicking at me. I pealed out of his driveway and headed back to mom's house.

Apparently in the meantime, he'd had a change of heart about calling the hospital and having her committed because as I pulled up to her yard, I saw her bound in a straight-jacket and being put into an ambulance by two medics while a couple of police officers stood with my siblings on the porch.

Megan and I followed the ambulance to the hospital. As mom was being processed through admissions, I was allowed to see her. She knew I was somehow responsible for her abduction and tearfully asked me why I was having her committed. I calmly explained how imperative it was for her to get serious medical treatment, for her own safety.

I visited her in the very accurately portrayed atmosphere of her *One Flew Over The Cuckoo's Nest* surroundings daily, and conferred with her doctors.

I was able to stay for only a week before my leave was up and I very reluctantly returned to base.

Not knowing what was happening to mom, and my now parentless siblings, I was back on base for only a few hours before I re-packed my duffle bag and grabbed a taxi to the airport. Upon my arrival back home, I headed for Megan's because I was a.w.o.l. and needed an untraceable address.

Rex's car was in Megan's driveway and I didn't want him to know I was illegally in town, so I sat in a field across the street until I watched him leave.

Megan was ecstatic to see me and instantly we were tangled together in a large bean bag chair near the front door, talking over my new situation.

Suddenly the front door partially opened and Rex saw us embraced. He quickly closed the door without coming in which gave Megan two seconds to leap out of the chair and strike an innocent pose on the couch, whereupon Rex entered.

We exchanged stilted pleasantries for a few moments and then Rex told Megan they needed to talk, and they got in his car and left. I figured she had no choice but to tell him the truth about us and waited with nervous anticipation. He knew I was a.w.o.l. and now he knew about Megan and me, surely he would turn me in to the military authorities if only to distance me from his wife.

He dropped Megan off a half hour later and she proudly told me that she'd convinced him she was only "comforting me" in our embrace, due to the recent distress of my mom's circumstances. Rex never said anything to me about it, but I could tell he wasn't buying her story.

I stayed in town for a month before mom was discharged from the psychiatric ward. She was being treated with Lithium and Thorazine, regularly seeing a psychologist, and entered group therapy.

Megan earnestly suggested that I apply for a Hardship Discharge in order to make sure things remained stabilized at home, and with a doctors written statement of mom's diagnosis as a: "Manic-Depressive, Paranoid Schizophrenic" along with the rest of the military required slew of accompanying paperwork, I was all set to begin the arduous process.

I returned to base and was immediately engulfed in months of government red tape. (Paaaper-wawk!!! Paaaper-wawk!!!) Getting the military machine to stay on top of my situation was a battle in itself but ultimately I was honorably discharged nine months later.

By then, stabilized on medication and re-defining herself in group therapy, mom had secured a job as a ward clerk at a local hospital. Her sanity, tenacity and courage intact, she was back on her leonine footing, and went on to successfully raise her remaining "pride of cubs" on her own.

She grew to experience profound joy and fulfillment in her new career, and in her hard won independence she found a whole new measure of happiness that for the remaining fourteen years of her life, reshaped her from a mentally ill person into a very sane and wise woman who accomplished so much in the face of overwhelming odds, and was loved, respected, and admired by many.

I on the other hand, allowed my psychological bondage to

continue as my return to civilian life facilitated Megan's relentless pursuit, and my eventual surrender. In the end, by leaving the confines of the military and submitting to her possessive control, I'd merely traded one set of manipulating circumstances for another.

If I'd been able avoid the Army draft altogether, breaking it off with Megan for good by living in Las Vegas longer than nine days, I wonder how different my life would've turned out? But of course, the river must run its course.

Now, twenty-four years later, after reading the Village Voice article on the steps of Saint Patrick's I found myself contemplating another move to Las Vegas. I loved the cultural aspects of living in Manhattan but decided that unless I had a lot of money, I didn't want to grow old here. I knew from experience that life in this city was much more grueling than it was on the West Coast, and as I looked at the newspaper cover again, the Sphinx seemed to be enticing me to solve my newly riddled dilemmas by moving to the desert.

With all of the new casinos and restaurants I knew I'd easily get a job. I also realized that I could still afford to buy a home in Nevada; there was no chance of that here. I could *drive* to the grocery store there, instead of walking through the city lugging my groceries in freezing snow or humidity drenched heat. I wouldn't have to haul my clothes to the Laundromat anymore; I could have a washer and dryer in my house! Such time saving luxuries that I used to take for granted, now tempted me back to my familiar side of the nation.

I also rationalized that I would be close enough to Los Angeles, the center of the Music Business on the West Coast. Nothing was happening for me here and possibly nothing ever would happen with the several hundred notebooks of song lyrics I'd written.

If that was going to be the case, I could live with it, but I preferred to do so in comfort. I didn't have to play the starving artist role in Nevada, and in New York, it wasn't so much a role as it was a required lifestyle.

I was sick of the outrageous rents for what barely passed as a tenement, I wanted a *real* home, with a kitchen bigger than a restaurant booth, several rooms instead of two, a couple of bathtubs/showers, and at least a small yard. That didn't seem like too much to ask, and by March 30th I was packed and ready for my cross country move.

On the night before I was to leave Manhattan behind, I attended the final dress rehearsal theatre performance of a new off-Broadway show titled: <u>New York Rock</u>, a musical with music and lyrics by Yoko Ono. It was only fitting that I would be seeing the show on the night before my departure, for so many obvious reasons, not the least of which it had been Yoko who'd sounded the call for me to move here.

While I was more than happy that I'd heeded her advice, I also knew it was time for me to say goodbye again, and I found my emotions were in between Yoko's <u>New York Rock</u>...and a hard place.

I assumed Yoko wouldn't be attending this rehearsal performance, to my knowledge she'd not directed or produced the play so I imagined she'd wait and attend the premier the following night. I had to be out of my apartment by then so the dress rehearsal was my only chance of seeing the show.

It was a clear, calm, slightly chilly evening. I put on my Walkman headphones and listened to Yoko's album: <u>It's Alright</u> as I walked the sixteen short blocks to the theatre.

As I entered the tiny, crowded vestibule, the low murmuring crowd of no more than fifty people, were finding their way to their seats in the theatres small, intimate setting. I looked at every face and wasn't surprised that Yoko was not among them. The lights were dimmed and the show began, and for the next ninety minutes, the familiar melodies and lyrics came to life through the lone actor and actress who sang Yoko's songs in staged vignettes.

Vocally they were on pitch, but emotionally they delivered the songs without genuine passion or conviction. I couldn't help thinking that these two actors were completely wrong for the roles. They were much too classically good looking to portray effectively the highly dramatic and often gritty emotions that Yoko's material required. They looked and moved like they belonged in a Vidal Sassoon Shampoo commercial rather than in a Yoko Ono retrospective.

While it was still mildly enjoyable to see and hear the music performed, it was all a bit fluffy for my expectations. Certainly this was the first time I'd been disappointed by an event artistically associated with Yoko.

Afterwards, as people milled about in the cubicle of the lobby, I overheard someone say that Yoko was upstairs in the building and had watched the show.

I supposed that she didn't want to be sandwiched in the cramped lobby quarters with the mingling crowd, and was waiting for the theatre to empty out before she made her exit. That was fine with me because for once in my life, I didn't want to face her. Certainly she would ask me if I enjoyed the show, I knew I wouldn't be able to effectively disguise my disappointment, and the thought of politely lying to her was beyond repugnant, she'd be able to see through me in a heartbeat.

Also, I was leaving the next day; I didn't want her to remember me as a critical voice. It had been nearly two years since our last meeting at the Mary Boone Gallery, and I was three weeks shy of being on our usual April meeting cycle.

The stars within me didn't feel right tonight, it was better if I didn't see her; I wasn't prepared to deal with a final bout of <u>Goodbye Sadness</u>.

Most of the audience had left the theatre and I was right on the heels of making my exit when Yoko came down the stairs. We spotted each other immediately, just as a small group of people rushed over to her. They excitedly engaged her in conversation and I stood solo by the doorway as I watched her answer questions and joke with them.

Standing only a few feet away, she looked at me through the crowd; her face lit up with smiling recognition as she noted my appearance with a nod. I smiled and nodded back at her. At that point I decided it was enough that she knew I'd attended and I slipped out the door.

Somberly I slowly walked to the corner a few yards away from the theatre, and leaned against a lamp post. I was relieved that I'd chosen not to feign accolades to her about the show, but saddened that more than likely I'd never be in this close proximity to her again.

Under the dim blue spotlight of the streetlamp, I looked up into the shimmering canopy of the galaxy, praying that I was doing the right thing by moving to Nevada. Searching the heavens for answers, I soon realized they would only materialize in the future destination I'd already committed myself to.

I sadly thought of my creative and amazing circle of friends, and how terribly I was going to miss them along with the cultural, artistic and spiritual magic that my time in Manhattan had lived and breathed in me. Could such a giant approaching void possibly be filled by the neon behemoth of plasticity in the "Left Coast" land of "Have a nice day!"??? I had no idea, but it was far too late to back out now. I was going to be officially homeless in a few hours and my rented moving truck was fully packed and waiting for me to get behind the wheel.

I looked back towards the theater and saw that people were leaving. Yoko must've already left without my noticing; I'd been too busy using her *"Keys to Open the Skies."* I remained leaning against the lamp post and watched the crowd disperse into the night.

The streets and sidewalks eventually cleared and I'd decided it was time to go when out of the theatre alone, stepped Yoko. Whether she saw me standing in the distance or not, I didn't know, but she stepped up to a car that was parked at the curb. Through the glare of the street light I saw the faint silhouette of a man through the rear window, sitting behind the wheel. Yoko stood on the sidewalk on the passenger side of the car. I could see her clearly, in profile; she didn't appear to be talking to him, just standing there. Was she waiting for him to open the door? Was she looking at me out of the corner of her eyes, waiting for me to address her? Should I take this last sudden opportunity to say goodbye?

"Let her go son, it's time for you to be..."Moving On."

Mother musically vibrated the phrase inside me with crystal clarity. Immediately I understood that she was purposely using a double-entendre to tell me I was making the right move to the desert; she did this by *singing* the title of Yoko's song: Moving On from the album: Double Fantasy.

I watched Yoko standing there a few moments more before she opened the passenger side door, got in and rode away.

I put my headphones on and started my walk home. Pushing the play button, Yoko's uplifting chorus: "It's alright/it's alright/it's alright/I know it's gonna be/alright" resounded in my head.

I knew everything *was* going to be alright, it *was* time for me to be: "Moving On." I had a newly improved: "Double Fantasy" of my own, and it included that Carole King song from her record: Fantasy about finding a quiet place, and a real home.

Driving across the country with a sixteen foot truckload of all my worldly possessions; I arrived in Las Vegas three days later.

Immediately I found an apartment and after settling in for a few weeks, I went job hunting. I purposely avoided going to The Four Queens because it held the memories of my brief employment there and the myriad of ways my life had been altered by that one phone call from mom about being drafted.

Surprisingly there weren't nearly as many job opportunities as I'd imagined, though I filled out many applications and left my resume with several casinos, a few weeks passed by and I'd only been called for one interview. Unfortunately it was a waiter position for a small restaurant, unassociated with any casino. It didn't seem like a busy enough place to make a living and though medical benefits were available, the plan was expensive.

I knew I had to find employment where at the very least medical benefits were provided. With that in mind, I had to push my pride aside and reluctantly answered an ad for The Four Queens Hotel and Casino requesting servers for a: "New Italian Bistro."

I was offered, and accepted the position, within an hour of making my application.

On the first day of my employment, I entered the back alley entrance of the casino the employees were required to use. I'd walked out of this same alley as a nineteen year old kid, into a whirlwind of a life I never could have imagined, and I was returning into this same portal twenty-four years later.

As if the obvious irony of an Oprah: "full circle moment" wasn't clear enough, the alley had a distinctly familiar smell. It wasn't offensive but it was completely identical to the one I remembered from so long ago, and the memories of my tortured youth washed over me like a tsunami.

The first year of my "rebirth" in Vegas was filled with renewed optimism, hopes, dreams, and new opportunities. Although I sorely missed my artistic friends and the cultural amenities of Manhattan, I easily made new friends and my income and living standards quickly improved.

I bought a strikingly beautiful brand new home in a remote and quiet suburb; with a very gorgeous panoramic view of Las Vegas from the front of the house and the endless natural beauty of The Rainbow Mountain Range in the back. Even the name of my street was beautiful, Skytop Drive. I felt like I *was indeed* touching the "sky top" and I'd *literally* ended up on the other side of The Rainbow.

My New York Carole King <u>Fantasy</u> of finding: "a quiet place to live" had far exceeded my desires and I even began living the <u>Double Fantasy</u> of John and Yoko's "Starting over…" because I too was: "falling in love again".

Every thing I'd asked for on the city steps of St. Patrick's Cathedral had quickly come to fruition with uncommon ease and it seemed as though the newspaper Sphinx had solved the riddles of my life after all.

I suppose I should've been wary of "Lady Luck" smiling down on me so rapidly because I ended up working at The Four Queens for almost two years before the Italian bistro was bought out and replaced by a Burger King. Suddenly the lion of winter was upon me again.

From: Carole King ... to Burger King? In what turn of twisted masochistic retrograde had my planets re-aligned? At the same time that I became jobless, my first "Left Coast" love affair gave my heart a left hook and was over after sixteen months. And, as if those two emotional asteroid collisions weren't enough, the IRS audited two years of back taxes and decided that I owed them nearly eight-thousand dollars.

As I applied for new employment and prayed for phone calls that were not forthcoming, the pressures of living off my small unemployment checks while at the same time remaining crippled inside by a broken heart, after several long months, eventually spiraled me into a serious depression.

I desperately petitioned mom for assistance but none was forthcoming. I finally came to accept the fact that either my torment was causing a cloud of: "unclearrr-rrrreception!" or she was simply M.I.A. Drowning in a pool of resigned futility I stopped even bothering to ask; "Mamma mia! Where *are* you?!"

I didn't need to see a medical doctor to diagnose my clinical depression, I was fully aware that my head of hopeless and eventually suicidal thoughts were symptomatic of my circumstances, but they consumed me nonetheless.

I knew I needed immediate treatment but I had no money or insurance. By chance I happened to read in Ann Landers column that November was National Depression Month. (My life was out of whack but at least I was in sync with the season of the witch!)

Ms. Landers urged all of her readers who were experiencing depression to seek counseling this month because many providers would be offering help at low or no cost.

I'd grown up strapped into a front row center seat to recognize mental illness, and blindly married into more of the same. Ann Landers was among the first of celebrities to admit a clinical depression in her own life so I figured she at least knew the ropes.

I decided to heed her sage advice and went to a well known, privately owned Mental Health facility where an admissions counselor asked me what my problems were.

I explained that I was four months unemployed, with credit cards, utilities, and a mortgage to pay, the IRS had cleaned out my bank account and was threatening to take my home, and emotionally I was romancing thoughts of suicide. I also lamented that though I'd been pursuing a song writing career since I'd moved here, nothing was happening on that front either.

The counselor replied; "Well you might as well play the slot machines instead of trying to get a recording contract, your odds are probably better at the casino."

As if I wasn't clearly depressed enough, her words slammed me into a deeper funk. She also quite curtly informed me that since I had no health insurance, the hospital wouldn't take me on as a patient. Apparently this was not a participating, sliding-fee merchant for National Depression month. Instead, she referred me to a mental health program at the University Of Nevada in Las Vegas where I was immediately asked to sign a waiver exempting the campus of any responsibility should I decide to kill myself while under their care.

When I'd seen the same insurance scene played out on television's *Alley McBeal* it had been funny, but that show was an adult comedy, there was absolutely nothing comedic about it happening to me now.

In and of it self, the waiver was disturbing, but even more perverse was that the so called "treatment" consisted of me sitting in a room alone, facing a two way mirror, where I was asked questions through a metal speaker in the wall, by a variety of people that I could not see. A loud metallic voice informed me that I was being videotaped and to: "Speak clearly into the microphone." Speak clearly?! Who were they kidding?! It was a monumental effort to speak at all! Seeing my own agonized facial expressions in the mirror as I replied to the disembodied, clinical questioning voices, was overwhelmingly surreal. No one on the other side of the wall offered any form of solace; they merely fired inane questions at me like I was a laboratory experiment.

I may've been mentally disturbed but I didn't have to be a rocket scientist to realize I wasn't being *treated* for depression, I was being studied.

I didn't bother to return for my next session, and no one called from the office. They never knew if I'd gone home and blown my brains out or not, and I guess it didn't matter since they had the suicide waiver…

Eventually, by the grace of God I was able to pull myself out of the depths of the mire on my own, and managed to get a job at a new casino that had opened up in my neighborhood.

I began working in the new Italian restaurant (of course…) but when *it* closed after 13 months I wondered if I'd started a trend! Three times in a little over three years I'd been working for Italian restaurants that closed their doors!

Fortunately I was promoted to a coveted spot in the same casinos' steakhouse, which appropriately for my Fire Sign of Leo, was named: Wildfire. I was <u>Starting Over</u> yet *again*, and the wild fires in my life continued to spread.

Baby Grand
(Part Two)

Speaking of new wild fires and starting over again, you'll remember that the beginning of this book unfolded with part one of Baby Grand where I described my un-landscaped yards, along with my latest broken hearted love affair, the absence of a white baby grand materializing in my house after nine years, my emergency spinal surgery and the continued paralysis in my hands that discarded my desire to own a baby grand in favor of landscaping my yards with the money I'd managed to save, and my new found solitary contentment that was quite suddenly shattered by the very imminent threat of my baby brother's desire to kill himself on the morning where this story began.

Initially I'd begun writing Baby Grand because I'd sent out the previous story: Angels for Christmas, in lieu of Christmas cards for the 2005 holiday season, and the positive response from family and friends was sincerely overwhelming. Several people told me it should be made into a movie. Everyone agreed that it should be published, and one lady in particular, one of my favorite restaurant patrons who unbeknownst to me was a published author, asked me if I'd allow her to take it to some publishing houses. She also asked me if I had more material. I told her yes and no. Yes, Angels for Christmas was hers to promote if she wanted to, and no I hadn't written any other stories, but I could most certainly do another one for her. Mother had very generously given me enough material over the years to choose from and the genesis of a new short story: Baby Grand, was born. I reasoned it would be easy enough to knock out this one particular "mother miracle" for my lady friend and so in mid-February of 2006, I began writing Baby Grand.

In the middle of the story, I'd been typing merrily along when mom decided to interrupt me. Just like that black and white scene in The Wizard Of Oz where Auntie Em's image is in the witch's crystal ball saying; "Dorothy, where *are* you??? Come home Dorothy!" Mother's face appeared in muted colors inside my head and wearing a sly, playful smirk, she said; *"So, you think you're getting off easy here huh buster? One story? Oh, no, no, no. We both know that you have more than enough material for a book and that's what this is going to be!"*

As per my usual mode of argument whenever she decided to intervene in my life, I instantly fired back: "A book?! I don't have time to write a book!!! I've been working six and seven days a week at the restaurant and I'm behind on my list of things to do as it is! Besides, I'm already half way through Baby Grand and now you want me to start over?!! What am I supposed to do with this story now?!! I've already written fourteen pages and you expect me to just throw it away…"

My cosmic arguments were interrupted by her next statement: *"I've not said anything about throwing it away have I?"*

Puzzled, I shut up for a moment before replying; "Well what else am I going to do with it, I can't *start* a book by telling this miracle, it's the most recent *big one* you've done! I'd have to start a book with your *first* miracles and eventually work my way up to Baby Grand. I don't see how I can salvage this work, what's your brilliant solution?"

I could see her facial expression of exasperation clearly in my mind as I impatiently gave her the chance to respond.

After she finished rolling her eyes, she retorted very calmly: *"It's quite simple dear, you open the book with Baby Grand part one and finish the book with part two. In between the two parts you can tell the other stories of the past twenty years since I've* *crossed over, and part two of <u>Baby Grand</u> will bring the reader currently up to date! Besides, it will look good on the book jacket: <u>Twenty years of one mother's Divine interventions!</u> Any questions?"*

I had... nothing. Humbled by the fact that she'd not only provided a solution, but had done so with an interesting and creative writing device, I consented with an embarrassed sigh of mea culpa, and then a very appreciative: "Okay, I get it. You win."

I saw her sly, playful smile again, and as her image dissolved into particles, her voice echoed: *"Was there ever a doubt I wouldn't?"*

Now, as I was saying in the middle of <u>Baby Grand</u> (Part One) before I was **so rudely**...uh...mmm...I mean...*"Divinely"* interrupted...

I was still the undisputed leader of landscape starved property in my neighborhood, but the circumstances of my life were on the upswing.

I'd begun the early morning laughing hysterically at my elderly neighbor bitterly complaining to his Irish Setter about my yards.

After sixteen months of frustrating attempts, I'd quit trying to play my keyboards because while the rest of the nerve endings in my body had been restored to normal after my nearly two year stint with paralysis, my hands, while useful in every other way, still lacked keyboard co-ordination. No need or desire for a Baby Grand any more.

No more fantasies of finding "The right one" in a piano, or a lover. I'd found the right "One" the wholly fulfilling One-ness vibrantly alive inside of me. I was more than happy with my solitary life, the last few years of living alone had taught me many, many, things, but the most important lesson was finding out that I am *already* a very, <u>*very*</u> rich man.

My physical, emotional, and spiritual sanity had been on the brink of extinction numerous times in my life, and maybe it's because I have five planets of Leo in my chart that I've been allotted more than the usual nine lives of a cat, or perhaps it's because my biological Mamma Leone is still protecting her cubs from The Other Side, or maybe it's a combination of both, with other celestial factors that I can't even imagine, thrown in. All in all, I believe the following Lennon lyrics summed up my newly contented awareness best: "I am he/as you are he/as you are me/and ***we are all together***." Ultimately *we are all together,* in the Oneness of creation.

I was getting excited about my desolate landscape finally coming alive. All set to spend my moderate savings account on plants, trees, and flagstones. You'll recall that I'd been in the middle of designing my Zodiac themed garden when my 42 year old "baby" brother called to ask for his portion of mom's Bank of New York stock inheritance so he could enjoy some exotic travel and leisure before he killed himself.

When he was a toddler, he always referred to me as "Bank". He called everyone else in the family by their correct names but he convinced himself for some reason that my name actually was: "Bank." Now he was asking me to use mom's money to finance his suicide.

It's true, I'd become the family "Bank" of mom's estate, but I wasn't about to use her hard earned money to bankroll his depression into a farewell good time before he ended his own life. I'm sure if he'd been listening, he could have heard mom calling out one of her most frequently used phrases in life, one of her sharper ways of saying no: ***"Don't bank on it!!!"*** I could clearly hear her, and this time, I swallowed the double entendre like a piece of stale bread.

I'd finally gotten my life back on track and was derailed in an instant by my brother's misguided answers to his problems. I managed to persuade him to move in with me; together we'd find solutions for creating a new life for him that was worth living. I'd already sent him money for his last months rent so he had a few weeks left to pack before I was to go to California with my truck and help him make the move.

I could tell that my brother and I were both going to need a miracle to get us through this. I hadn't lived with him in nearly thirty years and I'd become so accustomed to my comfortable solitary lifestyle that I was mourning the loss of it before he'd even arrived. I'd lied to him on the phone, saying that I wanted, in fact *needed*, the company. I knew it was a lie as it came out of my mouth but I'd have said anything to change his fatal ambitions. I was more than willing to share my sanctuary with him but I also knew it was not going to be easy.

Emotionally in need of some spiritual reassurance, I decided to take the twenty minute truck ride from my home on Skytop Drive to another rural "sky top" where I could get in touch with my higher self.

In the same way that I'd formerly used the triad of The NBC, The Triple Six Building and St. Patrick's Cathedral in Manhattan, I'd discovered a similar public area in Nevada shortly after moving here where my consciousness seemed to readily open up to the whispers of the Universe. (Note: The original definition of the word universe means: **One** song.)

I arrived at Hoover Dam and after parking my truck that bore the vanity plate RBRSOUL, I realized I was going to need an actual Rubber Soul to bounce back from the sadness I was feeling for my brother that at the same time was mixing with the reluctant surrender of my solitude.

I shuffled down the hill along the long winding sidewalk over looking the dam, and the heaviness in my heart slowed my gait with the uncertainties that were cluttering up my head.

Arriving at the main visitors' concourse, I stood at my usual place of benediction in front of the 142 foot flag pole bearing the American flag that was centered in between two 30 foot high bronze human winged figures that closely resembled Angels.

After saying my opening prayer, I lazily walked around the terrazzo floor that is inlaid with a detailed celestial map of planets and stars, finally coming to rest upon the three foot raised, large round concrete compass, which is framed with all twelve signs of the Zodiac.

When I first discovered this place, I found it extremely odd that such winged statues, a star map, and a Zodiac monument, were commissioned to commemorate the building of Hoover Dam, after all, this "occult" artwork was completed in 1935!

In those days, from what I've gleaned from the available media of the times, Americans seemed to be pretty much in the mindset of: "God, Country, and Apple Pie". There was no "Moral Majority" dividing the country, for the majority of citizens were already inherently moral, certainly more so then than today.

So, was that era in America, with its traditionally fundamental beliefs, really able to embrace and incorporate this homage to the Zodiac as relevant and credible knowledge in 1935?

The answer is apparently yes, for it was the venerable President Franklin D. Roosevelt who presided over the dedication ceremonies.

I really can't imagine such artifacts being commissioned on our tax dollars, and approved by our political and religious leaders today, for the reputation of Astrology has been too far maligned in our "enlightened" society.

Regardless, among other artwork at the site, is a concrete elevator tower that bears the inscription: "Since primordial times, American Indian Tribes and Nations lifted their hands to the Great Spirit from these ranges and plains..."

I was here now, doing as they had done, lifting my hands to the Great Spirit. I was opening my heart and soul to the "One song" supplicating for answers and strength, on my brother's behalf as well as my own. Though I spent over an hour meditating on the nuts and bolts of the new challenges I would soon be facing, I eventually left the dam with the same fearful uncertainties I'd arrived with.

Ode to Joia
(My rock n' roll rendition of Beethoven's Ninth)

When I got home I received a call from my dear friend Leslie who asked me if I could write a song for an upcoming special occasion. I told her I could very easily write the lyrics but because of the remaining numbness in my hands, I'd given up trying to play my keyboards altogether.

True, the numbness had lessened considerably, enough to do most things normally, and able to distinguish hot from cold, but the dexterity to play fluently had not returned the last time I'd attempted it; at least eight months ago.

Leslie and I good naturedly argued back and forth for several minutes about why I didn't want to attempt the music score, but no matter what I said, she wouldn't let me off the hook.

"Write the lyric, but at least *try* to compose the music too." she urged unrelenting.

Frustrated, I wearily replied; "I *seriously* don't think I can do the music Les."

She allowed me to savor my unwavering doubt for a brief moment before she firmly insisted: "Maybe not, but it won't hurt to try. Call me when you're finished, bye!"

I couldn't believe she'd just hung up on me!!! Evidently she expected more than I was capable of. She wouldn't let me off the hook, and now she'd hung up on me?! That was *off the hook!!!*

I've enjoyed writing song lyrics for the past twenty-plus years and for some reason my greatest gift to others has always been that I'm able to capture a moment, a circumstance, a thought, a person, place, or thing, with words that touch the heart and soul.

Friends have requested my writing talents on various occasions and I've always been happy to oblige. I love the challenge and the responses are always so positive; often the effusive praise seems embarrassingly overstated.

Putting words together seems like no big deal to me, like doing a crossword or jigsaw puzzle. It comes so naturally that I'm no longer surprised that I can write an entire song in twenty minutes, sometimes three songs in an hour, one right after the other. The process itself is second nature, what continues to amaze me is that I always have something write about! My friends know that all they have to do is give me a topic, and within 30 minutes or less, I'll have the piece completed. Much like comedian Mike Meyers <u>Saturday Night Live</u> character: "Linda Richmond" the middle aged, "Knew Yawk" Jewish "Toawk Show Host" of "<u>Koah-fee Toawk</u>" who gets so "vehclempt" at Barbra Streisands' voice "like buttah" that she's rendered nearly speechless, but gives her audience the instructions to: "Toawk amongst yoah-selves" and gives them a topic to: "discuss."

I very seldom get "vehclempt" when hearing a Streisand song, but like Linda Richmond, I can always easily find a topic to "discuss" in a song lyric. (Too bad there isn't an <u>American Idol</u> competition for lyricists, where the celebrity judges could include; oh I dunno...Cat Stevens or maybe... James Blunt...)

After Leslie's call, I immediately sat down and wrote a 32 line song, in 19 minutes. I know exactly how long it took because I always write the time down when I begin, and when the piece ends. I reached for the phone to call Leslie but then remembered she expected lyrics *and* music.

My double keyboards stared across the room at me like two

bratty children who'd just gotten away with something evil. I didn't want to go near their snickering faces, those pearly white, plastic sneering smiles that wore the black keys like a furrowed brow. I didn't want them to silently laugh at another one of my defeats while they sat defiantly still and soundless as I walked away from another frustrated attempt to "play nice" with them. I've endured my share of bullies in my day, but these electronic string and hammer voices, how deeply their endless taunts of inadequacy had subliminally echoed in my head for the past eighteen months.

My former keyboard skills were adequate but not exceptional and because I've taught myself how to play but do not read music, my music compositional style has always been bizarre, even to me! I used to just put whatever lyric I'd completed on the music stand, and begin playing whatever melody the words stirred in me.

Thank goodness the electronic keyboard was able to record my playing because I'd get so lost in *feeling* the new melody, that I'd play the song straight through without remembering how I'd done it! I'd then push the playback button and see if the music suited the words. Every time, though I'd try out other melodies, the first one I composed has been the one that stuck.

That was in the good old days before my paralysis, when my mind and Spirit connected with my fingers in a Zen orchestration of physical and spiritual fluidity. Now my previous talent mocked me from across the room, and out of defiance rather than belief, I sat down, balanced my lyric on the music stand, re-read the verse and chorus to familiarize myself with the cadence of the words, and began to play.

With utter disbelief I surprised myself by playing straight through the first verse and into the chorus, like I'd never stopped playing at all! By the time I moved into the second verse my chords were getting stronger and more complex without any effort! I could scarcely believe my eyes and ears as I continued playing completely through to the end of the song. I anxiously hit the playback button to see if what I'd just done was real. I'd gotten so lost in *feeling* the song, and the shocked excitement of playing it fluidly, that I wasn't sure the experience had sounded as good as I thought it had.

The music soared back at me through the amplified speakers, beautiful and graceful, like a band of Angels had just broken through the clouds, and as the tears of ecstatic joy burst from my eyes, I realized that indeed, my Angels had done exactly that.

It took me several minutes before the grateful and cleansing tears subsided. When I'd finally composed myself, with skyrocketing enthusiasm I played my very own rock and roll arrangement of the movement from Beethoven's Ninth Symphony: Ode to Joy.

Somewhere in the middle of the song, I could hardly see because of the elated tears that resumed streaming down my face, but I didn't need to see in order to play the music, I could *feel it* again!!!

Excitedly I picked up the phone to give Leslie the good news. She was equally delighted when I pushed the playback button and sang the lyrics over the phone. We both rejoiced at my new success and I was so incredibly grateful that I said a quick goodbye to Les, saying that I had to go back to the keyboard and see if I could do it again!

I grabbed another lyric from my notebook and the process returned as easily as it did the first time, as if there had never been a problem. From that day forward, though I'm still a mediocre pianist, I've been able to play *better* than I did before my surgery.

While my dream of owning a white baby grand returned, the reality of my stark landscape continued to beg for funding. Not only my piano dream, but the landscape also had to be put on hold again because my brother was coming to live with me and I'd be supporting another person. I'd have to be careful with my small savings because I had no idea how long he'd be out of work, nor how long he'd remain with me. As things turned out, he ended up staying a year and a half.

Financially it wasn't much of a stretch, but it was not an easy emotional eighteen months for either of us. While he struggled to find a suitable new career choice, I wrestled with having the constant presence of someone else's energy in my home. It wasn't that *he* was a burden, or to quote the sixties song by The Hollies: "He ain't heavy/he's my brother..." The burden was my own head. I was so spoiled by my previous solitary freedom; the relinquishing of it for this length of time had gotten me out of touch with my higher self again.

By the time our second February together rolled around, my brother was fine but I was on the borderline of letting the waves of depression that'd been crashing on my consciousness, take over. I retreated to my room more and more and wrote scores of dark lyrics.

My brother Tony is a very sensitive person and as much as I tried to hide my growing dissatisfaction, we didn't have to speak of it for him to recognize that I was on the verge of my last nerve. It was ironic that now I was the one succumbing to the abyss of emotional monochrome, just at the same time that his life was returning to living color.

He'd begun a new career in being a Blackjack Dealer, and while he'd had to work for low pay at some small casinos in the beginning, he'd landed a job at a larger one in the last six months and his finances had improved.

Everyone is familiar with the axiom: "What doesn't kill you, makes you stronger" and he was *living proof* of that, so much so that two weeks before Mothers Day in 2004, he informed me that he'd found an apartment and was ready to move.

Three weeks prior to his announcement, I'd been killing time on my day off and found myself peering through a storefront window where a large sign that read: "Piano Liquidation Sale" was posted. The store was closed and as I stood with my face pressed up against the glass, cupping my eyes from the glare of sunlight as I looked through the window, a piano mover's truck pulled up. Two large men got out of the truck and as they unlocked the door to the store I asked them what the store hours were. One of them told me the store wouldn't be opening today at all but he'd allow me to take a brief look inside.

I quickly made my way up and down the aisles, looking first at several white baby grand's that were far too expensive for me to consider and then at the lower priced spinets which I was not the least bit interested in. I knew I was just dreaming as I looked at them all and without the money to afford any of them, why was I wasting my time? I thanked the man who'd let me browse and left the store. Five weeks quickly passed and I'd forgotten all about it.

Three days before Mothers Day, my truck got a flat tire. The spare was put on and the following day I went to have the flat repaired.
As I stood waiting in line, I noticed a fresh, untouched copy of a weekend newspaper sitting on a chair. A small voice stirred within me saying; "When you're finished standing in line, read the paper." I assumed it was my own inner voice and barely registered its instruction. By the time I'd been waited on and told that the repair time was going to be an hour, I'd completely forgotten all about the newspaper and was on my way out the door to have a cigarette when mom's unmistakable voice entered my head: *"Read the paper!"*
I felt like I'd been spun around by some unseen force, and momentarily dazed, I registered her command and went to the chair where I picked up the paper and sat down. As I was looking through it I wondered what was *so* important for me to read. I skimmed the various headlines and columns; nothing was jumping out at me. I realized that maybe she just didn't want me to smoke and was using the paper to distract me. By the time I made it to the Classifieds, I'd forgotten all about her.
Indifferently I was browsing through the ads, and as usual, I looked at the <u>Musical Instruments for Sale</u>. For years I'd done this whenever I read the paper, and even though I'd spotted many bargains, they were still out of the realms of my finances. I never looked at the piano ads seriously, I was just curious as to the resale prices.
I came upon an ad that read: "Nearly new, white baby grand, mint condition, $4000 or best offer." Certainly it was a bargain; the cheapest white baby grand I'd seen over a month ago at the "Piano Liquidation Sale" had been fourteen-thousand!
Mother's voice firmly returned: *"Tear this out!"* I harrumphed disdainfully before I mentally replied; "For what? I don't have

that kind of money." At that moment a mechanic came up to me and said; "Excuse me Mr. Barone, your vehicle is ready." I looked up at him and started to close the paper when her voice insisted: ***"Tear it out!!!"*** Irritated by her useless intrusion, I hastily ripped the small portion of the newspaper out and stuffed it in my pocket as I made my way to the cashier.

Back on my wheels, I continued to run some errands and by the time I got home I'd forgotten all about the incident and was on my way upstairs to take a nap when mom's voice intruded again: ***"Call the number!"*** Annoyed by her directive, I froze on the stairs and argued back: "For *what*?! You *know* I don't have that kind of money and I have to take a nap before I go to work!

Her response was unyielding: ***"Call the number!"***
In a reluctant, passive trance, I reached in my pocket for the newspaper scrap. I stood and blankly stared at it for a moment until, wearily resigned, I stumbled back downstairs, picked up the phone and dialed.

A woman answered and cheerfully described the piano, saying that her mother had purchased it three years ago but she'd only had a chance to play it five or six times before she was diagnosed with a terminal illness and had passed away.

The woman asked; "Would you like to come and see it right now?" I really *didn't* want to; I'd been awake since 4am. I *wanted* to take a nap, but I found myself asking for directions.

She lived on the far opposite end of the valley and because it was Saturday I knew the traffic would be bad so I told her it would take me at least forty five minutes to get there.

The entire drive I kept wondering why I was on this wild goose chase at all. I didn't know exactly how much money was in my savings account; I rarely put money in but I figured it was $3200.00 at most. Part of that was earmarked for some minimal landscaping and the rest was for my "safety cushion". God forbid I should have some household emergency and not have the money to bail myself out. It was entirely doubtful that the piano woman would drop her price very much and even if she did, my savings would be wiped out, that alone terrified me.

Agitated by the busy freeway and my acceptance of this

pointless excursion, I reprimanded myself: "Why am I doing this? I don't have the money, I don't have the time and gas to waste and I don't even want to see her damn piano! I should be home sleeping before I have to go to work!"

My self recriminations boiled the entire ride and by the time I arrived at the piano woman's (she'd not told me her name) subdivision, I felt like an idiot for driving this long distance just to look at something I knew I couldn't afford.

Her directions had said to make the first left past the security gate on to Aspect Way, where her home was located. I was let through the gate and continued to look to the left for Aspect Way as I drove along on a street named Astral Avenue.

A wave of serenity immediately washed away my formerly anxious mood as I cruised slowly along the beautiful tree lined avenue. The neighborhood looked like a photo layout from: *Better Homes and Gardens*.

I wondered to myself about the significance of the street names. In Astrology, an "aspect" is a reference to the relative positions of the stars and planets and how a particular "aspect" influences human affairs.

Here I was driving along Astral Avenue, looking to make a left turn onto Aspect Way. Were my human affairs being influenced by a particular "aspect" in the cosmos? What "Astral Avenue" was I really traveling on? Was mom, along with the heavenly bodies, lined up for some miraculous intercession or was the "aspect" just fooling me into dreaming an impossible dream?

It took me a long time to find Aspect Way because I'd passed it coming into the subdivision. The piano woman hadn't told me it was the first left *behind* the security station. I realized that I wouldn't even have driven on Astral Avenue, or noticed that Aspect Way had an astrological connotation, if she had.

I parked in front of her home, walked to the door and rang the bell. A man answered and I explained that I'd come to see the piano. He invited me in and then he yelled for his wife: "*Joy-ce*!!! Someone is here to look at the piano!"

Joyce came to the entry hall and led me to a small room where the white baby grand practically filled the space. The moment I saw it I said; "It's very beautiful, it looks brand new!"

Proudly she responded; "It basically is brand new. As I told you on the phone, my mother bought it for herself and she was able to play it only a few times before she got sick and passed away. It's just been sitting here since then, it will need to be tuned. I'm moving to Arizona and I don't play piano, and my daughter already owns a baby grand so that's why the price is so low. Why don't you try it out?"

Reverently I sat on the gleaming lacquered Ivory colored bench and looked over the expanse of the perfectly white and black keys. Because I wanted to play something that really gave it a workout, I played my rock n' roll version of: Ode to Joy.

When I'd finished, Joyce clapped enthusiastically and then said to me: "So, you must've taken years of lessons huh?!"

Shaking my head I replied; "No, just a few lessons from a horrible nun when I was a child, and then later as an adult, I had three lessons with a weird guy who talked to his mother on the phone through my entire session and that's pretty much the extent of my training.

Joyce looked puzzled, with raised eyebrows she continued: "Well you must at *least* know how to read music then."

Again I shook my head and said; "No, I don't read music."

With a further startled look on her face she very curiously replied; "But... you know the names of the chords you're playing... right?"

I shrugged my head and shoulders, saying; "I have no idea."

Sheer amazement flourished across her face as she inquired; "How did you play that *so beautifully* then?! My daughter took lessons for twelve years and she can't play half as good as you! You have a special gift! You should be on stage! I know a lot about music, I've seen countless performances, and you're *incredible*! Have you ever thought of playing professionally?"

I realized Joyce had a piano to sell, and while I could see that she was sincere in her high praise, I didn't take her accolades seriously. I just shook my head no, and started to play a slow, regret filled romantic song, made famous by The Carpenters' but written by Leon Russell, one of my old favorites: Superstar.

I didn't have to sing the sad and longing lyrics: *"Don't you remember you told me you loved me baby..."* for the pensive heartache of my blues arrangement to perfume the air.

As the final notes delicately resonated, Joyce jumped up out of her chair reveling in renewed excitement: *"That was awesome!! How **on earth** are you doing this?! !"*

I paused for a moment to consider a sane and viable, *earthly* explanation. I wanted to tell Joyce that when I sat at a piano, I simply plugged my soul into the *One*-song.

Instead I said; "I don't really know how I do it; I never play the song exactly the same way twice. The arrangement depends on how I'm *feeling* the song at the moment."

In her eyes I saw the wheels of Joyce's brain struggling to comprehend my inexplicable method and I understood her confusion. I didn't understand it myself; I just knew it worked for me. I turned back to the keyboard and decided to give it a really tough workout this time. I'd warmed up enough by now to play a very challenging piece by Janis Ian titled: Between the Lines.

Afterwards, Joyce lauded me with more effusive and ebullient acclaim and offered to hook me up with some people who could assist me in finding places to perform. For several minutes she implored me to pursue a career on stage and as she prattled on, though I appreciated her enthusiasm, in my heart I no longer wanted to be a performer.

In my youth I would have had the nerve, but my confining years with Megan had effectively derailed my self-confidence in those days, along with any opportunities for reaching for those dreams.

In fact the moment that I *knew* our marriage was over was the day Megan said she'd "accidentally found" a notebook of song lyrics I'd written. She read through it while I was at work, apparently searching for hidden clues to my dissatisfaction in our marriage. I don't know why she needed *more* information; I'd been brutally honest in the past year, making it clear that living with her was killing me.

Among the bluesy ballads and sad love songs, there was a

Punk Rock lyric she took particular offense to in a piece titled: <u>Nazi Apostles</u>.

It was an obvious metaphorical commentary on the hypocritical actions of various religious sects who sanctimoniously preach love but spread hate.

Megan accusingly said that putting my negative thoughts on paper was "self destructive" and she urged me "for the sake of our marriage" to throw all of my notebooks away.

Somewhere I once read love described as: "That which promotes another's growth."

She'd never promoted my growth, unless it was to her explicit advantage, and now she wanted to censor my very thoughts.

Her dream had always been to be a published author, the next future poet laureate. She'd written scores of pieces inspired by the styles of her favorite manic depressive hero's Anne Sexton and Sylvia Plath (Both authors committed suicide, talk about "self-destructive"!) and Megan wasn't volunteering to trash *her own* work.

Here she was telling me that for the sake of our marriage (i.e. *her* dreams) I needed to destroy my songbooks. She might as well have asked me to put my soul in a paper shredder.

I didn't follow through with Megan's directive but by the time I'd finally begun to pursue a performers career, the doors were already closed because, as I was well aware, I was: "too old."

I recognized the prejudice, it's still alive and well today on <u>American Idol</u>. You cannot even audition for the show if you're older than 27 and I was more than two decades older than that!!!

Now I was content to remain behind the scenes and hoped to have other artists perform my songs. The kind of assistance Joyce was offering was not in that direction. I politely declined her offer, and thanked her for her kind and gracious compliments. As for buying the piano, I said I'd have to think about it.

I became extremely agitated on the drive home; I wasn't sure why. Of course I wanted to purchase the piano but as I added up the costs of the tuning, the moving and the piano itself, there was no way I could afford it. I'd not only be broke, I'd have to borrow some money on one of my credit cards and I didn't want to do that.

I kept telling myself to forget about it completely but something inside was persistently urging me otherwise. As the myriad of confusing thoughts wrestled inside my brain, I suddenly realized that I'd driven six miles away from town, in the wrong direction! As I searched for an opening to make a quick u-turn on the four lane highway, I was entirely upset with myself for getting so lost in thought about buying the piano that I'd just wasted more time and gas!

It took me over an hour to get home and by the time I did, I was filled with nervous frustration. I didn't want to think about buying the piano, but the image of it sitting in between the two white lions in my living room *finally,* after all these years, wouldn't leave me alone. Every nerve in my body was telling me not to buy it, but something else was prodding my spirit to throw caution to the wind...

When I was a small child, my dad's nickname for me on occasion was: "Marc Agony." Throughout my adult years I'd think of it and wondered why, and to this day I've never asked him. I couldn't imagine what his reasons for choosing such a disparaging moniker were and with the violence he exhibited throughout my childhood, I'm not sure I even want to know, but as I flung the keys on the kitchen counter in my anxiety ridden state, ready to go take my long overdue nap before I had to get ready for work, Mother broke through my simmering emotional froth, vibrating clearly inside me with: *"So, you've always wondered why your old man called you "Marc Agony"?! Well Marc Anthony, look at yourself! Why are you getting so worked up over <u>nothing</u>?"*

I was in no mood for being jerked around by her at the moment. I seethed with annoyance as I replied out loud: "*Nothing* is what I will have in my savings account if I let you have your way!"

She didn't miss a beat and calmly retorted; *"Oh, I see. You think you can find a better deal elsewhere? Fine! Go ahead... look in the classified section of <u>your</u> newspaper..."*

The paper at the flat tire repair shop was printed by a different publisher than the newspaper I had on my kitchen counter. I quickly leafed to the Classified ads in the back and scanned the Musical Instruments. I came upon an ad that read: Baby Grand, very good condition $1800.00. This was more in my price range; my savings wouldn't be wiped out.

"See, this is more like it, at least it won't leave me broke!" I said out loud in a superior tone.

Unenthusiastically she mockingly replied; ***"Go ahead, call the number…"***

I began dialing with a self satisfied smirk on my face, certain I'd thwarted mom's plans. If she was going to goad me into buying a piano, at least I'd find a better deal than she had in mind.

The woman who answered the phone described the piano as an antique, with vibrant sound, all strings and hammers in good condition, and the keyboard was original. She ended her description by saying that it had a walnut finish. I wasn't thrilled about the walnut finish; it would be stark in my all white living room.

Still, it was affordable, and since she lived nearby I told her I'd like to see it. She was unable to let me come by today so we made an appointment for tomorrow, Mothers Day.

After I hung up I heard nothing from mom regarding this new turn of events, smugly I figured she'd acquiesced to my way of thinking and as I raced up the stairs to take my nap, I snidely uttered under my breath a phrase my mom often used in life: "Case closed!"

Of course I ended up eating those words later that night when I described Joyce's piano to my co-workers and they all urged me to buy it. I was not swayed by their opinions; it was easy for them to decide, they weren't the ones shelling out four-thousand dollars! Besides, I had high hopes for the antique piano, maybe I could learn to live with the walnut finish…

The following morning I called the woman who I'd made the appointment with and she promptly told me she'd sold her piano the night before to some friends who'd dropped by. I was surprised but not even the slightest bit disappointed, actually I was relieved because now the case *was* closed. I assumed that was the end of it, the useless piano chase was dead in the water. I hadn't really been seriously shopping for a piano in the first place, I'd been getting a flat tire fixed when all this havoc started.

I had to go into work very early today because Mothers Day is the busiest day in the restaurant industry and our hours were extended. I was ready to get dressed and forget the whole piano affair when mom's voice reverberated inside me: *"Call Joyce and make her an offer."*

I stopped dead in my tracks, irritated I replied; "You're starting *this* again? I've already *told* you I can't afford it! Considering the moving costs and the tuning, the very most I could offer her would be $3300.00 and that's too far below her asking price! Besides, that will completely wipe out my savings; I'd have to get a cash advance on my credit card to pay the moving and tuning expenses, and what if I have some household emergency…"

Mom interrupted me before I could finish: *"Will you buy it if she's willing to go that low?"*

Afraid of backing myself into a corner, I heaved a sigh and gave myself a moment before I answered; "Well…Okay… I guess so, but I seriously doubt…"

She cut me off with: *"It won't kill you to ask. Call her."*

I was *so* tired of this game. In a last ditch effort to stop mom from hounding me, I picked up the phone and dialed Joyce's number.

"Hi Joyce, it's Marc, I looked at your piano yesterday…"

"Oh! Hi! I was hoping you'd call! A young girl and her father came by last night to look at the piano and they seemed really interested, they said they'd call me back this morning, but I didn't see nearly the musical passion or potential in the girl as you have! I was hoping you'd call before they did!"

I took a deep breath before I replied; "I appreciate that Joyce, thank you. The reason I'm calling is because your asking price is a bit out of my range and I was wondering just how much lower you'd be willing to go."

Joyce paused for a moment and then replied; "I know my mother would want me to sell it to someone with real talent and I really believe you *must* have a piano, so how about…$3200.00?"

I was stunned! That was nearly a thousand less than her asking price and one hundred less than I'd agreed with mom I would pay.

"Well Joyce, I don't see how I can refuse that offer, I guess I'll take it!"

Oh I'm so glad! I really think you should have it, it's meant to be!" She replied with remarkable conviction.

I told Joyce that I'd go to the bank tomorrow and because I didn't have a checking account, I'd be sending her money orders.

After our conversation, I hurriedly showered and went to work. It was most definitely **Mother's** Day alright; I could feel her in the air. I'd taken the drive on Astral Avenue and she'd taken me on a ride that I hadn't anticipated. Now I was going to have to come to grips with the very frightening "Aspect" of draining my savings.

The following morning I went to the bank. I didn't fill out a withdrawal slip because I wasn't sure if I even had $3200.00 in my savings account.

"Hi, I need to take some money out of my savings, here's my account number."

The teller smiled and after she looked up the account she said; "How much would you like?"

I hesitated with uncertainty: "Well… I'm not sure…how much money is in there?"

She turned back to her computer and said; "Six thousand four hundred dollars."

Her words stupefied me! "Are you… sure?!" I gasped in amazement.

She turned her computer towards me and replied; "That's what its showing, is there a problem?"

"A problem…? Um… no, I guess not. I just didn't realize I had that much!"

Smiling wide, she replied; "That's a nice surprise then huh!"

Astonished I concurred: *"Yeah* it is!"

"How much would you like today sir?"

I'd made really good tips on Mothers Day, enough to pay for the piano movers and the tuning. I needed just enough to send Joyce.

I said to the teller: "I guess thirty-two hundred will be enough."

After I got the cash, I stared at the receipt that showed my remaining balance of $3200.00 as I walked to my truck. I couldn't believe that I'd had <u>double</u> the amount than I thought I'd had! "When and how did *that much* get put in there?" I wondered in a state of honest confusion. At that moment, in a very sarcastic and lofty tone, mom's voice flooded my head: ***"Well… are you finally happy <u>now</u>???"***

I couldn't answer, I burst into blissfully relieved tears and shook my head yes. The shivering goose bumps began their rapid spreading throughout my body and then mom, in a smirking tone feigning irritation, replied; ***"Hallelujah! Jesus, Mary and Joseph it's about time…"*** and her voice echoed back into the ether.

I went to the store and promptly sent the money orders to Joyce. Then I went home to help my brother move across town to his new apartment. I could scarcely believe that a white baby grand was moving in and my brother was moving out. He was on firm footing again and I felt like a cat that'd been free falling through space for the last six months and had finally landed on all fours! I didn't tell him about the piano, I wouldn't really believe it myself until it was sitting in my living room.

On the day the piano movers were to arrive, as I was in the shower, I was nervously excited and still in awe with all of the mysterious chain of events in the four days that had led up to this moment.

First and foremost, I was grateful that my baby brother had received his "new wings" and was finding joy in living again. Secondly, that I hadn't had to give up my savings account "safety cushion" and still had money to buy some landscaping materials. And finally, I was overwhelmed that my dream of owning a white baby grand was going to be materializing in a few hours! I couldn't help but wonder why such good fortune was coming my way. I wasn't used to this kind of wonderful on such a large scale. I kept asking myself as I lathered my hair with shampoo: "Why is this happening? What have I done to deserve this? This is all too much! Why is this happening!?"

When mom was alive, as a child I could always tell she was in a good mood when she'd be sitting at the kitchen counter, painting her nails red, and sipping a vodka gimlet. In the "good old days" this meant that she was going out for the evening with my dad for dinner and dancing. As I rinsed my hair and body of soap, this image of her appeared in my head as clear as a bell. She was painting her nails red, with a gimlet on the counter, and smiling she said; ***"So now you have to know why? It's not enough that it just is?"***

I smiled at the image. I could smell the red nail polish, and in my mind I guiltily replied; "I was just wondering…"

She looked up from her nails, smiling, and with sparkling gimlet green eyes she looked at me and said; ***"Why? Okay, since you must know, I'll tell you why. It's very simple dear; you helped me to save my baby…so I'm giving you a baby of your own. Satisfied?"***

Her smiling statement annihilated my anxiousness and instantaneously I burst into tears. As my flesh prickled with goose bumps and rockets of energy raced up and down my spine, I sat on the shower bench and my tears mingled with the baptizing water spray for the longest time before I was able to turn the shower off, settle down, and sigh with an air of contented bliss.

An hour later, the doorbell rang and when I opened the door, the same piano mover that had let me into the building at the Piano Liquidation Sale five weeks earlier, looked at me and immediately said; "I remember you! So you got a piano after all! It's a real beauty! Even if you didn't buy it from us! Where would you like it?

I pointed to the white carpeted area in between the two white ceramic lions and said; "Right there."

After the piano movers left, I sat on the gleaming white bench, lifted the lid that covered the keyboard, and was shocked to find little flecks of red nail polish on several of the keys! "Omigod what's this!" I said out loud. I panicked, thinking that the red polish would be permanent, and then mom came through again: ***"Oh puh-leez! Don't freak!!! Just get out your micro-fiber*** *cloth and with a little bit of water it will come right out!"*

I ran to the kitchen, put some water on the cloth and raced back to the keyboard. The polish came off instantly. I breathed a heavy sigh of relief when I'd gotten all of the red spots removed. I smiled as I heard her sign off with a teasing: ***"Maybe I <u>should</u> have named you Marc Agony…"***

"And the beat goes on…"
(Sung by that "sunny faced deigo" and Cher)

There are many other instances, great and small, of mom's Divine interventions in my life, but she's already informed me that they are to be shared at another time. Believe it or not, there are *some* occasions when I don't argue with her instructions…

She has urged me however, to share a few song lyrics that were inspired during the writing of this book as well as some that I composed years ago, and of course I'm fine with that. Hopefully they will fill a need, answer a question, or touch your heart in ways that need to be touched today. And who knows, maybe mom will find a way to orchestrate a miracle or two out of them, in your own life.

Oh, and one more thing; I'm still the champion and unchallenged leader of the barest landscaped yard on the block! Not because I don't have the money, now it's because I can't seem to find the time! (As you've just witnessed, I've been a little busy…) However, one of my neighbors told me that he and his wife love to get out their lawn chairs, sit back with a glass of wine and listen, whenever they hear me playing, my baby. Grand!

Postscripts

Modern conventional wisdom, along with various media gurus; constantly tell us to: "Follow your passion." And, trite as the saying has become, it is still sage advice.

One of my many passions has always been song lyrics. What are the words trying to convey except, someone else's passion! Songs are mini passion plays, and the heart, mind, and spirit of every lyricist, is the script.

Perhaps that is why everyone loves whatever songs we love, because we can then identify and assimilate the composers' passion, and through their words and music, release our own.

Nevertheless, I've discovered while writing this book, that just because I do follow my passion for writing songs, it didn't mean that I was <u>fulfilling my purpose</u> in life.

I now truly believe that writing this book was the fulfillment of one of my higher purposes, and I believe we all have at the *very least*, one.

I hope you find additional enjoyment in reading the following mini passion plays. Perhaps some will inspire you to follow a few undiscovered passions and purposes, of your own.

Lyric note: This is the song in my heart, and the belief of my soul.

Love Is The Orchestra

Continuously the universe expands and unfolds
Creativity knows no bounds
Symphonies of ideas and theories remain untold
Our galaxy One chord of the sound

Chorus: Love is the orchestra we are the musicians
   Some play in tune, others off key
   From Atlantis to Zion my religious position
   believes that Love is the orchestra eternally

Every moment we are given a chance to create
whatever our human hearts desire
On this earth we reason, rule, plan and dictate
the sparks flying off of man kinds' bonfire

Chorus: Love is the orchestra we are the musicians
   Some play in tune, others off key
   From Atlantis to Zion my religious position
   believes that Love is the orchestra eternally

Whatever name you give as your savior
is between you and your holy one
Jesus said; "Love one another"
The Light of the World still shines on

Chorus: Love is the orchestra we are the musicians...
(Repeat)

Lyric note: This is for Patricia Artes, whose Light shines like the dawn.

Honesty In Your Eyes

I can be anything when I'm with you
Lady, my Queen, your wish is my rule
You smile so heavenly how can I resist
such shining light, infinite bliss

> **Chorus:** This is what I see when I look in your eyes
> the wide open skies, sun, moon, and stars on the rise
> Flourishing Angelic spirit, worldly wise
> I see cosmic honesty in your eyes

Dream big or small, state your desire
together we'll spread like wild fire
Anytime, anyplace, anywhere you want to go
I'm complete there, in the warmth of your soul

> **Chorus:** This is what I see when I look in your eyes…
> (Repeat)

> **Bridge:** Everything you are is everything I need to be a very
> very happy man
> Apart or together our love guaranteed is touched
> by an Angels hand

> **Chorus:** Here is what I see when I look in your eyes…
> (Repeat)

Lyric note: The inspiration for this will be obvious once you read it. What wasn't obvious to me as I wrote it was that "It's a good thing" is a familiar catchphrase of Martha Stewart's, that **Leo** doyenne of everyday good taste.

It's A Good Thing

Like an echo reverberating through the canyons
her voice calls from across The Great Divide
I'm usually resistant to her instructions
Though I run there is nowhere to hide

   1ˢᵗ Chorus: It's a good thing I can't get away
                  from all of the blessings she brings my way
                  With the best intentions she leads me along
                  to the golden intersections of her One song

Love is her armor, shield and sword
Love is why she fights for me
The love of a mother is beyond words
it lives among the holiest of holies

   1ˢᵗ Chorus: It's a good thing…
   (Repeat)

   Bridge: There is nothing as strong as a mother and child bond
              even when things go wrong her love marches on
             We are all imperfect even mothers' have flaws
             but before we sit in judgment take a breath and pause

   Final Chorus: It's a good thing, come what may
                    Even if my wildest dreams fade away
                    I'll always have one thing I can be proud of
                    I answered her callings, with love

Lyric Note: Uh…you've read the book right?

My Mary Kay

What that woman did to me no boy should ever have to learn
Making love guilty of her neurotic twists and turns
Storing her shame and blame in me drilling holes in my heart
Her Jezebel spirit rampantly trampled my soul and tore it apart

   Chorus: Back in the day my Mary Kay
              never spent a minute in jail
              She got away with no price to pay
              for molesting a teenage male

She lied care free and manipulated me into being her foolish slave
Her adultery casually threw my innocence into an early grave
Fanning the flames of her own desires playing my body and mind
cajoling me into her hell fire I was a kid running blind

   Chorus: Back in the day my Mary Kay…
   (Repeat)

   Bridge: I wasted too many years of my precious youth
              being exploited by her manic highs and lows
              as for her sexual and emotional abuse
              she denies the truth but God and I know

One day I finally woke up to see my freedom was now or never
Though she begged and pleaded her words were no longer clever
The slick veneers of her selfish tears gathered like moss over stone
She almost buried me in lies but I got wise and I'm happier, alone

Lyric note: Sometimes words can fall on a page in place of tears.

This Tear

Today I feel like crawling right out of my skin
I don't like the state of mind my spirit is in
I couldn't sleep, Lord knows I've tried
I couldn't keep it locked up inside
I couldn't weep, but I finally cried
my heartache cried out right here
when I wrote down this tear

Chorus: This tear it belongs to me, this tear is mine and mine alone
This tear holds a painful memory; this tear is water from a stone
It came from my heart where love used to be
when you were a part of my destiny
This song is my tear; it's all I could cry
This tear came out of a heart that's bone dry

You think it was roses for me and thistles for you
but you always lived in a fantasy that could never come true
I couldn't compete although I tried
I lived in deceit to save your pride
I couldn't keep on being denied
so the truth spilled out right here
when I wrote down this tear

Chorus: This tear it belongs to me, this tear is mine and mine alone…
(Repeat)

They say "time heals all wounds" but time's moving slow
Maybe someday inner peace will blossom and grow
It would be sweet to feel that side
whole and complete no pain to hide
until that feat reverses this tide
one thing remains crystal clear
only one thing, this tear

Lyric note: I've always considered this a direct Angelic message and I recorded it musically as a lullaby, for broken spirited adults.

My Darling One

Heartbeats on clean sheets
motionless desire
Mean streets, deceits
missiles set to fire
Day and night, darkness and light
perfect love so rare
Black and white, wrong or right
it hurts being aware

Chorus: Go to sleep my darling one dream a brand new dream
Every troubled storm passes on so run in your meadows of green
Go to sleep my darling one let your heartaches rest
and with the mornings rising sun remember your spirit is blessed

Bridge: Lying there thinking of yesterday frozen by a failure from the past
The love you gave was blown away you're still suffering from the blast

Wishing well broken, hell
you wonder if it ever worked
Prison cell fire bell
rang, but you never even jerked
Day and night, darkness and light
Perfect Love somewhere
For tonight my darling sleep tight
dream away your despair

Chorus: Go to sleep my darling one…
(Repeat)

Lyric Note: Love **has** returned many times in my life since I wrote this piece seventeen years ago, but I still attract the emotional whack jobs! Maybe I should write the flip side and title it: **Freak Magnet!**

Love Will Return

Chorus: Love will return in my life one fine day
Love will return sweet and pure
All of my heartache will be washed away
Love will return with a cure

Looking back I understand where I went wrong the first time
With both of my hands I placed my open heart on a fault line
and when the earthquake struck
Old Lady Luck charmed me with a pair of snake eyes
I was foolish then, but when love comes again
I'll listen to my heart instead of pretty lies

Chorus: Love will return in my life one fine day…
(Repeat)

Bridge: I've danced in the flames of love and lost my way to paradise
so the next time love returns you can bet I'll surely think twice

Final Chorus: Love will return in my life one fine day
Love will return sweet and pure
All of my heartache will be washed away
Love will return with a cure
All of my heartache will be washed away
Love will return oh yes I'm sure

Lyric note: The following was written from a true life event that happened on the street corner of 23rd and 6th Avenue in New York City, in the winter of 1990.

Lost In Your Eyes

The streetlight changed from red to green
a December moon made love to the night
I've been blessed with a vision for I've clearly seen
the purest form of Heavenly Light
As soon as I saw you standing there
instantly I was immobilized
Forgive me please I can't help but stare
at this moment I'm so lost in your eyes

    Chorus: Standing here on this corner/ I'm so lost in your eyes The temperature has gotten warmer/ in your face I see sunny skies/ Though the frozen winds of winter are slicing all around me like knives/ next to you the sun shines and shimmers/ I'm so lost in your eyes

You returned my gaze and smiled
I felt the blood rush up to my face
and all at once there was a helpless child
standing on the corner in my place
You nodded and said hello
I thought I'd die right then and there
What I've replied I'll never know
and at this moment I don't even care

Chorus: Standing here on this corner I'm so lost in your eyes...
(Repeat)

Bridge: Please don't walk on alone/let me be the one at your side Without your love I'll aimlessly roam/oh Venus don't let me be denied/ Please stay right where you are/this chance may not happen again/ I'll stand with you forevermore/our romance will never know an end

My heart changed from blue to red
its empty halls have filled up with love
I may well be in way over my head
still I thank my lucky stars up above
Time won't stand still I'm told
I've also heard how fast it flies
but I could stand here and never grow old
and forever be lost in your eyes

Chorus: Standing here on this corner I'm so lost in your eyes…
(Repeat)

Lyric note: Inspired by the "shower of love" I received in the shower when mom explained why she'd arranged for me to buy my Baby Grand.

Showers Of Love

Showers of love are washing over me
I'm swimming in a sea of Cosmic energy
Whatever I desire, dare to dream or deem to be
there's a powerful beam of loves light guiding me

>**Chorus:** Showers of love washing over me
>from The Powers That Be over sun, moon, and stars
>Awakening my spirit, giving me insight
>showers of love reigning over me tonight

Sometimes we trip, stumble and fall
everyone's bound to make a slip up
we're human after all
But with each mistake we learn
and hope next time to get it right
until our souls return
to the source of Divine Light

>**2nd Chorus:** Where we shall always be in showers of love
>with The Powers that be over sun, moon and stars
>Eternally refreshed in One Perfect Light
>Showers of love emptying into white

Lyric note: In loving memory of my wonderful "Deigo Paisan" Joey Ciadella, the kindest man I've ever known, who was like a Father to me. This lyric was written for Joey's wife Stella, their son Carl and his wife, Sue.

Ciao Bella
(Goodbye Beautiful One)

A kinder man I've never found
His smile always lit up the room
He spoke with a symphonic joyous sound
His laughter was springtime in full bloom

He lifted me up whenever I was down
Touched my heart like no one else I've ever known
It's gonna be hard to get along with out him around
I wasn't ready when God called him home

Chorus: Ciao Bella, sleep peacefully
Under the starlight umbrella your twinkling eyes shine on me
So long "good fella" I miss you more than I can say
but I know I'm gonna see you again in Heaven one day

A huge piece of my soul is missing since you've gone
and my heart has turned a whiter shade of pale
No other choice but to learn how to carry on
I'm gonna need an army of Angels to prevail

Chorus: Ciao Bella, mi amore, paisan
Back to The Garden where your light shines on
Thanks for loving me in this life we shared together
One day our love will be reunited, forever

M&M's Thank You Notes
(Mother's & Mine of course!)

On Mother's behalf I'm instructed to first thank The Father, The Son and The Holy Spirit, along with all of the heavenly hosts of the "Other Side" who moment by moment, gather us into the swell of the "ONE-song" with unconditional and everlasting love.

Mom also lovingly thanks all of the countless human instruments she's orchestrated in *my* life who have allowed her to use them to bring me "Immeasurable Joy!" (Quotation marks and pun are hers, and I can see her smiling wide at this moment ...)

As for *my* thanks, ditto what mom said... with everlasting gratitude and love. I'd also like to especially thank ***all*** of the musicians quoted in this book whose music has been my constant source of comfort and inspiration, with ***very special thanks*** to Yoko Ono whom I must quote here: **"You gave me my life/ like a gush of wind in my hair...".** Thank you Ocean Child, for the always magnificently fragrant sea breeze.

I most gratefully thank all of the participants in this book whose real names were used, please know that I used them to honor you and thank you, in print, for being the ***imprints*** of my life. And yes, I admit *that* pun was mine...

I'd like to thank all of the people at Outskirts Press, with special thanks to Christina Brett for her friendship, laughter, and Miss

Moneypenny skills. I'd especially like to thank Cheri Reinhart for getting this project finished on time! (Mom thanks them too!)

Special thanks to Jim McAdams for his book jacket design and for unconsciously picking up mom's whisperings in the "ears" of the waving Italian flag.

To all of my friends and supporters of my art who are unmentioned in the story; please rest assured you are honored always, in my heart. These include: Christina Javied, Sal Mascolo, my Mamma Leone Family, Lee and Linda Weiss, Mr. and Mrs. Billy Bell, Polly Bell D'Addabbo, The Douris Family, Steve and Jane Detora, The Ciadella Family, my Fuego Family and patrons (Saints and otherwise!) and to all of those who remain unmentioned due to space, you all have a very special place of gratitude, in my spirit.

Oh yeah, and thanks mom, for giving me this story to live, and tell. I know *you* have already started the sequel, but could I catch my breath from this book before we begin?
You know how much I'd appreciate it!

With very special love,

Marc

Write to Marc Barone:

Lions Pride Press
P.O. Box 92132
Henderson, NV. 89009-2132
Phone: (702) 568-8706

Or Visit His Website

www.outskirtspress.com/italianmothers

See pictures from the stories in this book, listen to an excerpt read by the author, order copies for family and friends,

and

<u>Free</u>: Download 2 songs from this book written and performed by the author.

Printed in the United States
76870LV00004B/229-234